Knowledge
Manageme
Organizat.
Design

Knowledge Management and Organizational Design

Edited by Paul S. Myers

Butterworth-Heinemann

Boston Oxford Johannesburg Melbourne New Delhi Singapore

Library of Congress Cataloging-in-Publication Data

Knowledge management and organizational design / edited by Paul S.
  Myers.
      p. cm.—(Resources for the knowledge-based economy)
    Includes bibliographical references and index.
    ISBN 0-7506-9749-0 (pbk.)
    1. Organizational learning. 2. Organizational effectiveness.
  I. Myers, Paul S., 1964– . II. Series.
HD58.82.K66 1996
658.4′03—dc20   96-18403
                                                                      CIP

British Library Cataloguing-in-Publication Data
A catalogue record for this book is available from the British Library.

The publisher offers discounts on bulk orders of this book.
For information, please contact:
Manager of Special Sales
Butterworth–Heinemann
313 Washington Street
Newton, MA 02158-1626
Tel: 617-928-2500
Fax: 617-928-2620

For information on all Business publications available, contact our World Wide
Web home page at: http://www.bh.com/bh/bb

10 9 8 7 6 5 4 3 2 1

Printed in the United States of America

Table of Contents

Acknowledgements

The Ernst & Young Center For Business Innovation in Boston supported my work on this anthology, and I thank Larry Prusak for inviting me to participate in this project. Terrence Boyle provided valuable assistance in securing permission to re-print the thirteen selections. I thank the authors and copyright holders for their willingness to share their ideas with a diverse audience of practitioners, managers, and academics.

Introduction to Series— Why Knowledge, Why Now?

Why is there such an upsurge of interest in Knowledge? In 1996 there will be at least six major conferences on the subject; there are plans to add three new journals focusing on Knowledge, sometimes loosely called Intellectual Capital or Organizational Learning), and many major firms, in the United States and (more slowly) Europe, are adding positions such as Chief Knowledge Officer, or Organizational Learning, and even a few Vice Presidents for Intellectual Capital!

How come all this focus on a subject that, at some levels, has been around since the pre-Socratic philosophers? Is it yet another one of the multitudinous management enthusiasms that seem to come and go, with the frequency of some random natural phenomena? We don't think so! Many of us doing research on this subject have seen the rise and fall of many of these varied nostrums—all of which attempted to offer to firms a new road to achieving a sustainable competitive advantage. However, when much of the shouting dies down, we have concluded that, excluding monopolistic policies and other market irregularities, there is no sustainable advantage other than what a firm knows, how it can utilize what it knows, and how fast it can learn something new!

However, this still does not answer the question, why Knowledge, why now? Let us try to list some very broad trends that seem to be playing a significant role in the playing current in Knowledge.

A) The globalization of the economy which is putting terrific pressure on firms for increased adaptability, innovation, and process speed.

B) The awareness of the value of specialized Knowledge, as embedded in organizational processes and routines, in coping with above pressures

C) The awareness of Knowledge as a distinct factor of production, and its role in the growing book to market ratios within Knowledge based industries.

D) Cheap networked computing which is at last giving us a tool to work and learn with each other.

While many can argue for and against these trends we feel that the preponderance of the evidence points to the increasing substitution of brain for brawn within our organizations and social lives. Yet we have delayed few conceptional tools to better work with "wetware."

It is with these forces in mind that we offer the following volume to you. While there are, as yet, few agreed upon standards and analytic frames and definitions, there are enough serious articles and books to help managers get some real traction in dealing with the crucial yet elusive subject of Knowledge.

After all, we have had about 500 years of thought concerning the other major factors of production (e.g., land, labor, and capital). Let these volumes start the process of codifying knowledge about knowledge in order for us to better manage in the twenty-first century.

Laurence Prusak

1

Knowledge Management and Organizational Design: An Introduction

Paul S. Myers

For more than a decade, management thinkers have heralded the arrival of the new information economy characterized by globalization, increased complexity, and rapid change. "Do more with less!," "Don't automate, obliterate!," and "Get innovative or get dead!"[1] are but a few of the leading words of advice for meeting the newly shaped competitive environment. Underlying many of these prescriptions is the need to explicitly manage the intellectual capital and other knowledge assets of a firm. Corporate success in today's economy comes from being able to acquire, codify, and transfer knowledge more effectively and with greater speed than the competition.

But, managers and practitioners sensibly ask, how do we get there from here? Fortunately, for now we can draw on decades of research and ideas developed by social scientists and management consultants as a starting point for understanding how to manage organizational knowledge. Research on decision-making, innovation, and work design, to name but a few subjects, has a lot to say about the contemporary concerns and practical problems of knowledge management. This present volume is a collection of articles and book excerpts selected for their insight into the relationship between organizational design and knowledge management. It is the first anthology of its kind to draw together the work of leading economists, sociologists, psychologists, management thinkers, and practitioners, each with a unique contribution to our understanding of how the form and management of organizations shapes their levels of knowledge transfer, innovation, and learning.

While much of the work in the field of organization design done prior to the 1990s discusses "information" and "expertise" rather than "knowledge" per se, its distinctive perspective is readily applicable to knowledge management issues. These connections become clearer, of course, once we have a working definition of

[1]Rosabeth Moss Kanter, *When Giants Learn To Dance*, (NY: Simon & Schuster), 1989; Michael Hammer, *Harvard Business Review* (July–August) 1990; Tom Peters, *California Management Review* Winter & Spring, 1991.

organizational knowledge. We can define organizational knowledge as processed information embedded in routines and processes which enable action. At its core, knowledge must be seen as tied to the personal or human element. Knowledge, as we generally understand it, resides in peoples' heads; for, after all, individuals must identify, interpret, and internalize knowledge. The representation of knowledge, however, can be mechanical, digital, visual, and so forth. For knowledge to provide a company with sustainable competitive advantage, such knowledge must be independent from any given individual. For this reason, we can identify—and then manage—organizational knowledge only to the extent it has been captured by an organization's systems, processes, products, rules, and culture.

ORGANIZATION DESIGN AND KNOWLEDGE MANAGEMENT

Organizational performance is the result of the interaction of strategy, organizational context, and individual behavior. At the risk of over-simplification, this means managers need to choose the right approach to the right markets, create processes to deliver quality goods and/or services to those markets, and motivate people to act in line with the company's objectives. Volumes have been written about business strategy, including some recent books on the centrality of knowledge management to successful strategies (e.g., Nonaka & Takeuchi, 1995; Davis & Botkin, 1994). The high level of attention fueled by the "reengineering" movement has added the language of business processes to every manager's vocabulary for structuring work and organizations (e.g., Hammer & Champy, 1993; Davenport, 1993). Many recent management books and articles emphasize creating empowered teams and valuing diversity as ways to motivate high performance in knowledge-intensive businesses (e.g., Nevis, Lancourt, & Vassallo, 1996; McGill & Slocum, 1994).

Organizational design takes into account all three critical performance factors: strategy, organization, and motivation. At its base, the approach presumes that a person's actions are influenced by his or her situation.[2] Most practices derived from this tradition are based on the belief that firms achieve effective performance by aligning, or making consistent, various organizational features. Organization design interventions deal with modifying elements of an organization's structure, including the division of labor, allocation of decision rights, choice of coordinating mechanisms, delineation of organizational boundaries, and networks of informal relationships (see Cash, et al, 1994).

The impetus for this collection of articles is the belief that businesses will find it increasingly difficult to succeed in a knowledge-intensive economy without leveraging the power of organizational design for effective knowledge management. Organizational design is about enabling a group of people to combine, co-

---

[2]As this introduction is not intended as a comprehensive synthesis of the field, interested readers may wish to look toward recent work by Galbraith (1995), Mohrman, Cohen, and Mohrman (1995), and Nadler, et al (1992) for additional insights.

ordinate, and control resources and activities in order to produce value, all in a way appropriate to the environment in which the business competes. In this view, design is more a process than a structure in that the resulting organization should be intended as constantly adapting and evolving, not fixed forever in some pre- determined form. Recent empirical work provides evidence for this view. Mohrman and her colleagues concluded from their study of knowledge work in eleven Fortune 500 companies that "appropriate organizational design enables an organization to execute better, learn faster, and change more easily" (1995:7). The task for leaders is to implement (by using the various structural levers) the mix of factors which increases the likelihood that individual and organizational knowledge acquisition, codification, and transfer will occur regularly, appropriately, and productively.

The increased importance of organizational design for business performance challenges the current paradigm and experience of many managers who may be quick to propose a technological ("We need better databases!") or a personnel-related solution ("Hire smarter people! Fire the laggards!"), rather than a structural one, to address business performance issues. As part of their respective training, doctors study the basic structures of the human body, engineers and architects understand the fundamentals of physics and materials science, auto mechanics learn how a combustion engine works. Only when they understand the underlying concepts, phenomenon, and variables in their field and how they interrelate, can these professionals deal with specific issues and identify solutions. Similarly, managers need to raise to a conscious, actionable level their understanding of the fundamental behavior, processes, and dynamics of the organizations they lead.

THE SELECTIONS

This collection draws on fifty years of management thinking to present a useful introduction to key issues facing knowledge-intensive organizations. The articles have been selected from among classic works which have influenced the field of organizational design as well as from more recent contributions which describe contemporary leading practices in knowledge management.

Even the most cursory review of writings on the subject of organizational design during this century reveals an enormous array of approaches and perspectives, topics of interest, underlying assumptions, research methodologies, and levels of analysis. On one side the field is anchored by social science discipline-based researchers who strive to understand society and organizations as they are and who treasure that knowledge for its own sake. On the other end of the spectrum are action-oriented consultants who are interested in providing solutions to practical problems of administration, but who pay scant attention to any higher-order or more generally applicable learning. Located between these two groups are those practitioners and management thinkers who seek to combine theory and practice, to understanding social systems in order to change and improve them.

This volume, I hope, falls squarely in the middle of that spectrum. The selections are clearly written and concise and reflect the mix of empirical data and conceptual richness which makes their message for practitioners both credible and actionable while being suitable for further testing and refinement by academic researchers. Arranged thematically, the chapters discuss decision-making, organization structure, innovation, strategic alliances, managing knowledge workers, and power relations.

The anthology begins with a pair of theoretical pieces to introduce a perspective that is useful when reading the remaining selections. Theories allow us to identify critical variables and their relationships in a particular situation and then to generalize those findings to wider applicability. Without a theory of action—an explanation of cause and effect or a prediction about likely outcomes—a manager's anecdote or an office's experiment cannot be a reliable and sustainable source of leveragable knowledge or replicable learning.

Hayek's classic essay provides an economic theory of the link between knowledge and organizational structure. He provides a taxonomy which distinguishes between two kinds of knowledge by pointing out the importance of context and interpretation to its value. While Hayek addressed issues at the macro-economic level, fifty years later Jensen and Meckling have written a companion piece to Hayek's which places his ideas in an organizational context. They expand on Hayek's ideas about the cost of transferring knowledge and argue that organizational design is about more than simply choosing between centralization and decentralization in the allocation of resources. Rather, they posit a framework for understanding the links between knowledge, decision making, and organization design which identifies the choices managers must make about their organizations in order to align individual behavior with corporate objectives.

Not surprisingly, the vast majority of management writing on organization design has dealt with industrial age organizations. The dominant factor influencing design choices, as the contingency theory approach posits, is the external environment of markets, technologies, and regulations. Pinchot and Pinchot describe the familiar, traditional bureaucratic organization and explain why it is no longer suited to the knowledge era. They focus their analysis on the changing nature of work and argue that the old model is being replaced by an interdependent set of structures and practices which better fits the demands of today's environment. Bahrami's research in high technology companies suggests that flexible, agile firms with "novel organization structures and management processes to accommodate them" may be the leading organizational form of the next decade. He points out that this new form presents managers with a fresh set of dilemmas and tensions to be addressed on an on-going basis, rather than resolved ex ante through a single design choice.

Innovation requires applied knowledge, and highly innovative organizations are adept at knowledge acquisition, codification, and transfer (see Nonaka & Takeuchi, 1995; Kanter, 1983). Burns and Stalker give an historical review of how innovation became organized in this century. While the book from which this selection has been excerpted, *The Management of Innovation,* is best known for introducing the concepts of "organic" and "mechanistic" organizations and linking their respective desirability to the stability of the external environment, this early chapter helps us understand how conditions at the societal level influence levels of innovation. They emphasize that invention is a social phenomenon relying in great part on the diffusion of information through professional relationships and suggest that an organization's design can hinder or facilitate that process. In a thorough review of the field, Kanter fully fleshes out Burns and Stalker's ideas about the importance of organizational context in producing innovation. Breaking down the innovation process into four sets of tasks, she describes the structural, collective, and social conditions which enhance the flow of information and knowledge, facilitate and strengthen relationships, and support individual and group creativity.

Kanter's article touches on the importance of inter-organizational relationships as an important source of input for the innovation process, and the growing numbers of business alliances and joint ventures over the past decade suggests that companies are well aware of this benefit from partnerships (e.g., Lewis, 1995; Yoshino & Rangan, 1995). Badaracco studied the variety of alliances created by IBM and General Motors and found that among their main benefits were the creation of knowledge and learning new practices. This was particularly true regarding "embedded" knowledge; for Badaracco, embedded knowledge is a more social notion than Hayek's "particular knowledge" for it "resides primarily in specialized relationships among individuals and groups and in the particular norms, attitudes, information flows, and ways of making decisions that shape their dealings with each other" (1991: 79). Although such knowledge is difficult and costly to transfer, alliances create an arena for building ties which will facilitate learning over time. Pucik provides some guidance for practitioners in how to increase the chances that such learning actually occurs. He outlines a role for the human resource function in supporting organizational learning, which requires transforming HR from an administrative unit to a valued business asset. Drawing on the alliance experiences of firms which demonstrate high levels of learning, he also offers specific advice for human resource professionals.

The need to manage knowledge more consciously raises more direct human resource implications: how can firms attract and retain knowledge workers? The rise of the "intelligent organization," in Pinchot's phrase, has placed a premium on human assets rather than natural resources or financial capital which reigned supreme in earlier eras. Handy explores this phenomenon by reviewing the global demographic shifts which are occurring simultaneously with the emergence of the information-intensive economy. If Handy suggests that finding workers prepared for knowledge-era businesses will be a limiting factor for corporate success in the years ahead, Tampoe reminds us that motivating excellent performance presents challenges as well. More and more, companies must meet the expectations of their knowledge workers in terms of work environment and quality of life issues or else face lower productivity or even turnover of their most highly valued assets. Addressing the personal and social objectives of employees to build effective and "empowering" workplaces, he argues, is the key to motivating knowledge workers.

The final group of articles deal with the nexus of knowledge, work, and power. Organizational design shapes the flow of information, resources, and support within a firm, and in this way strongly determines the powerholders. Crozier's classic description of the French cigarette factory demonstrates the power that can accrue to holders of technical knowledge, especially when few or no others possess that knowledge. The transformation of the shop floor through computerization, however, threatens to diminish or even eliminate such expert power for some individuals. The excerpt detailing the experience of paper mills workers from Zuboff's insightful ethnographic study of the effects of technological change illustrates how power is shifting from workers to college-trained process engineers. Clearly, some employees gain while others lose power as a result of the increased value placed on organizational knowledge. Baker provides some guidance about how to exploit one's position in the organization structure to create opportunities and advantages for individuals and firms. He points out that not merely knowledge, but social capital—who one knows and how one handles those relationships—are critical assets for business and personal success.

Taken together, these thirteen selections connect organizational design concepts and ideas to the exigencies of knowledge management for today's corporations. They are intended as a catalyst to management action, whether by sparking a conversation among colleagues, providing a solution for a project team, or inspiring a leader to try an innovative design. While this anthology represents only an introduction to the work of researchers and practitioners which focuses on the role of organizational form in business performance, it makes clear that the organizational design approach offers valuable insights for those charged with helping their organizations acquire, codify, and transfer knowledge.

REFERENCES

Cash, James I., Jr., Robert G. Eccles, Nitin Nohria, and Richard L. Nolan. 1994. *Building the Information-Age Organization: Structure, Control, and Information Technologies.* Homewood, IL: Irwin.

Davenport, Thomas H. 1993. *Process Innovation.* Boston: Harvard Business School Press.

Davis, Stan and Jim Botkin. 1994. *The Monster Under The Bed.* New York: Simon & Schuster.

Galbraith, Jay R. 1995. *Designing Organizations.* San Francisco: Jossey-Bass.

Hammer, Michael and James Champy. 1993. *Reengineering the Corporation.* New York: Harper Business.

Kanter, Rosabeth Moss. 1983. *The Change Masters.* New York: Simon & Schuster.

Lewis, Jordan D. 1995. *The Connected Corporation.* New York: The Free Press.

McGill, Michael E. and John W. Slocum, Jr. 1994. *The Smarter Organization.* New York: John Wiley & Sons.

Mohrman, Susan A., Susan Cohen, and Allan M. Mohrman, Jr. 1995. *Designing Team-Based Organizations: New Forms for Knowledge Work.* San Francisco: Jossey-Bass.

Nadler, David A., Marc S. Gerstein, Robert B. Shaw, and associates. 1992. *Organizational Architecture.* San Francisco: Jossey-Bass.

Nevis, Edwin C., Joan Lancourt, and Helen Vassallo. 1996. *International Revolutions: A Seven Point Strategy For Moving Beyond Resistance.* San Francisco: Jossey-Bass.

Nonaka, Ikujiro and Hirotaka Takeuchi. 1995. *The Knowledge-Creating Company.* New York: Oxford University Press.

Yoshino, Michael Y. and U. Srinivasa Rangan. 1995. *Strategic Alliances.* Boston: Harvard Business School Press.

2

The Use of Knowledge in Society

Frederick A. Hayek

Many of the current disputes with regard to both economic theory and economic policy have their common origin, it seems to me, in a misconception about the nature of the economic problem of society. This misconception in turn is due to an erroneous transfer to social phenomena of the habits of thought we have developed in dealing with the phenomena of nature.

What is the problem we wish to solve when we try to construct a rational economic order? On certain familiar assumptions the answer is simple enough. *If* we possess all the relevant information, *if* we can start out from a given system of preferences, and *if* we command complete knowledge of available means, the problem which remains is purely one of logic. That is, the answer to the question of what is the best use of the available means is implicit in our assumptions. Stated briefly in mathematical form, it is that the marginal rates of substitution between any two commodities or factors must be the same in all their different uses.

This, however, is emphatically *not* the economic problem which society faces. And the economic calculus which we have developed to solve it, though an important step toward the solution of the economic problem of society, does not yet provide an answer to it. The reason for this is that the "data" for the whole society, from which the economic calculus starts, are never "given" to a single mind.

The peculiar character of the problem of a rational economic order is determined precisely by the fact that the knowledge of the circumstances which we must use never exists in concentrated or integrated form but solely as the dispersed bits of incomplete and frequently contradictory knowledge which separate individuals possess. The economic problem of society is thus not merely a problem of how to allocate "given" resources—if "given" is taken to mean given to a single mind which deliberately solves the problem set by these "data." It is rather a problem of how to secure the best use of resources known to any of the members of society, for ends whose relative importance only these individuals know.

Or, to put it briefly, it is a problem of the utilization of knowledge which is not given to anyone in its totality.

This character of the fundamental problem has, I am afraid, been obscured rather than illuminated by many of the recent refinements of economic theory, particularly by many of the uses made of mathematics. Though the problem with which I want primarily to deal in this paper is the problem of a rational economic organization, I shall be led again and again to point to its close connections with certain methodological questions. Many of the points I wish to make are indeed conclusions toward which diverse paths of reasoning have unexpectedly converged. But, as I now see these problems, this is no accident.

In ordinary language, we describe by the word "planning" the complex of interrelated decisions about the allocation of our available resources. All economic activity is in this sense planning; and in any society in which many people collaborate, this planning, whoever does it, will in some measure have to be based on knowledge which, in the first instance, is not given to the planner but to somebody else, yet somehow will have to be conveyed to the planner. The various ways in which this knowledge on which people base their plans is communicated to them is the crucial problem for any theory explaining the economic process, and the problem of what is the best way of utilizing knowledge initially dispersed among all the people is at least one of the main problems of economic policy—or of designing an efficient economic system.

The answer to this question is closely connected with that other question which arises here, that of *who* is to do the planning. It is about this question that all the dispute about "economic planning" centers. This is not a dispute about whether planning is to be done or not. It is a dispute as to whether planning is to be done centrally, by one authority for the whole economic system, or is to be divided among many individuals. Planning in the specific sense in which the term is used in contemporary controversy necessarily means central planning—direction of the whole economic system according to one unified plan. Competition, on the other hand, means decentralized planning by many separate persons. The half-way house between the two, about which many people talk but which few like when they see it, is the delegation of planning to privileged industries, or, in other words, monopolies.

Which of these systems is likely to be more efficient depends mainly on the question under which of them we can expect that fuller use will be made of the existing knowledge. This, in turn, depends on whether we are more likely to succeed in putting at the disposal of a single central authority all the knowledge which ought to be used but which is initially dispersed among many different individuals, or in conveying to the individuals such additional knowledge as they need in order to enable them to dovetail their plans with those of others.

UNCOMMON KNOWLEDGE

It will at once be evident that on this point the position will be different with respect to different kinds of knowledge. The answer to our question will therefore largely turn on the relative importance of the different kinds of knowledge: those more likely to be at the disposal of particular individuals and those which we should with greater confidence expect to find in the possession of an authority made up of suitably chosen experts. If it is today so widely assumed that the latter will be in a better position, this is because one kind of knowledge, namely, scientific knowledge, occupies now so prominent a place in public imagination that we tend to forget that it is not the only kind that is relevant. It may be admitted that, as far as scientific knowledge is concerned, a body of suitably chosen experts may be in the best position to command all the best knowledge available—though this is of course merely shifting the difficulty to the problem of selecting the experts. What I wish to point out is that, even assuming that this problem can be readily solved, it is only a small part of the wider problem.

Today it is almost heresy to suggest that scientific knowledge is not the sum of all knowledge. But a little reflection will show that there is beyond question a body of very important but unorganized knowledge which cannot possibly be called scientific in the sense of knowledge of general rules: the knowledge of the particular circumstances of time and place. It is with respect to this that practically every individual has some advantage over all others because he possesses unique information of which beneficial use might be made only if the decisions depending on it are left to him or are made with his active co-operation.

We need only to remember how much we have to learn in any occupation after we have completed our theoretical training, how big a part of our working life we spend learning particular jobs, and how valuable an asset in all walks of life is knowledge of people, of local conditions, and of special circumstances. To know of and put to use a machine not fully employed, or somebody's skill which could be better utilized, or to be aware of a surplus stock which can be drawn upon during an interruption of supplies, is socially quite as useful as the knowledge of better alternative techniques. The shipper who earns his living from using otherwise empty or half-filled journeys of tramp-steamers, or the estate agent whose whole knowledge is almost exclusively one of temporary opportunities, or the *arbitrageur* who gains from local differences of commodity prices—all are performing eminently useful functions based on special knowledge of circumstances of the fleeting moment not known to others.

It is a curious fact that this sort of knowledge should today be generally regarded with a kind of contempt, that anyone who, by such knowledge, gains an advantage over somebody better equipped with theoretical or technical knowledge is thought to have acted almost disreputably. To gain an advantage from better knowledge of facilities of communication or transport is sometimes regarded as almost dishonest, although it is quite as important that society make use of the best opportunities in this respect as in using the latest scientific discoveries. This prejudice has in a considerable measure affected the attitude toward commerce in general compared with that toward production. Even economists who regard themselves as immune to the crude materialist fallacies of the past constantly commit the same mistake where activities directed toward the acquisition of such practical knowledge are concerned—apparently because in their scheme of things all such knowledge is supposed to be "given." The common idea now seems to be that all such knowledge should as a matter of course be readily at the command of everybody, and the reproach of irrationality leveled against the existing economic order is frequently based on the fact that it is not so available. This view disregards the fact that the method by which such knowledge can be made as widely available as possible is precisely the problem to which we have to find an answer.

THE PLANNER'S DILEMMA

If it is fashionable today to minimize the importance of the knowledge of the particular circumstances of time and place, this is closely connected with the smaller importance which is now attached to change as such. Indeed, there are few points on which the assumptions made (usually only implicitly) by the "planners" differ from those of their opponents as much as with regard to the significance and frequency of changes which will make substantial alterations of production plans necessary. Of course, if detailed economic plans could be laid down for fairly long periods in advance and then closely adhered to so that no further economic decisions of importance would be required, the task of drawing up a comprehensive plan governing all economic activity would be much less formidable.

It is, perhaps, worth stressing that economic problems arise always and only in consequence of change. As long as things continue as before, or at least as they were expected to, there arise no new problems requiring a decision, no need to form a new plan. The belief that changes, or at least day-to-day adjustments, have become less important in modern times implies the contention that economic problems also have become less important. This belief in the decreasing importance of change is, for that reason, usually held by the same people who argue that the importance of economic considerations has been driven into the background by the growing importance of technological knowledge.

Is it true that, with the elaborate apparatus of modern production, economic decisions are required only at long intervals, as when a new factory is to be erected or a new process to be introduced? Is it true that, once a plant has been built, the rest is all more or less mechanical, determined by the character of the plant, and leaving little to be changed in adapting to the ever changing circumstances of the moment?

The fairly widespread belief in the affirmative is not, as far as I can ascertain, borne out by the practical experience of the businessman. In a competitive industry at any rate—and such an industry alone can serve as a test—the task of keeping costs from rising requires constant struggle, absorbing a great part of the energy of the manager. How easy it is for an inefficient manager to dissipate the differentials on which profitability rests. A great variety in costs of production, even when using the same technical facilities, is commonplace in business experience but does not seem to be equally familiar to many economists. The very strength of the desire, constantly voiced by producers and engineers, to be allowed to proceed untrammeled by considerations of money costs, is eloquent testimony to the extent to which these factors enter into their daily work.

One reason why economists are increasingly apt to forget about the constant small changes which make up the whole economic picture is probably their growing preoccupation with statistical aggregates, which show a very much greater stability than the movements of the detail. The comparative stability of the aggregates cannot, however, be accounted for—as the statisticians occasionally seem to be inclined to do—by the "law of large numbers" or the mutual compensation of random changes. The number of elements with which we have to deal is not large enough for such accidental forces to produce stability. The continuous flow of goods and services is maintained by constant deliberate adjustments, by new dispositions made every day in the light of circumstances not known the day before, by B stepping in at once when A fails to deliver. Even the large and highly mechanized plant keeps going largely because of an environment upon which it can draw for all sorts of unexpected needs: tiles for its roof, stationery or its forms, and all the thousand and one kinds of equipment in which it cannot be self-contained and which the plans for the operation of the plant require to be readily available in the market.

I should also briefly mention the fact that the sort of knowledge with which I have been concerned is knowledge of the kind which by its nature cannot enter into statistics and therefore cannot be conveyed to any central authority in statistical form. The statistics which such a central authority would have to use would have to be arrived at precisely by abstracting and then lumping together items which differ as regards location, quality, and other particulars in ways that may be very significant for the specific decision. It follows from this that central planning which is based on statistical information cannot by its nature take direct account of these circumstances of time and place. The central planner will have to find some way to make decisions by leaving them to be made by the "man on the spot."

If we can agree that the economic problem of society is mainly one of rapid adaptation to changes in the particular circumstances of time and place, it would seem to follow that the ultimate decisions must be left to the people who are familiar with these circumstances, who know directly of the relevant changes and of the resources immediately available to meet them. We cannot expect that this problem will be solved by first communicating all this knowledge to a central board which, after integrating all knowledge, issues its orders. We must solve it by some form of decentralization.

But this answers only part of our problem. We need decentralization because only thus can we insure that the knowledge of the particular circumstances of time and place will be promptly used. The "man on the spot" cannot, however, decide solely on the basis of his limited but intimate knowledge of the facts of his immediate surroundings. There still remains the problem of communicating to him such further information as he needs to fit his decisions into the whole pattern of changes of the larger economic system.

USEFUL INDIVIDUAL KNOWLEDGE

How much knowledge does the individual need in order to make these decisions successfully? Which of the events beyond his own horizon of immediate knowledge are of relevance to his immediate decision, and how much of them need he know?

There is hardly anything that happens anywhere in the world that *might* not have an effect on the decision he ought to make. But he need not know of these events as such, nor of *all* their effects. It does not matter for him *why* more screws of one size than of another are wanted at the particular moment, *why* paper bags are more readily available than canvas bags, or *why* skilled labor, or particular machine tools, have for the moment become more difficult to obtain. All that is significant for him is *how much more or less* difficult to procure they have become compared with other things with which he is also concerned, or how much more or less urgently wanted are the alternative things he produces or uses. It is always a question of the relative importance of the particular things with which he is concerned, and the causes which alter their relative importance are of no interest to him beyond the effect on those concrete things of his own environment.

It is in this connection that what I have called the "economic calculus" (or the Pure Logic of Choice) helps us, at least by analogy, to see how this problem can be solved and is being solved by the price system. Even the single controlling mind, in possession of all the data for some small and self-contained economic system, would not—every time some small adjustment in the allocation of resources had to be made—go explicitly through all the relations between ends and means which might possibly be affected. It is indeed the great contribution of the Pure Logic of Choice to have demonstrated conclusively that even such a single mind could solve this kind of problem only by constructing and constantly using rates of equivalence (or "values," or "marginal rates of substitution"); that is, he would have to attach to each kind of scarce resource a numerical index which cannot be derived from any property possessed by that particular thing, but which reflects, or in which is condensed, its significance in view of the whole means-end structure. In any small change he will have to consider only these quantitative indices (or "values") in which all the relevant information is concentrated; and, by adjusting the quantities one by one, he can appropriately rearrange his dispositions without having to solve the whole puzzle *ab initio* or without needing at any stage to survey it at once in all its ramifications.

Fundamentally, in a system in which the knowledge of the relevant facts is dispersed among many people, prices can act to co-ordinate the separate actions of different people in the same way as subjective values help the individual to co-ordinate the parts of his plan.

"MIRACLE" OF THE PRICE SYSTEM

It is worth contemplating for a moment a very simple and commonplace instance of the action of the price system to see what precisely it accomplishes. Assume that somewhere in the world a new opportunity for the use of some raw material, say, tin, has arisen, or that one of the sources of supply of tin has been eliminated. It does not matter for our purpose—and it is significant that it does

not matter—which of these two causes has made tin more scarce. All that the users of tin need to know is that some of the tin they used to consume is now more
profitably employed elsewhere and that, in consequence, they must economize tin.
There is no need for the great majority of them even to know where the more urgent need has arisen, or in favor of what other needs they ought to husband the
supply. If only some of them know directly of the new demand and switch resources over to it, and if the people who are aware of the new gap thus created in
turn fill it from still other sources, the effect will rapidly spread throughout the
whole economic system. This influences not only all the uses of tin but also those
of its substitutes and the substitutes of these substitutes, the supply of all things
made of tin, and their substitutes, and so on. All this takes place without the great
majority of those instrumental in bringing about these substitutions knowing anything at all about the original cause of these changes. The whole acts as one market, not because any of its members surveys the whole field, but because their
limited individual fields of vision sufficiently overlap so that through many intermediaries the relevant information is communicated to all. The mere fact that
there is one price for any commodity—or rather that local prices are connected in
a manner determined by the cost of transport, etc.—brings about the solution
which (if conceptually possible) might have been arrived at by one single mind
possessing all the information which is in fact dispersed among all the people involved in the process.

We must look at the price system as such a mechanism for communicating
information if we want to understand its real function—a function which it fulfills
less perfectly as prices grow more rigid. (Even when quoted prices have become
quite rigid, however, the forces which would operate through changes in price still
operate to a considerable extent through changes in the other terms of the contract.) The most significant fact about this system is the economy of knowledge
with which it operates, or how little the individual participants need to know in
order to be able to take the right action. In abbreviated form, by a kind of symbol,
only the most essential information is passed on, and this is passed on only to
those concerned. It is more than a metaphor to describe the price system as a kind
of machinery for registering change, or a system of telecommunications which enables individual producers to watch merely the movement of a few pointers, as an
engineer might watch the hands of a few dials, in order to adjust their activities to
changes of which they may never know more than their reflection in the price
movement.

Of course, these adjustments are probably never "perfect" in the sense in
which the economist conceives of them in his equilibrium analysis. But I fear that
our theoretical habits of approaching the problem with the assumption of more or
less perfect knowledge on the part of almost everyone has made us somewhat
blind to the true function of the price mechanism and led us to apply rather misleading standards in judging its efficiency. The marvel is that in a case like that of
a scarcity of one raw material, without an order being issued, without more than
perhaps a handful of people knowing the cause, tens of thousands of people
whose identity could not be ascertained by months of investigation, are made to

use the material or its products more sparingly; that is, they move in the right direction. This is enough of a marvel even if, in a constantly changing world, not all will react so perfectly that their profit rates will always be maintained at the same "normal" level.

I have deliberately used the word "marvel" to shock the reader out of the complacency with which we often take the working of the price mechanism for granted. I am convinced that if it were the result of deliberate human design, and if the people guided by the price changes understood that their decisions have significance far beyond their immediate aim, this mechanism would have been acclaimed as one of the greatest triumphs of the human mind. Its misfortune is the double one that it is not the product of human design and that the people guided by it usually do not know why they are made to do what they do. But those who clamor for "conscious direction"—and who cannot believe that anything which has evolved without design (and even without our understanding it) can solve problems which we cannot solve consciously—should remember this: the problem is precisely how to extend our utilization of resources beyond the span of the control of any one mind; and, therefore, how to dispense with the need of conscious control, how to provide inducements which will make the individuals do the desirable things without anyone having to tell them what to do.

The problem which we meet here is by no means peculiar to economics but arises in connection with nearly all truly social phenomena, including language and most of our cultural inheritance, and constitutes really the central theoretical problem of all social science. As Alfred Whitehead has said in another connection, "It is a profoundly erroneous truism, repeated by all copy-books and by eminent people when they are making speeches, that we should cultivate the habit of thinking what we are doing. The precise opposite is the case. Civilization advances by extending the number of important operations which we can perform without thinking about them." This is of profound significance in the social field. We make constant use of formulas, symbols, and rules whose meaning we do not understand and through the use of which we avail ourselves of the assistance of knowledge which individually we do not possess. We have developed these practices by building upon habits and institutions which have proved successful in their own sphere and which have in turn become the foundation of the civilization we have built up.

The price system is just one of those formations which man has learned to use (though he is still very far from having learned to make the best use of it) *after he had stumbled upon it without understanding it.* Through it, not only a division of labor but also a co-ordinated utilization of resources based on a similarly divided knowledge has become possible. The people who like to deride any suggestion that this may be so usually distort the argument by insinuating that it asserts that by some miracle just that sort of system has spontaneously grown up which is best suited to modern civilization. It is the other way round: man has been able to develop that division of labor on which our civilization is based because he happened to stumble upon a method which made it possible. Had he not done so, he might still have developed some other, altogether different type of civilization, something like the "state" of the termite ants, or some other altogether unimaginable type. All that we can say is that nobody has yet succeeded in designing an alternative system in which certain features of the existing one can be preserved which are dear even to those who most violently assail it—such as particularly the extent to which the individual can choose his pursuits and consequently freely use his own knowledge and skill.

It is in many ways fortunate that the dispute about the indispensability of the price system for any rational calculation in a complex society is now no longer conducted entirely between camps holding different political views. The thesis that without the price system we could not preserve a society based on such extensive division of labor as ours was greeted with a howl of derision when it was first advanced by von Mises in the early 1920's. Today the difficulties which some still find in accepting it are no longer mainly political, and this makes for an atmosphere much more conducive to reasonable discussion. When we find Leon Trotsky arguing that "economic accounting is unthinkable without market relations"; when Professor Oscar Lange promises Professor von Mises a statue in the marble halls of the future Central Planning Board; and when Professor Abba P. Lerner rediscovers Adam Smith and emphasizes that the essential utility of the price system consists in inducing the individual, while seeking his own interest, to do what is in the general interest, the differences can indeed no longer be ascribed to political prejudice. The remaining dissent seems clearly to be due to purely intellectual, and more particularly methodological, differences.

3

Specific and General Knowledge, and Organizational Structure

Michael C. Jensen and William H. Meckling*

Specific knowledge is knowledge that is costly to transfer among agents and *general knowledge* is knowledge that is inexpensive to transmit. Because specific knowledge is costly to transfer, getting it used in decision-making requires decentralizing many decision rights in both the economy and in firms. Such delegation in turn creates two problems: the rights assignment problem (determining who should exercise a decision right), and the control or agency problem (ensuring that self-interested decision agents exercise their rights in a way that contributes to the organizational objective).

Capitalist economic systems solve the rights assignment and control problems by granting *alienability* of decision rights to decision agents. A right is alienable if its owner has the right to sell it and capture the proceeds offered in the exchange. Indeed, we define "ownership" to mean possession of a decision right along with the right to alienate that right, and we believe that when people use the word ownership that is what is they mean. This combination of a decision right with the right to alienate that right is also what is generally meant by the term "property right" that is so often used in economics.[1]

In contrast to markets, organizations generally do not delegate both decision rights and the alienability of those rights to the agent. A machine operator might be delegated the rights to operate and maintain a machine, but not the rights to sell it and pocket the proceeds. In the absence of alienability, organizations must solve both the rights assignment and control problems by setting up alternative systems and procedures. We discuss the critical role that alienability plays in the market system and some of the substitute control mechanisms used in firms.

*This article is a slightly revised version of an article by the same title that was published as Chapter 9 in *Contract Economics,* Lars Werin and Hans Wijkander, eds. (Oxford: Basil Blackwell Ltd., 1992). Our research has been supported by the Managerial Economics Research Center, University of Rochester, and the Division of Research, Harvard Business School. We are grateful for the comments and criticisms of George Baker, Robert Eccles, Lars Werin, and Karen Wruck.

From *Journal of Applied Corporate Finance,* Vol. 8, No. 2 (Summer): 4–18. Copyright © 1995 Journal of Applied Corporate Finance. Reprinted with permission.

COLLOCATION OF KNOWLEDGE AND DECISION AUTHORITY

F. A. Hayek was among the first economists to note the importance of knowledge and its distribution to a well-functioning economy. In his seminal article, "The Use of Knowledge in Society," Hayek argues that most economists, as well as advocates of centralized planning, misunderstand the nature of the economic problem. "The economic problem of society . . . is not merely a problem of how to allocate 'given' resources—if 'given' is taken to mean given to a single mind. . . . It is rather a problem of how to secure the best use of resources known to any of the members of society . . . a problem of the utilization of knowledge which is not given to anyone in its totality."[2] Hayek's insight was that an organization's performance depends on the collocation of decision-making authority with the knowledge important to those decisions.[3] He argues that the distribution of knowledge in society calls for decentralization:

> If we . . . agree that the economic problem of society is mainly one of rapid adaptation to changes in the particular circumstances of time and place . . . decisions must be left to the people who are familiar with these circumstances, who know directly of the relevant changes and of the resources immediately available to meet them. We cannot expect that this problem will be solved by first communicating all this knowledge to a central board which, after integrating all knowledge, issues its orders. We must solve it by some form of decentralization.[4]

Hayek's pioneering work provides a point of departure for analyzing how the distribution of knowledge affects organizational structure and its critical role in the development of a theory of organization. Hayek assumes that markets automatically move decision rights to the agents with the relevant knowledge, and that those agents will use the decision rights properly. Unfortunately, he never discusses how this occurs. We show how understanding this issue provides insights into the organizational and managerial problems of firms.

In the second section of this paper, we discuss the limits of human mental capacities and their implications for the costs of transferring knowledge. The third section defines the characteristics of decision rights and the different systems by which such rights are allocated. The fourth discusses the role of alienability in solving the rights assignment and control problems in markets, and the implications of this market solution for the internal problems faced by firms and other large organizations that cannot use alienability to solve the rights assignment and control problems. The fifth section discusses the problems of the firm in collocating decision rights and specific knowledge, the sixth discusses the technology for partitioning decision rights within the firm, and the seventh discusses corporate internal control systems.

KNOWLEDGE

The opportunity set confronting an individual or a firm is a function of the individual's knowledge. Decision-makers confront the limits of their knowledge at two levels. One is "technological feasibility," by which we mean the limits to human knowledge about physical laws. Most economic analysis effectively sidesteps this issue by assuming a given, fixed level of technological knowledge.

The second limitation on knowledge, and the one of primary concern here, arises from those limitations that are specific to each individual.[5] Humans have limited mental capability. The computers and sensory systems with which we are individually endowed are a scarce resource with limited storage and processing capability, as well as limited input and output channels. The limitations on human mental and sensory faculties mean that storing, processing, transmitting, and receiving knowledge are costly activities.

This limited capacity of the brain means that knowledge possessed by any individual decision-maker or group of decision-makers is thereby limited to a minuscule subset of the knowledge known to humanity. While decision-makers seldom, if ever, possess all available knowledge, they are constantly creating new knowledge. In maximizing their own objective functions, decision-makers deliberately seek out knowledge (including knowledge about what decisions to consider).

When knowledge is valuable in decision-making, there are benefits to collocating decision authority with the knowledge that is valuable in making those decisions. There are two basic ways to accomplish such a collocation of knowledge and decision rights. One is by moving the knowledge to those with the decision rights; the other is by moving the decision rights to those with the knowledge. The process for moving knowledge to those with decision rights has received much attention from researchers and designers of management information systems. But the process for moving decision rights to those with the relevant knowledge has received relatively little attention in either economics or management science.

In a market system, collocation of decision rights and knowledge is accomplished either when those with decision rights spend time and resources to acquire the knowledge or when those with knowledge buy the decision rights. When the cost of moving knowledge is higher than the cost of moving decision rights, knowledge holders will value the decision rights more highly and will thus tend to purchase them. In this way, optimizing behavior on the part of individuals causes the distribution of decision-making rights in the economy to reflect the limitations of human mental and sensory systems.

Knowledge and the Cost of Transfer

The cost of transferring knowledge depends on factors such as the nature of the knowledge, the organizational environment, and technology. We use the terms "specific" and "general" knowledge to distinguish between knowledge at the extremes of the continuum measuring transfer costs. The more costly is knowledge to transfer, the more specific it is; the less costly to transfer, the more general.

"Transfer," as we use it, means *effective* transfer, not merely "communication." The recipient of knowledge is assumed to understand the message well enough to act on it. The simple purchase of a physics book is not sufficient to transfer the knowledge to the purchaser (as evidenced by students who regularly pay thousands of dollars for help in acquiring such knowledge). Thus, transfer involves the use of storage and processing capacity as well as input/output channels of the human brain. Moreover, knowledge transfers are not instantaneous: it takes people time to absorb information. These delays are costly; and for some decisions such costs can be high, including even the complete loss of opportunities.

Hayek's 1945 article takes the distribution of knowledge in the economy as given and thus never mentions the costs of transferring or producing knowledge. Nevertheless, the significance of such information costs are the logical foundation of his analysis.[6] Writing during the 1940s' debate in Britain over central planning, Hayek attacks central planners on the grounds that they will make bad decisions because they will not (indeed they cannot) have the knowledge of "particular circumstances of time and place" necessary to make the best decisions. As examples of such "idiosyncratic" knowledge, he cites knowledge of the existence and location of the following: a not-fully-employed machine, someone's particular skills, surplus stock, empty or half-filled freighters, temporary opportunities in real estate, and commodity price differences.

As Hayek points out, conveying knowledge of such particular circumstances to a central authority in statistical form is impossible. Aggregating or lumping together items such as location or quality destroys their usefulness for specific decisions. Adding up the quantity of empty spaces in steamers or logs in widely scattered wood piles, for example, eliminates the information about time and location that is so valuable in periods of transportation or energy shortages.

Specific knowledge—of which such "idiosyncratic" knowledge of particular circumstances is an example—is often acquired jointly with the production of other goods. When knowledge is a by-product of activities that will be performed anyway, the cost of that knowledge to the acquirer is nil. Other examples of idiosyncratic knowledge include knowledge of the specific skills or preferences of individuals, of the peculiarities of specific machines, of particular unemployed resources or inventories, and of arbitrage opportunities. Such knowledge, almost by definition, is difficult or impossible to aggregate and summarize.

Thus, while the initial costs of acquiring idiosyncratic knowledge tend to be modest, the costs of transferring such information are likely to be high relative to the benefits. Because time is often important in taking advantage of opportunities for arbitrage or for exploiting knowledge of unemployed resources, delays in actions are costly.

Uncertainty about what specific piece of idiosyncratic knowledge will prove valuable also enlarges transfer costs in a subtle way. After the fact, it is often obvious that a specific piece of knowledge critical to a decision could have been transferred at low cost (for example, particular quirks of an organization, person, legal rule, or custom). But transferring this specific piece of knowledge in advance requires knowing in advance that it will be critical. Without such clairvoyance, transfer of the fact must occur as part of a larger and more costly-to-transfer body of knowledge, most of which will never be used. The expected cost of transferring that larger body of data, not the particular fact, is the relevant transfer cost.

Although knowledge of particular circumstances of time and place and idiosyncratic knowledge cannot be summarized in statistics, they can be transmitted to other locations in the decision-making structure. The question is not *whether* knowledge can be transferred, but at *what cost* it can be transferred, and whether it is worth it to do so. Transfers yield benefits when the additional knowledge enables the decision-maker to make better choices. The issue is whether decisions will be improved enough to warrant the transfer costs.

Quantities and prices are good examples of general knowledge. Unlike idiosyncratic or other specific knowledge, quantities are easily aggregated and transferred among agents at low cost. Prices, which are also easily communicated among agents, are signals that communicate a large amount of information inexpensively. When a price rises, people know it is appropriate to conserve the commodity—and they need not know why its relative supply has shrunk.

Of course, we do observe situations in which collocation of knowledge and decision rights is achieved by transferring knowledge. Formal educational programs and the collection, analysis, and dissemination of data are obvious examples. United and American Airlines achieved a major competitive advantage with computerized reservation and pricing systems that reduced the cost of transferring knowledge about prices, empty seats, and schedules. Particularly challenging information transfer problems arise in situations where optimal decision-making requires integration of specific knowledge possessed by different individuals performing traditionally quite separate corporate functions. One good example is integration of the specific knowledge of marketing, manufacturing, and R&D personnel required to design and bring a new product to market. The fairly recent move to cross-functional teams by many large corporations is a response to such high information-transfer costs.

While the general applicability of scientific knowledge distinguishes it from idiosyncratic knowledge, scientific knowledge is also costly to transfer and thus it too falls in the category of specific knowledge. Science creates order out of chaos by abstracting from particulars and providing general rules of cause and effect. Scientific knowledge is an essential ingredient in decisions because it provides the basis for predicting the outcomes of alternative courses of action.

At the level of the firm, scientific knowledge plays a central role in resolving the key questions that economists address from a macro or economy-wide perspective—notably, what to produce and how to produce it. For example, the design and development of products from machinery and buildings to household appliances and drugs depend critically on scientific knowledge.

In addition to scientific and idiosyncratic knowledge, knowledge produced by assembling and analyzing knowledge of particular circumstances (through time and/or across circumstances such as location, income, education, age) is a significant input to decision-making. For example, the entrepreneur who wants to capitalize on a particular half-filled freighter must be able to identify the freighter, its location, and its cargo capability. On the other hand, someone deciding whether to found a business to increase the utilization of freighters will want to assemble knowledge about how many partially-filled freighters there are, what routes they follow, what kinds of cargo capacity they have, and so on—knowledge that abstracts from the particular circumstances crucial to making full use of a particular freighter. Assembled knowledge includes, but is not limited to, that generated by formal statistical methods.

Assembled knowledge also includes knowledge gained from experience. The exercise of skills such as machine operation, writing, mathematics, or statistics are examples. Knowledge of law, of accounting practices, of contracting practices, and of the rules that govern the operation of organized exchanges are all potentially important inputs to decision-making. Assembled knowledge can be either general (as is likely to be true of the output of statistical manipulation of basic data) or specific (as is likely to be true of knowledge from experience).

RIGHTS SYSTEMS

A decision right is the right to decide on and take an action. Decision rights are the basis for saying that individuals have the "power" to make decisions and to take actions with resources. Power means that a decision made by a party will be operative. In modern societies, the ultimate source of this power is the police powers—the threat of physical violence by the state. An entity or person has the right to take an action with a specific object if the police powers of the state will be used to help ensure its ability to take the action. The right to choose what action will be taken is an important part of possessing a right. (The word "right" in this context, incidentally, has no normative content.)

In any developed social system, the right to take actions with specific physical objects, including our persons, is assigned to specific individuals or organizations. In a private property capitalist system, most of these rights are assigned to private individuals or organizations. In a socialist or communist system, most of these rights are assigned to the state or the governing party.

Although rarely emphasized,[7] the usual economic analysis of the price system is founded on the existence of a system of privately "owned" rights. There are two actions of special importance that are an integral part of ownership of a right in a resource: the right to sell the resource (more accurately, to sell rights in the resource) and the right to capture the proceeds of the sale.[8] Thus, the objects of exchange in markets are not physical articles per se, but bundles of rights attached to those articles.[9] It is this system of *alienable rights* (almost universally mislabelled "the price system" in our profession) that extends the efficient utilization of resources beyond the capacity of any single mind. It provides incentives to make individuals take appropriate actions without anyone having to direct them.[10] This is what Adam Smith meant by the "invisible hand," and his fundamental insight was that control of human behavior is inherent in the operation of markets.

The assignment of decision-making rights in modern societies is largely a matter of law.[11] But once assigned, rights are regularly reshuffled by contracts, by purchase and sale, and by managerial assignment within firms. In the United States, the body of law that spells out the assignment of rights is the product of hundreds of years of law-making of three sorts: court decisions (common law), legislative enactments (statutory law, including constitutions), and administrative decrees (administrative law).

The private-property capitalist mechanism is the product of thousands of years of evolution. It is highly complex and embraces a multitude of actions, objects, and individuals. Most important, however, it functions as a free-standing system. It is automatic; there is no central direction. With minor exceptions, rights to take almost all conceivable actions with virtually all physical objects are fixed on identifiable individuals or firms at every instant of time. The books are kept up to date despite the burden imposed by dynamic forces such as births and deaths, dissolutions, and new technology. Disputes arise, but evolution has provided a sophisticated arbitration service—namely, the courts—to deal with that problem as well. The extent to which the legal system enforces property rights (that is, once again, the security of decision rights and the right to alienate them) is a major determinant of the effectiveness of markets.

The failure of socialist and communist economies (whose distinguishing characteristic is the absence of private property rights) is now the topic of headlines throughout the world. The difficulties that Eastern bloc countries are having in attempting to establish capitalist market systems to replace their failed systems is testimony to the complexity and value of market systems.[12] These economies provide vivid evidence of the inefficiency and poverty that result from the waste of specific knowledge and the lack of control in the absence of alienable decision rights. Without the assignment of private alienable rights, there can be no true market system. Thus, given the failure of most Eastern bloc countries to establish alienable private rights in resources, it is not surprising that many of them are failing in their attempt to create effective market systems.

THE FUNCTIONS OF ALIENABILITY

Alienability is the effective combination of two rights: the right to sell or transfer rights and the right to capture the proceeds of exchange.[13] Alienability is not only a necessary condition for exchange, it is the foundation of markets and the institutional device by which markets both (1) collocate knowledge with decision rights and (2) exercise control over decision makers. The alienability of rights deserves special attention in analyzing both markets and organizations because understanding the function of alienability in markets clarifies several critical functions that must be performed inside organizations.

Alienability Solves the Rights Assignment Problem. When decision rights are alienable, voluntary exchange creates a process in which the purchase and sale of rights by maximizing individuals collocates knowledge and decision rights. It does so by conveying decision rights to the site of knowledge.

In a market system, decision rights are acquired through exchange by those who have knowledge. Voluntary exchange ensures that decision rights will tend to be acquired by those who value them most highly, and this will be those who have specific knowledge and abilities that are most valuable to the exercise of the right.

Alienability Solves the Control Problem. By the word "control" we mean the process and the rules that govern both the measures of performance used to evaluate individuals' actions, and the rewards and punishments meted out to those individuals as a consequence. Control and knowledge are complements in the analysis of organizations. The knowledge and decision rights possessed by the individual, together with the state of the world, define the opportunity set from which individual decision-makers can choose. The control system plays a major role in determining which choices individuals make from their opportunity sets.

By collocating decision rights with rights to their capital value, alienability provides both a measure of performance for individual decision-makers and the rewards and punishments to motivate them to use those decision rights efficiently. Market prices for alienable rights reveal the value of assets in alternative uses to current as well as potential holders of those rights. In cases where resources produce future flows of revenue or consumption services, and rights to those flows are alienable, prices represent the present value of claims to those future flows. These capitalized values perform two important functions in controlling human behavior.

- They provide a measure of the performance of the parties who have the rights to decide how the asset or assets will be used.
- They provide the reward or punishment that accrues to the owners of the rights as a result of their decisions.

The collocation of decision rights with rights to their capital value accomplished by alienability thus both measures the performance of individuals and brings the (capitalized) wealth consequences of an individual's decisions to bear upon that person. The decision-maker who chooses an action that lowers the value of rights assigned to him or her bears the costs of so doing. When the decision-maker chooses actions that enhance the value of the rights, he or she captures the increased value.

The major problems with the market control system occur when the legal or technological environments create "externalities" by not allowing for the definition and assignment of rights that cause an individual to bear the full costs or to capture the full rewards of his or her actions. Pollution and non-patentable inventions are two good examples of situations in which decision-makers do not bear the full costs or receive the full benefits of their actions.

The problems that arose in organizing production in Eastern bloc countries without alienability highlight the importance of alienability to issues of organizational design and efficiency. But the internal organization of the capitalist firm is also an example of the suppression of alienable decision rights. Indeed, we distinguish activities within the firm from activities between the firm and the rest of the world by whether alienability is transferred to agents along with the decision rights.

In this view, transfers of decision rights without the right to alienate those rights are *intra-firm* transactions. While firms can sell assets, workers in firms generally do not receive the rights to alienate their positions or any other assets or decision rights under their control. They cannot pocket the proceeds. This means there is no automatic decentralized process that tends to ensure that decision rights in the firm migrate to the agents who have the specific knowledge relevant to their exercise. It also means there is no automatic performance measurement and reward system that motivates agents to use their decision rights in ways that promote the interests of the organization. Explicit managerial direction and the creation of mechanisms are required to substitute for alienability.

The Existence of Firms

Pushed to its logical extreme, our focus on specific knowledge implies more or less complete atomization of the economy. There is no room for the firm. Firms as we know them would not exist if alienability of all decision rights were granted to each agent along with the rights. There would be nothing left over for the residual claimants in the enterprise, be they entrepreneurs, partners, or stockholders.

Firms must obtain advantages from the suppression of alienability that are large enough to offset the costs associated with its absence, or they could not survive open competition with independent agents. Such advantages could come from economies of scale or scope, or from the reduction of transaction costs that could not be obtained by independent contracting agents.

Knowledge considerations are one reason for the emergence of firms.[14] By bringing diverse kinds and sources of knowledge to bear on decisions, the existence of a firm significantly expands the collective opportunity set for all because no one person is likely to possess the entire set of knowledge relevant to a particular decision.

In principle, it's true, an entrepreneur could assemble the relevant knowledge by individual exchanges, and knowledge transfer on a *quid pro quo* basis is not an uncommon phenomenon. Consulting and legal services provide obvious examples of such outsourcing, and so do the network organizations growing in the U.S. that contract out most internal functions common to organizations.[15] But where the production, transfer, and application of knowledge are the primary goods being offered, exchanges tend to take the form of long-term relationships. The most common of these is employment contracts. Such contracts tend to be general in nature—the contents of the exchange are not precisely specified—and they are seldom alienable. Transaction costs are one reason for the prevalence of such contracts.[16] Single proprietors who contract on a case-by-case basis for production and application of all knowledge would soon find themselves swamped by transaction costs in all but the smallest-scale firms.

The value of proprietary knowledge to competitors or potential competitors is another reason for long-term employment relationships. Longer-term contracts reduce the costs of restricting the flow of valuable knowledge to outsiders. Finally, longer-run relationships encourage individual participants to invest in firm-specific knowledge that has little or no value except within the particular organization.

The suppression of alienability, while necessary for the existence of a firm, does impose costs. Nevertheless, we believe that those costs can be reduced by thorough understanding and analysis of the functions performed by alienability.

The franchise organization, a rapidly growing sector of the American economy, is a good example of a mixture of firm and market systems that uses alienability of rights as part of the control system. A franchise contract sells the right to manage a divisional profit center to a manager for a franchise fee. The manager receives the capital value right to the residual cash flows, subject to an annual royalty payment and contractual provisions limiting his decision rights in various areas.[17] Most important for our purposes, the manager receives the right to alienate the franchise contract by sale to others. The contract often restricts alienation rights in various ways—for example, by the right of the franchiser to approve the purchaser.

The advantage of alienability as a control device is that it rewards and punishes agents by imposing on them the capitalized value of the future costs and benefits of their decisions. In the absence of arm's-length transactions, this is difficult to accomplish inside a firm. Nevertheless, there are mechanisms for providing within companies the functions that alienability normally provides in markets. We turn now to a discussion of these substitute mechanisms and how they help to solve the organizational problems of the firm.

THE ORGANIZATIONAL PROBLEMS OF THE FIRM: TRADE-OFFS BETWEEN INFORMATION COSTS AND AGENCY COSTS

We have seen how alienability solves the rights assignment and control problems in the economy. Recognizing that firms, by definition, can make relatively little internal use of alienability enables us to see clearly the problems faced by every firm in constructing substitute mechanisms. The assignment and enforcement of decision rights in organizations are a matter of organizational policy and practice, not voluntary exchange among agents.

In principle, the modern corporation vests all decision rights in the board of directors and the chief executive's offices. Decision rights are partitioned out to individuals and to organizational units by the rules established by top-level management and the board of directors. The chief executive's office enforces the rules by rewarding those who follow them and punishing those who violate them. These assignment and enforcement powers are constrained in important ways by the laws and regulations of the state and by social custom.

Every CEO, including a benevolent despot with the power to direct the economy, confronts the rights assignment and control problems of organizational structure discussed above. The limitations of his or her own mental and communication abilities make it impossible for the CEO to gather the requisite information to make every detailed decision personally. Any CEO attempting to do so in a large, complex organization will commit major errors. In delegating authority to maximize survival, the CEO wants to partition the decision rights out among agents in the organization so as to maximize their aggregate value.

Ideally, as we have seen, assigning decision rights to maximize value means collocating decision responsibility with the knowledge that is valuable in making particular decisions. In practice, however, accomplishing such collocation of decision rights with knowledge within organizations is more difficult than in markets. In markets, as we have seen, those with the most knowledge tend to acquire the decision rights by purchasing them. In organizations, by contrast, assigning decision rights requires consideration of the costs of generating and transferring knowledge in the organization, and how the assignment of decision rights affects incentives to acquire information.

Because they are ultimately self-interested, the agents to whom the CEO delegates authority have objective functions that diverge from his or her own. The costs resulting from such conflicts of interest in cooperative behavior are commonly called "agency costs." Because agency costs inevitably result from the delegation of decision rights, the CEO must devise a control system (a set of rules) that fosters desirable behavior.

It is generally impossible, however, to structure an incentive and control system that will cause agents to behave exactly as the CEO wishes. In addition, control and incentive systems are costly to design and implement. Agency costs are the sum of the costs of designing, implementing, and maintaining appropriate incentive and control systems as well as the residual loss resulting from the difficulty of solving these problems completely.[18]

Figure 3-1 provides an intuitive way to think about the trade-offs associated with assigning a particular decision right to different levels in the organization's hierarchy. The vertical axis measures costs and the horizontal axis measures the distance of the decision right from the CEO's office (measured by levels of hierarchy) in a simple, hierarchically-structured organization. For simplicity, Figure 3-1 abstracts from the decision regarding where the right is assigned within a given level of the hierarchy,[19] and thus deals with the age-old debate over centralization versus decentralization in organizations.

Determining the optimal level of decentralization requires balancing the costs of bad decisions due to poor information and those due to inconsistent objectives. The costs attributable to poor information plotted in Figure 3-1 measure the costs of acquiring information plus the costs of poor decisions made because it is too expensive to acquire all relevant information. In the extreme case of a completely centralized organization (located at the origin on the horizontal axis), the costs owing to poor information are the high while the agency costs owing to inconsistent objectives are zero.[20]

The costs owing to poor information fall as the CEO delegates the decision right to lower levels in the organization. They fall because the decision right is exercised by agents that have more specific knowledge relevant to the decision. We

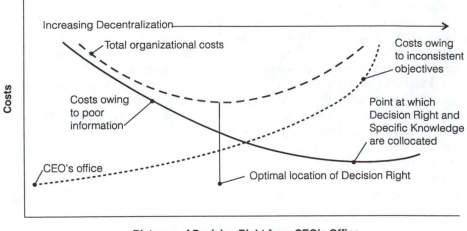

Distance of Decision Right from CEO's Office

FIGURE 3-1   Determining the optimal level of decentralization.

assume for simplicity that the hierarchy and both cost functions are continuous. We assume the costs owing to inconsistent objectives increase monotonically and at an increasing rate as the right is assigned to lower levels, and that these costs are conditioned on optimal controls at each alternative rights assignment. We also assume that the cost owing to poor information has a unique minimum. By definition this minimum must occur where the right is collocated with the specific knowledge relevant to the decision.

Total organizational costs plotted in Figure 3-1 are the sum of the costs owing to poor information and the costs owing to inconsistent objectives. They are high at the completely centralized allocation and decline as the right is moved down in the hierarchy to where more relevant specific knowledge is located. In Figure 3-1 the vertical line marks the optimal location of the decision right. It occurs where the decrease in the cost owing to poor information just offsets the increase in the cost owing to inconsistent objectives (the point where the absolute values of the slopes of the two curves are equal).

Specific knowledge exists at all levels of the organization, not just at lower levels. For example, a machine operator often has specific knowledge of a particular machine's operating idiosyncrasies, but the chief financial officer is likely to have the specific knowledge relevant to the capital structure decision. The CEO may often have the best specific knowledge of the strategic challenges and opportunities facing the firm. The key to efficiency is to assign decision rights to each agent at each level in such a way that minimizes the sum of the costs owing to poor information and the costs owing to inconsistent objectives. Figure 3-1 illustrates that, even at the optimum, an organization will be making poor decisions due to both poor information and the conflicts that arise from inconsistent objectives.

Factors Affecting the Degree of Decentralization

The optimal degree of decentralization depends on factors like the size of the organization, information technology (including computers, communications, and travel), the rate of change in the environment, government regulation, and the control technology. In general, as the size of a firm increases, the sum of the cost owing to poor information and the cost owing to inconsistent objectives rises. When the marginal costs owing to poor information rise more rapidly with size than the marginal costs owing to inconsistent objectives, the optimal degree of decentralization rises.

Changes in information technology have an ambiguous effect on the optimal degree of decentralization. The direction of the effect depends on which kinds of information are most affected. When improved technology makes it easier to transfer specific knowledge effectively from lower to higher levels in the organization, there will be a shift toward centralization. Mrs. Fields Cookies is an example of a firm where technological development made it possible for headquarters to obtain detailed and timely information on store operations and to provide very detailed day-by-day, even hour-by-hour, directions on operating decisions in its company-owned stores.[21]

Conversely, when improved technology makes it easier to transfer to lower levels in the organization information that was formerly specific to higher levels in the organization, there will be a shift toward decentralization. J. C. Penney's investment in satellite communications provided the firm with closed circuit TV that made it possible to decentralize much of the store purchasing decisions from corporate headquarters to the local store managers. The TV system made it possible for central buyers in New York to display and "market" the goods to local store managers, who could then use their specific knowledge of local tastes and fashions in stocking their stores.[22]

Increased governmental regulation tends to increase centralization. It does so by increasing the amount of specific knowledge in the headquarters office dealing with the regulatory agency. Improvements in control technology—such as communication and measurement techniques that reduce the marginal agency costs associated with delegating decision rights—will tend to increase decentralization in an organization.

Our characterization of decision rights so far has been overly simple. It is relatively uncommon in large organizations for agents to have the total rights to make any major decision in the way we normally think about decisions. Instead, decisions are normally made by a process in which *decision management* and *decision control* rights are assigned to different individuals within the firm. Decision management rights are the rights to initiate and implement recommendations for resource allocations. Decision control rights are the rights to ratify initiatives and to monitor the implementation of resource commitments.[23] Although we do not have space to pursue the issue here, the analysis portrayed in Figure 3-1 can be applied to the assignment of both decision management and decision control rights. For example, when the relevant specific knowledge for decision control lies at a lower level in the organization (such as the knowledge that would be used in the performance evaluation and bonus-setting process for lower-level managers), some decentralization of control rights is optimal.

In sum, the CEO in the typical firm cannot generally use alienability to solve the firm's organizational problems. He cannot delegate the alienability of decision rights to decision agents without thereby converting them into independent firms. Organizational problems within the firm must therefore be solved by substitute means. This is accomplished by devising a set of internal "rules of the game" for the firm that:

- partition out the decision-making rights to agents throughout the organization;
- create a control system that
    provides measures of performance;
    specifies the relationship between rewards and punishments and the measures of performance.

This is a simple but remarkably powerful list. While there are many factors that determine the behavior of any individual organization, our empirical observations indicate that knowledge of these "rules of the game" enables one to make good predictions about an organization's behavior and effectiveness. We now consider common organizational devices for implementing these organizational rules of the game.

THE TECHNOLOGY FOR PARTITIONING DECISION RIGHTS IN THE FIRM

The techniques available for structuring activities within the firm are a product of evolution, as is the system of rights for the economy as a whole. What has evolved is a complex body of managerial technology that is employed in assigning decision rights and in controlling behavior within the firm. Scientific understanding of that technology is rudimentary, but we can describe some of its major components and their use.

Job Descriptions and Internal Common Law

Decision rights are allocated to agents within firms in various ways. Many are allocated directly to individuals or positions through job descriptions (and these descriptions are often the best source of written documentation of the assignment of decision rights in an organization). Examples include the right to make pricing, hiring, or promotion decisions, the rights to initiate recommendations for resource allocation, to ratify or monitor the initiatives of others, or to implement particular programs.[24] The allocations of decision rights to individuals change over time as the organization and individuals change. These rights assignments occur both formally and informally, and are associated with committee memberships and project assignments as well as the organization's internal "regulatory" and "common law" traditions.

Budgeting

Physical and monetary budgets are common techniques for partitioning decision rights in firms. Agents can be given decision rights over the use of physical resources, such as capital equipment or building space. The rights allocated through such physical budgets are less complete and therefore more constraining than are decision rights allocated by the grant of monetary budgets. Dollar budget authorizations tend to be used when the intent is to grant some discretion in the choice of inputs. When rights are allocated through monetary budgets without side constraints, decision agents have the opportunity to sell or exchange assets, and therefore to substitute among them. The organization is better off to the extent that managers use their specific knowledge to make substitutions that increase the efficiency of the organization.

Nevertheless, budgets denominated in money terms are frequently constrained in ways that deny managers the opportunity to substitute. These "line" budgets, which are commonly used in government as well as industry, are broken down in great detail and the recipient is specifically forbidden from transferring funds from one category to another. Under such budgets the manager's ability to use his or her specific knowledge to increase efficiency is obviously restricted. Such restrictions can be optimal if the specific knowledge relevant to making these substitutions lies at a higher level in the organization. This occurs, for example, when there are external effects on other parts of the organization that cannot be incorporated in the manager's performance measure, but can be incorporated in the performance measure at a higher level of the organization.

Budgets can be fixed or variable. They are fixed if the amount of authorized spending is independent of the level of activity or of performance. Under a variable performance budget, spending authority is a specified function of performance or activity levels—for example a fraction of revenues. (The "each tub on its own bottom" budgeting systems of some universities are examples of variable performance-related budgets.) While variable budget allocations have substantial incentive effects (because most agents prefer to have control over more resources), these incentive effects often seem to be ignored in practice.

Budgets are usually accompanied by side constraints. Physical resource budgets, for example, are commonly restricted to use rights; that is, the recipient is not allowed to sell the resources and retain the proceeds. Diversion of dollars or physical resources to personal use (except that specified as compensation) is also prohibited. Manpower or head count limitations that are independent of the dollars available are another example of a separate constraint.

Rules, Regulations or Fiat

The rules and regulations that accompany budgets are examples of regulatory constraints on behavior that exist because employees are self-interested. Such constraints imposed by fiat are the most primitive form of control technology. Like line budgets, they control behavior by circumscribing in advance the opportunity set from which a decision-maker can choose. But unless the regulator is omniscient, such rules will eliminate superior as well as inferior courses of action because they are made without the specific knowledge that lies at the local level. In this sense, control by regulation tends to disregard the advantage of collocating knowledge and decision rights at the local level. Regulations are efficient control devices when the budget office has the relevant specific knowledge or where the prohibited behavior—for example, theft or embezzlement—is clearly not consistent with the objectives of the CEO.

THE CONTROL SYSTEM

Because all individuals in a firm are self-interested, simply delegating decision rights to them and dictating the objective function each is to maximize is not sufficient to accomplish the objective. A control system that ties the individual's interest more closely to that of the organization is required. The control system specifies (1) the performance measurement and evaluation system for each subdivision of the firm and each decision agent, and (2) the reward and punishment system that relates individuals' rewards to their performance.

In a real sense, specification of the performance measurement and evaluation system *is* specification of the objective function, although a surprising number of organizations seem to fail to recognize this point. Self-interest motivates individuals to discover and understand the performance measures and evaluation system on which their rewards and punishments depend. It does not take them long to discover when the rewarded objective is different from that which is stated.

Cost Centers and Profit Centers as Performance Measurement Systems

Cost centers and profit centers embody two widely used divisional performance measurement rules. Cost centers are subdivisions that are directed to minimize the total cost of providing a specified quantity of service. Manufacturing divisions are frequently organized as cost centers. Mathematically (and in the absence of information or agency problems), minimizing total cost for a given quantity of output is equivalent to maximizing output for a given total cost. In addition, both are consistent with maximizing the value of the firm if the correct output constraint is chosen.

In the presence of information and agency problems, however, the two formulations are not equivalent. Minimizing cost for given total output often seems to degenerate into a system where managers are rewarded for minimizing *average* cost per unit of output. And, in the absence of a quantity constraint, measuring performance by average cost per unit of output will virtually never be consistent with firm value maximization. A decision manager with such an objective will strive to achieve the output quantity that minimizes average cost even though it bears no relation to the value-maximizing quantity.

The tendency of firms to divisionalize along product lines appears to be influenced by control considerations. Product subdivisions are often operated as profit centers, where the measure of performance is the difference between some measure of revenues and costs. Profit centers are more independent than cost centers: their budgets are more likely to be variable than those of cost centers, and this generally means fewer knowledge demands on the CEO. The scale of operations of the center then varies directly with revenues, and does not require the same forecasting accuracy as a fixed-dollar budget would require.

The reduction in knowledge required to monitor a division organized as a profit center is particularly evident where the products are sold in outside markets. Here the CEO can use competition in outside markets as a part of the control system. Competition and the ability of the division's customers to purchase from others provide the CEO with a performance measure for the product division—namely, profits—that incorporates consumers' assessment of quality, timeliness, and value. Internal transfer pricing systems in which buyers have the right to purchase from any source also allow the CEO to decentralize to the buyers an important part of the control system. Such decentralization is optimal to the extent that specific knowledge of product and service quality lies with the buyers and is costly to observe from higher in the hierarchy.

But neither profit centers nor cost centers are panaceas for the CEO's organizational problems. Cost centers, for example, tend to lead to problems of quantity and quality control. Measured on the cost of output for a fixed quantity, division managers are motivated to reduce cost by reducing quality. Preventing this requires quality to be cheaply observable from higher in the hierarchy. To the extent that quality is easily observable, cost centers will tend to be more desirable. Divisions where quantity is difficult or impossible to measure (such as computer services) are difficult to run as cost centers because the manager can simply reduce the quantity of service to lower cost.

The Role of Budgets in Performance Measurement

Budgets are related to performance measurement in several ways. Budgets are sometimes used to delegate decision rights, but they are also used as targets in the performance measurement system—for example, as expenditure or revenue targets. In these cases, the amount by which expenditures are less than the targets and by which revenues exceed targets are favorable performance measures.

We have two major points about the use of budgets in performance evaluation. The first is fairly straightforward: When budgets are used to delegate decision rights, measures of violations of budgeted expenditures must be part of performance measurement if expenditure limits are to have meaning. Indeed, violations of any rules, regulations, or fiat must affect performance measures and rewards and punishments if the constraints are to affect behavior.

Our second point is that the use of some kinds of budgets can cause major problems for large organizations. Take the case of the budget-target system known as *strategic business planning*. In this widely-used system, performance is measured by how close the results are to a plan whose targets are typically "negotiated" between corporate headquarters and division heads.

Such a budget-target system poses problems because its success depends critically on setting correct plans or targets for each division and decision agent. This in turn imposes enormous knowledge requirements on the central staff that must do the planning. When much of the required specific knowledge is located at lower levels in the organization and involves high cost to transfer to the central planning staff, strategic business planning will be inefficient. When such knowledge is important, the result of centrally devised targets will be poor plans and strategic business planning will generate large organizational costs.

In short, strategic business planning is the private organizational version of central planning in the market system. And much as central planning has failed in most countries, the practice of strategic business planning (at least as defined as a system that measures performance against pre-set targets) has contributed to the failure of many large American corporations over the past two decades.[25]

Measuring, Rewarding, and Punishing Individual Performance

The performance measurements discussed previously are all *group* measures. But the CEO's measurement problem is not simply one of measuring group performance. In the end, he or she must reward and punish individuals.

For a sizable organization, the CEO cannot literally either review the performance of every individual or decide on his or her specific rewards. Inevitably, the CEO will delegate much of the responsibility for measuring and rewarding performance and will promulgate rules or policies that control the decisions of those to whom authority is delegated. The CEO can, for example, tie individual rewards to individual performance by direct pay-for-performance systems (and here the sensitivity of the relation between pay and performance is a major decision variable), or by promotions that depend on performance. Individual rewards can be tied to group performance by creating bonus pools that are a function of group performance or by setting up profit-sharing plans, employees stock ownership plans, stock option plans, or phantom stock plans.

We have observed a longstanding tendency for large organizations to avoid pay-for-performance incentive plans and to rely instead on promotion-based rewards.[26] Although this phenomenon is as yet poorly understood by economists, our belief is that promotion-based systems will turn out to be a relic of an older era of centralization and technological stability. Factors such as more rapid technological change and more intense global competition—when coupled with the long-term tendency of most organizations to become even larger (even as the need increases for downsizing and exit in maturing industries)—have made decentralization of corporate decision-making a more valuable strategy in the past decade or so. And as decentralization of corporate decision rights becomes more valuable, our prediction is that many firms will choose (or be forced) to replace their promotion-based systems with significantly greater use of the incentives held out by profit-sharing and stock ownership.

CONCLUSIONS

This paper analyzes the relations between knowledge, control, and organizational structure, both in the market system as a whole and in private organizations. The limited capacity of the human mind and the costs of producing and transferring knowledge mean that knowledge relevant to all decisions can never be located in a single individual or body of experts. Thus, if knowledge valuable to a particular decision is to be used in making that decision, there must be a system for assigning decision rights to individuals who have the knowledge and abilities or who can acquire or produce them at low cost. In addition, self-interest on the part of individual decision-makers means that a control system is required to motivate individuals to use their specific knowledge and decision rights properly.

The rights assignment and control problems are solved in a capitalist economy by a system of voluntary exchange founded on a system of alienable decision rights. Voluntary exchange of alienable decision rights tends to ensure that those agents with the relevant knowledge and abilities will place the greatest value on a decision right, and will therefore acquire it. This solves the rights assignment problem of collocating decision rights and specific knowledge.

In the absence of externalities, alienable decision rights also solve the control problem; they motivate individual decision agents to use their decision rights efficiently. Alienability does this by providing an effective system in which the market price or capital value of the right measures the effectiveness with which any individual uses a decision right. Alienability also means that the individual can capture the value of the right in exchange. In this sense, alienability provides an effective reward and punishment system that places the capitalized value of the costs and benefits of an individual's actions on his or her own shoulders.

Why Firms Are Different from Markets

Alienable rights cannot generally solve the control problem inside firms because firms cannot generally assign alienability along with the decision rights without turning each individual agent into an independent firm. Indeed, the characteristic that distinguishes such organizations from markets is the fact that alienability of the rights is not delegated to individual decision agents in the organization.

Because of the limited computational capacity, storage, and input/output channels of the human mind, it is often desirable for groups of individuals to exercise decision rights jointly. Private organizations are widespread examples of such joint exercise of decision rights. In such organizations, independent individuals coordinate their actions through contracts with the legal fiction that serves as the firm's nexus. The bundle of decision rights owned in the name of such an organization is vested nominally in its board of directors and CEO, and the rights are then partitioned out among decision agents in the organization. Those organizations that accomplish this partitioning in a fashion that maximizes their value will tend to win out in the competition for survival.

The inalienability of decision rights within an organization means that the exchange mechanisms that serve to collocate decision rights with the relevant knowledge and skill are not operative. Furthermore, the inalienability of rights within an organization means that the control problems must be solved by alternative means. Organizations solve these problems by establishing internal rules of the game that provide:

- a system for partitioning decision rights out to agents in the organization; and
- a control system that provides:
  a performance measurement and evaluation system; and
  a reward and punishment system.

In general, because of their inability to simulate true capital value claims, these substitute organization "rules of the game" will not perform as effectively as alienable rights in a market system. Therefore, survival requires that the firm must realize benefits from the joint exercise of rights that are large enough to offset the disadvantages incurred by sacrificing alienability. Economies of scale and scope, information advantages, and specialization are potential sources of such benefits.

The creation of a science of organization is still in its infancy. We believe that the structure outlined in this paper provides a view of organization that yields important insights for both social scientists and managers. Knowledge of an organization's rules of the game, along with a surprisingly small amount about its technology or opportunity set, enables one to make accurate predictions about its behavior.

REFERENCES

1. See, for example, Ronald H. Coase, "The Problem of Social Cost," *Journal of Law and Economics,* 3, (1960), pp. 1–44; and Armen Alchlan and William Allen, *Exchange and Production Competition, Coordination & Control* (Wadsworth, Belmont, CA., 1983), p. 91.

2. F. A. Hayek, "The Use of Knowledge in Society," *American Economic Review,* No 35 (September, 1945), pp. 1–18.

3. This principle is also recognized in Milton Harris, C. H. Kriebel, and Artur Raviv, "Asymmetric Information, Incentives and Intrafirm Resource Allocation." *Management Science,* No. 28, (June, 1982), pp. 604–620.

4. Hayek (1945).

5. A condition described as "bounded rationality" by J. March and Herbert Simon in their book. *Organizations* (New York: John Wiley and Sons, Inc. 1958). See also H. A. Simon, "A Behavioral Model of Rational Choice," *Quarterly Journal of Economics,* No. 69 (1955), pp. 99–118; and H. A. Simon, "Theories of Decision Making in Economics and Behavioral Science," *American Economic Review,* Vol XLIX, No. 3 (June, 1959), pp. 253–283.

6. Like Hayek, economists have generally taken the costs of information transfer to be prohibitively large, and, therefore, taken the distribution of knowledge as given. They have analyzed extensively the effects of "information asymmetry" (as it is known in the principal/agent literature) on contracting relations. In his study of institutions, Oliver Williamson defines the concept of "information impactedness" to deal with the organizational implications of transactions where information is "known to one or more parties but cannot be costlessly discerned by or displayed for others." (See Oliver E. Williamson, *Markets and Hierarchies: Analysis and Antitrust Implications* (New York: The Free Press, 1975), p. 31. Explicitly recognizing the costs of transferring knowledge is more useful analytically.

7. A notable exception to this generalization is Alchian and Allen (1983, and earlier editions dating back to 1969).

8. Including the right to sell the rights in output that an individual or firm creates with the resource.

9. It follows that the values established in exchanges are values of bundles of rights, not prices of physical objects. Property whose use is restricted by regulatory constraints or private covenants will sell at different prices from identical property with full-use rights. Goods are sometimes alienated illegally, e.g. theft, black markets, drugs and prostitution. When the police powers are not 100% effective, rights are not 100% secure, and the lower value of such rights will reflect the probability that the rights will be taken (either illegally, or legally through political action such as confiscation or nationalization).

10. In the absence of externalities or monopoly, of course. But externalities are themselves a result of an incomplete definition and assignment of rights. See Coase (1960).

11. Customs and mores not embodied in law also confer decision-making powers and constraints on individuals or groups, especially in primitive societies. The social sanctions imposed on those who take actions in violation of social or group norms can have substantial impact on the decision rights of individuals—an impact that is distinct from that of the formal legal sanctions of the state. Alternatively, individuals

sometimes possess decision-making powers without having legal rights in those re-sources, e.g., possessors of stolen goods. Those engaged in illegal activities themselves employ threats of physical violence to preserve powers.

12. For an excellent survey, see Clive Crook, "Perestroika: And Now for the Hard Part. *The Economist* (April 28, 1990), pp. 1–22.

13. Alienability includes the right to sell or transfer alienability itself.

14. Indeed, one economist has argued that "conservation of expenditures on knowledge" determines the vertical boundaries of the firm. See Harold Demsetz "The Theory of the Firm Revisited," *Journal of Law, Economics, & Organization*, No. 4 (1988), pp. 159.

15. See John W Kensinger and John D. Martin, "Financing Network Organizations," *Journal of Applied Corporate Finance*, Vol. 4 No. 1 (Spring, 1991), pp. 66–76.

16. This point is emphasized by Ronald H. Coase in "The Nature of the Firm," *Economica* (1937). New Series, IV, 386–405. See also Williamson (1975).

17. For a description and analysis of the nature of the franchise contract, see Paul H. Rubin, "The Theory of the Firm and the Structure of the Franchise Contract," *Journal of Law and Economics*, No. 21 (April, 1978), pp. 223–233. Like so much of the literature on franchises, this analysis ignores the critical role of alienability in the functioning of this organizational form.

18. For our original formulation of agency theory, see Michael C. Jensen and William H. Meckling, "Theory of the Firm: Managerial Behavior, Agency Costs and Ownership Structure," *Journal of Financial Economics*, No. 3 (1976) pp. 305–60.

19. We can assume for simplicity that the right is optimally assigned within each level in the hierarchy.

20. Assuming the CEO does not have agency problems with himself or herself. See Richard H. Thaler and H. M. Schefrin, "An Economic Theory of Self-Control," *Journal of Political Economy*, Vol. 89, No. 2 (April, 1981), pp. 392–406.

21. See Tom Richman, "Mrs. Fields' Secret Ingredient," *Inc. Magazine*, (October, 1987).

22. See Hank Gilman, "J. C. Penney Decentralizes its Purchasing: Individual Stores Can Tailor Buying to Needs," *Wall Street Journal*, May 8, 1987.

23. See Eugene F. Fama, and Michael C. Jensen, (1983a). "Agency Problems and Residual Claims," *Journal of Law and Economics*, No. 26 (June 1983), pp. 327–349; and Eugene F. Fama and Michael C. Jensen, (1983b), "Separation of Ownership and Control," *Journal of Law and Economics*, No. 26. pp. 301–325.

24. For further discussion of the breakdown of the decision process into initiation, ratification, implementation, and monitoring rights, see Fama and Jensen (1983b).

25. See Walter Kiechel, "Corporate Strategists Under Fire," *Fortune* (December 27, 1982); and Robert H. Hayes, "Strategic Planning—Forward in Reverse?," *Harvard Business Review*, Vol. 63, No. 6 (November–December, 1985), pp. 111–119.

26. See George P. Baker, Michael C. Jensen, and Kevin J. Murphy, "Compensation and Incentives: Practice vs. Theory," *Journal of Finance*, Vol. 43, No. 3 (July, 1988), pp. 593–616; and Kevin J. Murphy, "Performance Measurement and Appraisal: Motivating Managers to Identify and Reward Performance," in William J. Bruns, Jr., ed., *Performance Measurement, Evaluation, and Incentives*, Harvard Business School Press, 1992.

4

The Rise and Fall of Bureaucracy

Gifford & Elizabeth Pinchot

Given that bureaucracy is in such ill repute today, it is hard to remember that it once was considered a great organizational innovation. By organizing the division of labor, by making management and decision making a profession, and by providing an order and a set of rules that allowed many different kinds of specialists to work in coordination toward a common end, bureaucracy greatly extended the breadth and depth of intelligence that organizations could achieve. Begun as a system of organizing government activities, it has spread to big businesses and large organizations of all kinds.

Max Weber, who launched the systematic study of bureaucracy as its role in Western society began to explode in the late nineteenth century, saw bureaucracy as both the most efficient possible system and a threat to the basic liberties he held dear. Weber predicted the triumph of bureaucracy because of its greater efficiency: "The purely bureaucratic form of administrative organization, that is the monocratic variety of bureaucracy, is, as regards the precision, constancy, stringency and reliability of its operations, superior to all other forms of administrative organization."[1]

Weber would have been surprised (even frightened) by how accurate his prediction of bureaucracy's triumph has proven. During the last hundred years, the landscape of society has changed dramatically as large bureaucratic organizations replaced small family enterprises in retailing, manufacturing, and services. Many not-for-profits, from Blue Cross to the Audubon Society, have adopted the bureaucratic form. Even family entrepreneurship has taken a step toward bureaucracy with the shift from hosting a hometown diner to owning a franchise.

Bureaucracy created a system capable of effectively managing the massive investments, division of labor, and large-scale mechanized production of capitalism. Its organizational power drove the initial rapid growth of the steel, chemical, and automobile industries. Bureaucracy united AT&T as it established a peerless national communication network with rank on rank of managers structured by the Bell System Practices—a set of policy manuals that provided detailed and explicit instructions for every task. IBM added customer focus to bureaucracy and created an organization effective enough to give it forty years of preeminence in the new computer industry.

Despite all these successes, respect for bureaucracy is declining. As in so many other areas of life, what brought great success in the past has become the limitation of today. Suddenly everyone knows that bureaucracy is slowing us down and keeping our organizations internally focused and uncreative. It is time to question bureaucracy. What is the basis of its success? Why is it suddenly less useful than it was? What can we do about it? What are the alternatives to bureaucracy?

WHAT BUREAUCRACY IS AND WHY IT CONQUERED ALL

Bureaucracy gained preeminence because it worked for many of the needs of the industrial age. It increased the effectiveness of hierarchy by reducing some of the worst abuses of power and by providing a rational way to manage tasks too complex for any one person to comprehend. Let us look more closely at why it worked so well. There is consensus among social scientists that the six characteristics of bureaucracy, all part of Weber's original description, are roughly as follows:

A hierarchical chain of command
Specialization by function
Uniform policies covering rights and duties
Standardized procedures for each job
A career based on promotions for technical competence
Impersonal relations[2]

To this list we add an operating principle of bureaucracy suggested by Fred Emery:

All coordination done from a level or more above the work being coordinated[3]

A Hierarchical Chain of Command

The bureaucratic organization is structured as a pyramid with an absolute boss on top who divides up the overall task of the organization and gives responsibility for each subtask to subbosses who divide responsibility yet more finely and so on through an unbroken chain of sub-subbosses that stretches down to every employee. In the 1980s, huge organizations such as General Motors, Sears, IBM, and the U.S. government had as many as twelve layers of management between the CEO and the worker—too many, as it has turned out.

The establishment of a clear chain of command was a powerful way to bring order to large groups in a common enterprise. The chain of command resolved potential conflicts by granting clear responsibility, authority, and accountability for each potential decision. Each boss and subboss in the chain of command was given an absolute monopoly of power over a task or function and then held accountable for it. This greatly simplified the boss's task of making sure the organization executed commands.

Limitations of Prebureaucratic Autocracy. Autocratic organizations without a clear chain of command run out of steam at about a hundred persons. Many entrepreneurs fall into this trap by assuming the role of a "craftsman entrepreneur," a person who maintains control of a growing organization like a fine craftsman with many assistants. Rather than establish an effective chain of command, he or she tries to be everywhere making all decisions throughout the organization for a big group of helpers. The result is the classic growth curve of the

FIGURE 4-1 Bureaucracy.

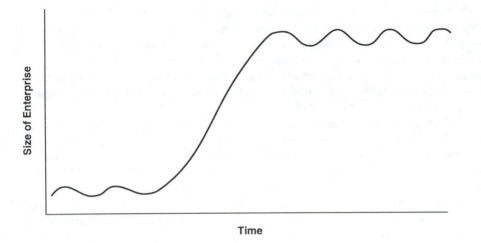

FIGURE 4-2   The craftsman entrepreneur.

craftsman entrepreneur: rocky start, smooth expansions, rocky leveling out as if bumping against a ceiling.

Such entrepreneurs might explain all the ups and downs of their business as changes in the market, but in fact they are suffering from the limitations of the prebureaucratic form of autocracy. To the extent the entrepreneur continues to be an absolute ruler, he or she cannot go beyond the scope of business that can be understood and managed by a single omnipresent manager. Some entrepreneurs caught in this craftsman role appoint subordinate managers, but by continually countermanding the orders of those managers, they fail to respect the chain of command they establish and thus disempower their managers.

Delegation and Empowerment. Those entrepreneurs who succeed in expansion commonly introduce a chain-of-command structure, which by its nature delegates power and increases the thinking power of the organization by empowering more brains to take action. The business may grow when supervisors and middle managers are empowered in a limited but significant way to make decisions about their areas and to establish procedures and issue orders. Postbureaucratic entrepreneurships are growing just fine with decentralized teams and lateral networking taking the place of chain of command. Nonetheless, the innovations of bureaucracy, including the divestiture of some of an owner's power to a hierarchy beneath, served the goal of growth in earlier eras.

Specialization by Function

Bureaucracy achieves efficiency through specialization of labor. In fact, the organizational structure of a bureaucracy is created by dividing the overall task into a series of well-defined specialties or functions. Each function is given responsibility for a defined set of tasks and given the tools needed to accomplish that task. The boss gives orders and assigns tasks in such a way that all the parts add up to a coherent whole.

With specialization, different varieties of engineers study exactly why efficiency is lost in each of many steps in the production process and then design equipment and procedures to raise yields. Salespeople perfect their selling skills, and financial professionals manage the liquidity and profitability of the business with increasingly sophisticated tools. In general, specialization leads to more effective ways of doing each aspect of the organization's overall task.

Before the specialization of bureaucracy, each craftsperson learned all of blacksmithing or all of barrel making and performed all aspects of the job from start to finish. Craft production can often be satisfying and have artistic merit, but in the Industrial Revolution it worked against the mechanization and economies of scale that specialization and division of labor made possible. As organizations moved from craft production to division of labor, the strict hierarchy of bureaucracy provided the clout to set aside the traditions and concerns of craftsmen and to make each new innovation part of the rules and procedures of the organization.

Specialization can contribute to organizational intelligence by allowing people to concentrate on each little aspect of what the organization does. With many specialists, each good at his or her special area, the organization can bring great intellectual pressure and ingenuity to bear on each of the many different aspects of the business.

Uniform Written Rules and Policies

A bureaucracy is governed by uniform written rules and policies that in a corporation, profit or not-for-profit, are set by the board and the management. These rules define the rights and duties of employees and managers. The most basic rules concern who can give orders to whom.

In a bureaucracy, the boss is responsible for the actions of all the people under him or her and has the right to give them orders that they must dutifully obey. The employee's primary responsibility is not to do what is right or what needs to be done but only to follow exactly the orders of his or her immediate boss.

The written policies of a bureaucracy also guarantee employees regular wages as long as they are employed and, in some cases, even a pension for long-term service. These forms of compensation are quite different from those of the feudal systems, in which each level in the hierarchy, from serf on up to the local lord, often took a piece of the action, however paltry, in their domain.

Written rules concerning rights and duties partially offset some of the worst aspects of chains of command by reducing the potential power of any petty tyrants at the supervisory and middle management levels. Supervisors disciplining employees have more precisely defined powers, which both empower them to a degree and limit arbitrary behavior.

Standardized Procedures Defining Each Job

In a bureaucracy, fixed procedures govern how employees are to perform their tasks, sometimes to an astonishing degree. Frederick Taylor, an engineer who became known as the father of scientific management for his work in the early part of this century, recorded and then taught the exact motions of the most productive workers in a factory so that everyone else doing that task could make the same motions.[4] This reliance on established procedures is in stark contrast to the system of "make it up as you go along," characteristic of an entrepreneurial start-up or, at worst, the arbitrary personal whims of a feudal lord and his powerful minions.

Uniform rules and procedures written down and stored as official documents increased the intelligence expressed in organizations by instituting a crude "memory" of lessons learned. Written rules and procedures extended the power of the commands, standardizing the actions to be learned through frequent turnover of employees. Change could be accommodated if it could be written down and not bump into an existing rule. Standardized procedures could serve to make lessons learned in one part of the organization more broadly effective and to overcome irrational resistance to more effective ways of doing things.

The Professional Career

Success in the bureaucratic organization is defined as a lifetime career of advancing to higher levels in the chain of command. Rising in the ranks provides both power and symbols of status. Promotion is achieved through technical competence in one's specialty and efficiency in carrying out orders.

The professional career provides a "contract" between employee and organization: In its simplest form, a person devotes him- or herself to the organization in exchange for secure work and wages. The full-time professional manager was married to the organization for life. In return, the organization promised a stable or rising salary, a pension, lifetime employment, and a chance to rise in the hierarchy.

Before bureaucracy, favoritism and nepotism destroyed the efficiency of organizations more than they do today. Even today, there are many cultures in which a boss confronted with a choice between promoting an incompetent relative or another employee has no culturally acceptable alternative but to opt for the incompetent relative. In its ideal form, bureaucracy subordinates these family loyalties and other sympathies to the goals of the organization through a policy of promotion for measurable technical competence. In a government bureaucracy, in the civil service and the police and fire departments, for example, this policy is often manifest in exams that are prerequisites for moving to higher level positions. The promise of a good bureaucratic career allowed organizations to recruit, train, and retain highly skilled specialists.

The lure of rising in the hierarchy and the security of a professional career was an important element in bureaucracy's success, providing a strong motivation for long-term loyalty to the organization. Yet most will not make it in a bureaucracy, since the only success is moving upward. This carries the seeds of disappointment later in one's career when the pyramid has narrowed and only a few can move up to the next level.

Impersonal Relations

In a bureaucracy, relationships are from role to role rather than from person to person. The organizational structure and job description define what is expected of an individual in each role, and the holder of a particular role is expected to carry out its responsibilities in a rational and unemotional manner. Therefore, emotions are not to be displayed: The coolly analytical win, and the open and caring lose.

Impersonal relations helped move bureaucracy beyond nepotism and favoritism by preventing family feeling or friendship from getting in the way of enforcing rules and making tough decisions. It kept managers' sentiments from getting in the way as they wrenched workers away from the satisfactions of craft production and toward the bureaucratic routines and unthinking work of the assembly line.

All Coordination from a Level or More Above

In a bureaucracy, workers do not figure out how to coordinate their work with their peers. The boss divides up the work and defines each person's job so that added together those jobs produce the output that is the boss's responsibility to manage. The boss's boss then provides coordination between units, and the units, therefore, do not need to coordinate with one another. All coordination must rise up and pass through the next higher boss.

Employees are not paid to think broadly; their job is to stay within the "boxes" defined by their job descriptions and the standardized procedures. Above all, they are forbidden to coordinate with their peers, who are either subordinates of the same boss or of another one elsewhere in the organization. To do so would rob the bosses of their authority.

Coordination from above worked well during the early Industrial Revolution when huge numbers of employees unskilled in the mechanical arts had to be quickly fitted to a job in the "satanic mills."[5] Turnover could be extraordinary. Near the turn of the century, Ford Motor Company's Highland Park, Michigan, plant had to hire fifty-four thousand workers a year just to keep thirteen thousand working.[6] With such rapid turnover, workers had little time to understand the whole and needed a simple and clearly defined assignment.

WHY BUREAUCRACY NO LONGER WORKS

The world no longer needs the machinelike organizations bureaucracy produces. The challenges of our times call for lively, intelligent organizations. Bureaucracy was efficient for certain kinds of repetitive tasks that characterized the early Industrial Revolution. It no longer works so well, because its rules and procedures are often diametrically opposed to the principles needed for workers to take the next step toward greater organizational intelligence. These principles include more responsibility to define and direct one's own job, more responsibility to coordinate with others, and a shift in authority from one's boss to one's "customers."

From Unskilled Work to Knowledge Work

Peter Drucker has been telling us for decades that more and more of work, both technical and nontechnical, is knowledge-based. We no longer need many unskilled assembly-line workers; most of the jobs in factories involve technical knowledge and training. What is more, few of the jobs in a manufacturing organization are in the factory. Most "manufacturing" jobs are in functions such as marketing, design, process engineering, technical analysis, accounting, and management, which require professional expertise and mastery of a large body of knowledge. This same trend toward more knowledge workers is present in service industries, not-for-profits, and government. Drucker estimates that one-third of all jobs are already filled by the highly paid and productive group he calls knowledge workers.[7]

The very nature of knowledge work, which involves information gathering, imagination, experiment, discovery, and integration of new knowledge with larger

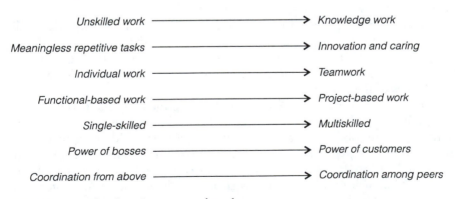

FIGURE 4-3 The changing nature of work.

systems, means that bosses cannot order about knowledge workers like the ditch diggers or assembly-line bolt turners of yore. If knowledge workers are any good at all, they soon learn more about what they are doing on a specific project than their boss. Knowledge work inherently has a large component of self-direction and teamwork and is hampered by remote control from distant bosses. As we move beyond bureaucracy we will find ways to organize so that all work is knowledge work, bringing everyone's native intelligence and collaborative abilities to bear on constantly changing ways of achieving shared goals.

From Repetitive Tasks to Innovation and Caring

Since the passing of craft production, management has been responsible for organizing people to work efficiently at narrow, boring jobs. This has meant that the managerial role was as much to limit the intelligence and potential of employees as it was to elicit talent. Now the mindless repetitive jobs that bureaucracies were designed to manage are rapidly disappearing. Machines do more of the routine work, and the work that is left requires initiative and flexibility. As a result, the job of leaders is more nearly to bring out people's talents around a common vision.

What sort of work will be left as machines get smarter? What do people do so much better than machines that it will provide human work for the foreseeable future?

People are much better than machines at innovating, at seeing new possibilities within fluid and imperfectly defined systems and knowing what to do. Innovation in this sense includes the creative salesperson who sees what the customer really wants and bends the system to get it. It includes the member of a quality action team who makes an intuitive leap that exposes the real root cause of a problem to measurement and analysis. It also includes the intrapreneur who sees how to use company assets to generate more revenues and thus create more jobs.

Another apparently irreplaceable human talent is caring. As more work becomes service, caring about and for others becomes increasingly important. People do not generally sue doctors just because they make a mistake. They sue them because they make a mistake and relate to patients in a way that says they do not care. Good salespeople keep customers because the customers can sense that they genuinely care. Good intrapreneurs are able to break through barriers within the organization when others sense that they care more about the result than about personal success. Good leaders spread intrapreneurial zeal when it comes from inner values that all can get behind. Leaders elicit commitment when their people sense that they care about them, the group's success, and their mutual contributions.

The rules of bureaucracy forbid caring and, in particular, acting on the basis of the inner values one holds dear rather than out of strict obedience and loyalty to the boss. We find no examples of innovation where the intrapreneur did not break some bureaucratic rules. Most often the intrapreneurs and team members were carried away by a passion for an idea that aligned with deeper values—that promised at least in some small way a better world. We know few con artists who can long fool the alert into thinking they care when they do not.

Caring, like innovation, must come from the inside: We cannot order people to innovate or to care. We also cannot order people to use their intelligence; people engage their intelligence when they have reason to care, when they are part of something bigger than themselves and see that their wider interests are served by the work at hand. Bureaucracy is too autocratic and rule-driven to motivate and manage the intelligence that is brought to innovation and caring. Creativity and connecting with others require engaged relationships, personal responsibility, and flexible thinking and acting. Thus, as the rules of bureaucracy block both innovation and caring, they block the essence of modern work.

Education, Innovation, and Caring

The Tofflers pointed out in *The Third Wave* that universal public education had the purpose of teaching obedience, punctuality, and the ability to sit still a long time and do mindless, repetitive work.[8] In the early industrial era the ability to endure boredom was a key survival skill. Although education has improved a bit, bureaucracies have done little to prepare the average worker for the innovation, teamwork, and caring that constitute much of modern work.

For years corporations have used effective training in creativity and innovation (for a chosen few), but these lessons are generally remedial. They seek to restore what was destroyed by education. We need educational systems today that preserve "childlike" curiosity and give practice in teamwork, initiative, and collaborative big-picture responsibility.

Many of our current practices in education not only block innovation, they also blunt one's ability to care, to engage heart and mind in one's work. People who act on what they care about jump out of their seats. They fail to follow the lesson plan and ask too many questions. They help their fellow students rather than maximizing their own grades. Many schools are getting better at teaching children to care about one another and to treat one another with respect, but still follow the bureaucratic model in the way both teachers and students are treated—forced to measure up to defined procedures rather than pursue goals with creative innovations, evaluated on individual performance instead of teamwork and collaboration, taught compliance rather than participative self-management and democratic processes.

From Individual Work to Teamwork

Bureaucracy replaces the natural ability of humans to find ways to work together with the more sterile discipline of the chain of command. It is not rich and lively enough for today's fast-paced changes and challenges. Virtually every recent management innovation that works relies in part on the power of teams. A "Total

Quality" program gives power to teams to examine processes and make them work better, a task that until recently belonged exclusively to managers. Because knowledge workers cannot produce much of value alone, their work takes them across organizational boundaries to search for integrated information. In reengineering, case teams replace isolated functions. In lean manufacturing, ordinary workers take responsibility for the whole and run for help whenever trouble shows up.

When three members of a thirty-two-person work team at Hoechst Celanese's Salisbury plant left the team, the remaining team members had authorization to replace them but decided not to do so.[9] As is so often the case, the people doing the work knew more than the bosses about where work and expense could be saved. Organizations become more intelligent when they find ways to bring the intelligence of every member into supporting the purpose and goals of the organization.

From Functional Work to Project Work

As knowledge workers shift from static jobs to solving a series of problems or seizing opportunities, they do so in work organized as projects. Each project in this complex world generally requires a cross-disciplinary team. These teams then learn together as the project evolves. Soon, their bosses in the functions they "report" to become too distant from the work to manage the decisions for the teams. As a consequence, control shifts from the functional organization of bureaucracy to project teams.

Specialization will continue to be a critical part of every complex organization. But because of the interconnection of issues in a complex world, more and more work will involve integrating the viewpoints and activities of specialists, and less and less will be performing tasks completely within those specialties. As a result, each employee will have to be both a specialist and a generalist.

The 1956 Pontiac was designed with a concave sculpted panel with many vertical ribs indented between the two taillights. The door to the gas cap was neatly hidden between two of the vertical ribs. Because the cracks at the edge of the gas door fell where the eye already expected a vertical line, the door did not break up the uniform sweep of the design.

The design worked aesthetically, but a senior manager reviewing it was afraid car owners would be unable to figure out where to find the gas cap. Rather than raising the concern with the designers and asking them to deal with it in a thoughtful way, he ordered the gas cap door chromed, ruining the whole sweep of the design with an anomalous chrome square.

Managers cannot bring out the intelligence of everyone in the organization if they pretend they can do better thinking in a few hours than a project team that has wrestled with the problem for months. Instead of issuing arbitrary orders, they need to raise concerns and trust the project team to find a way of handling them that integrates with all the other issues guiding the design. Paradoxically, as issues become more complex and specialties more differentiated, it becomes increasingly necessary for teams of diverse specialists to themselves integrate their work with the work of other teams. Management can never understand all the trade-offs and creative solutions that get the team where it is. Heavy-handed intervention leads to inconsistencies—or worse. In an intelligent organization, participation is widespread to help expose all the issues as early as possible. Individuals with multiple skills are brought together to cover more viewpoints in a team of manageable size, and the team does its work guided by feedback, not commands.

From Single-Skilled to Multiskilled

As Fred Emery has pointed out, no system can exist without redundancy to provide reserve capacity when something does not exactly follow the plan.[10] Bureaucracy gets its margin of safety from extra bodies. If extra work of one kind appears because customers ordered a different mix of products than expected, a bureaucracy has extra workers of that exact type waiting in the wings, or it falls short of meeting the orders. The same situation arises if someone is sick: Another "identical" worker needs to be waiting to do the job. This system of narrowly defined skills and extra bodies is expensive and inflexible.

In a typical multiskilling program, responsibility shifts to teams, and employees get raises for each new skill they acquire. At Lechmere, Inc., a twenty-seven-store retailer, cashiers at the Sarasota, Florida, outlet get pay raises by learning to sell products, and sporting goods staff get raises by learning to operate the forklift. With a multiskilled workforce, when bottlenecks appear, whether through absenteeism or a sudden rush of one kind of work, someone can step in and get things moving.[11]

Bureaucratic relationships between organized labor and management prevent multiskilling by adherence to numerous contractually defined job classifications. Unions today do well to negotiate for more training and education to make members more widely employable. Unionized companies as entrenched as National Steel and General Motors "have improved morale, speed, and efficiency by loosening job classifications and developing a broader more flexible workforce through cross-training employees."[12]

From the Power of Bosses to the Power of Customers

For an organization to be responsive, customers' wishes have to have a strong influence on the people doing the work. Relaying this sort of information through bosses is too slow—and besides, they may not be there to hear what customers want.

This sort of thinking applies to internal customers or "users" of a unit's output as much as to external customers. In a rapidly changing world, if internal customers cannot get what they need promptly and flexibly, the system will not be able to serve external clients promptly and flexibly. Freedom of choice between alternative suppliers gives users of internal services the power enjoyed by real customers—the power to say no to one and yes to another. Once internal customers have this power, the attention of those internal suppliers shifts from pleasing their bosses to winning customers. If they have customers, the boss can be pleased; without customers, they had better find new work.

From Coordination from Above to Coordination among Peers

Clearly, new systems of coordination and control are needed. In a bureaucratic system, employees are not responsible for coordinating their work with others at their level; that is their boss's job. They need not think about the big picture beyond doing their specialty well—to do so would be presumptuous. It is the job of senior management to figure out how it all fits together, so cross-functional concerns are referred up to a level of management that can resolve them. When coordination is the boss's job, cross-functional, or horizontal, communication with one's peers is frowned upon as either a waste of time or a usurpation of the boss's authority.

In postbureaucratic organizations, most of the coordination between functions and even businesses is done by teams. In 1988, John Hanley, vice president for product development at AT&T, needed to cut in half the product development time for cordless phones. The old product development system was a series of handoffs from R&D to Manufacturing to Marketing to Sales. Hanley formed teams that included people from each of these functions and gave the teams authority to make decisions about almost everything except their deadline: They would be finished in one year. Rather than wrestle with the bureaucracy, the teams worked together as intrapreneurial generalists. They did market research, decided how much each product should cost, what its features would be, what it should look like, and how it should work. The result: half the development time, better quality, lower cost.

Reality has become so complex and multidimensional that there is no way of dividing the organization into chains of command that will work for all aspects of the challenges faced. As a result, integration is achieved through peer-level cross-organizational communication rather than through the hierarchy. Huge volumes of cross-functional communication are needed because every important process crosses the boundaries of the organization. The general manager does not have time enough in the day just to relay communications; the process is not fast enough. Besides, as you may remember from the childhood game of "telephone," in which a verbal message is whispered from person to person down a long line of kids, communications relayed through too many humans get garbled. In the intelligent organization, communications whenever possible are direct, without intermediaries.

In the industrial era, the large-scale but stable means of production pushed us toward distant, formal, and unequal relationships at work. Today, our complex and intelligence-intensive tasks push us toward relationships that are close, open, honest, and more nearly equal. Because "organization" is about how we structure

TABLE 4-1 Revolutionary Change in the Structure of Our Relationships

What Bureaucracy Is	Why It Once Triumphed	Why It Fails Now	What Replaces It
Hierarchical chain of command	Brought simple large-scale order Bosses brought order by dominating subordinates	Cannot handle complexity Domination not best way to get organization intelligence	Visions and values Teams (self-managing) Lateral coordination Informal networks Choice Free intraprise
Specialization Organization by function	Produced efficiency through division of labor Focused intelligence	Does not provide intensive cross-functional communication and continual peer-level coordination	Multiskilling specialists and intrapreneuring Organization in market-mediated networks
Uniform rules	Created a sense of fairness Clearly established power of bosses	Still need rules, but need different rules	Guaranteed rights Institutions of freedom and community
Standard procedures	Provided crude organizational memory Able to use unskilled workers Overcame old ways	Responds slowly to change Does not deal well with complexity Does not foster interconnection	Self-direction and self-management Force of the market and ethical community
A career of advancing up the ladder	Bought loyalty Furnished continuity of elite class of managers and professionals	Fewer managers needed and more educated workforce expects promotions; therefore, not enough room for advancement	A career of growing competence A growing network to get more done More pay for more capabilities
Impersonal relations	Reduced force of nepotism Helped leaders enforce tough discipline and make tough decisions	Information-intensive jobs require in-depth relationships	Strong whole-person relationships Options and alternatives Strong drive for results
Coordination from above	Provided direction for unskilled workers Furnished strong supervision required by rapid turnover in boring jobs	Educated employees are ready for self-management	Self-managing teams Lateral communications and collaboration

our relationships, these new realities will completely change our ideas about methods and patterns of organization.

The nature of work in modern high-tech workplaces calls on people in many positions in the organization to take responsibility for processes and services that intimately affect the customer and the wider community. Even in small service businesses and government agencies, the goods and services produced are knowledge- and information-intensive by virtue of the skills and intelligence of the people with their hands on the work processes. When a medical unit delivers life-saving help to patients, its members must intelligently apply hundreds of technical instruments, drugs, and procedures to a variety of unique customers—and learn anew as the knowledge and technology are continually updated. This is as true of the technicians as the physicians. What works in a society of knowledge workers will be completely different from what worked before.

REFERENCES

1. Wolfgang J. Mommsen, *Political and Social Theory of Max Weber,* p. 112.
2. R. H. Hall, "The Concept of Bureaucracy: An Empirical Assessment," *American Journal of Sociology* 69 (1963): 33. See also Warren Bennis, *Beyond Bureaucracy* (San Francisco: Jossey-Bass, 1993), p. 5; and Gerald Zaltman, Robert Duncan, and Jonny Holbeck, *Innovations and Organizations* (Malabar, Fla.: Robert E. Krieger Publishing, 1984), pp. 122–123.
3. Fred Emery, "The Management of Self-Managing Groups," unpublished paper, November 1989.
4. Weisbord, *Productive Workplaces,* p. 24.
5. William Blake (1757–1827).
6. John Case, "A Company of Business People," *Inc.,* April 1993, p. 81.
7. Peter Drucker, *Post-Capitalist Society* (New York: Harper Business, 1993), p. 64.
8. Alvin Toffler, *The Third Wave* (New York: William Morrow, 1980), p. 45.
9. D. Keith Denton, "Multiskilled Teams Replace Old Work Systems," *HR Magazine,* September 1992, p. 49.
10. As Fred Emery has pointed out, no system can exist without redundancy to provide reserve capacity when something does not exactly follow the plan.
11. Denton, "Multiskilled Teams Replace Old Work Systems," p. 49.
12. Ibid., p. 48.

5

The Emerging Flexible Organization: Perspectives from Silicon Valley

Homa Bahrami

Many enterprises are in the midst of fundamental changes in organizational designs and management practices. Pioneering and traditional companies alike are experimenting with novel organizational structures and management processes in order to accommodate the fast pace of technological change, global competition, and the emergence of a knowledge-based economy. These developments are collectively precipitating a move away from monolithic and rigid organizational designs which were geared for repetitive transactions and routine activities. The resulting impetus is toward flexible and agile organizational forms which can accommodate novelty, innovation, and change.[1]

This article describes some of the organizational features of the emerging flexible enterprise and is based on field studies of 37 high-technology firms in California's Silicon Valley.[2] These firms are experimenting with new organizational arrangements and are at the forefront of experiencing the challenges of the information era. Their business foundations are anchored in knowledge-based industries. Many compete in global markets and face global competition. They employ educated, young, and mobile professionals with high expectations. Some enter, or even, create pioneering markets and develop as yet untested products without the benefit of existing role models and blueprints for success. Moreover, they must manage novelty and continuous changes in products designs, competitive positions, and market dynamics. As Bill Joy, a co-founder of Sun Microsystems, observes:

> *"High-technology obeys the iron law of revolution... the more you change, the more you have to change ... you have to be willing to accept the fact that in this game the rules keep changing."*[3]

THE CHANGING ORGANIZATIONAL LANDSCAPE

An extensive array of organizational experiments have been under way in many firms during the past decade. Some of these developments have turned out to be transient fads, whereas others point to fundamental shifts in organizational design and management practice. Some of the more prevalent developments include delayering, team-based networks, alliances and partnerships, and a new employer-employee covenant.

The delayering and down-sizing trend was initially triggered by the need to reduce costs. However, it also reflects the administrative impact of information and communication technologies. Increased use of technologies, such as electronic mail, voice mail, and shared databases, has, over time, reduced the need for traditional middle management, whose role was to supervise others and to collect, analyze, evaluate, and transmit information up, down, and across the organizational hierarchy. The potential consequences of delayering are intended to be, in part, faster response to competitive and market changes, larger spans of control, increased workloads, and a broader range of assignments and roles for individuals and groups. One of the expected benefits of flatter hierarchies is the organization's ability to become flexible and responsive by reducing the time lag between decision and action—enabling faster response to market and competitive dynamics.[4]

In an attempt to manage cross-unit projects and to reduce time-to-market, many firms are increasingly relying on multi-functional, multi-unit teams. Indeed, during the last decade "teams" and "groups" have become part of our managerial vocabulary and are now viewed as a central organizational building block.[5] A key advantage of teams is their intrinsic flexibility. They can be formed, re-formed, and disbanded with relative ease; they can by-pass the traditional hierarchy; and their composition can evolve over time in order to blend different skills and address changing priorities.

Reliance on sub-contracting has been prevalent in a number of industries for some time.[6] Recently, however, there has been a substantial increase in alliances which affect core business activities—such as product development, distribution, and financing. This trend is giving rise to complex organizational forms and business relationships. A number of reasons have been put forward to explain the rapid diffusion of such "hybrid" organizational forms. These include "changing environmental conditions, the limits of large-scale organization, and the importance of speed and information."[7] As Evans suggests, collaborative partnerships are a flexible mode of blending capabilities, sharing risks, and generating options.[8]

Recently, we have also witnessed a major re-assessment of the implicit lifetime contract between employers and employees. Many firms have reexamined their employment policies—initiating early retirement programs and other incentives to reduce the size of their workforce. As pointed out in other studies, the critical tradeoff in this context is between "corporate flexibility and individual security."[9] Many corporations rely on temporary workers, specialized vendors, and consultants in order to flexibly deal with unique contingencies. Additionally, this trend points to a fundamental shift in the foundation of employer-employee relationship, away from the traditional patriarchal orientation toward what may be characterized as a peer-to-peer relationship. This sentiment is echoed in the following comment which encapsulates the implicit relationship between Apple Computer and its employees: "You own your own careers; we provide you with the opportunities."[10]

Collectively, these and other changes point to a somewhat radical reshaping of the traditional organizational landscape.[11] As current trends indicate, contemporary firms need flexible and agile organizations that can effectively function in environments of continuous and kaleidoscopic, rather than periodic and paradigmatic, change.

FLEXIBILITY: THE EMERGING IMPERATIVE

Historically, the term "flexibility" has been used rather loosely—referring to a blend of capabilities and attributes that facilitate adjustments to change. However, as suggested in previous studies, flexibility is a polymorphous concept whose meaning varies according to the situational context.[12] For example, flexibility means "being agile"—fast on one's feet, able to move rapidly, change course to take advantage of an opportunity or to side-step a threat. This capability is critical for enabling "time-based" competition, facilitating rapid response, and reducing product development cycles. It also refers to the ability to quickly redefine a position and re-focus in the midst of a dynamic engagement—such as an acquisition, new product introduction, or legal proceedings.

Flexibility, however, is not just synonymous with agility. It also implies the ability to be "versatile"—able to do different things and apply different capabilities depending on the needs of a particular situation. For example, employees with diverse capabilities are versatile in that they can readily switch between different assignments.

On the "defensive" side of the spectrum, flexibility also refers to qualities which enable an enterprise to endure when negatively affected by change. This attribute is reflected in concepts such as "robustness" or "resilience." The former characterizes the capability to absorb shocks and withstand perturbations—for example, by having excess slack or liquid assets. The latter refers to the ability to come back from the brink of disaster without bearing permanent scars or disabilities.[13] Sometimes the events which trigger the need to change can be anticipated ahead of time. More often than not, however, firms need to respond to changes which are typically unexpected.

The point is that all these different attributes—spanning both offensive and defensive qualities—are needed in a truly flexible enterprise. The concept of flexibility, in an organizational context, refers to the ability to precipitate intentional changes, to continuously respond to unanticipated changes, and to adjust to the unexpected consequences of predictable changes. Put simply, strategic flexibility "is the ability to do things differently or do something else should the need arise."[14]

All the different senses of flexibility are critical for the survival and success of high-technology companies. Indeed many of these firms are at the forefront of both, inflicting and responding to continuous change. Such environments exhibit a high propensity for what the economist Shackle termed "kaleidoscopic" change, where a small, apparently insignificant, change can dramatically alter the entire context.[15]

Due to short product life-cycles, technology firms have to quickly capitalize on narrow windows of market opportunity, introduce new products in rapid succession, and respond, in real time, to competitive and market dynamics. Organizational problems are further exacerbated by rapid and volatile growth patterns. Early success is no guarantee of long-term survival. An incumbent pioneer can be quickly eclipsed by a technological breakthrough, an unexpected spin-off, or a sudden shift in market conditions. Managing kaleidoscopic change is an everyday fact of life and a criteria for survival; it is not a one-time, periodic adjustment, or simply a corrective move following a crisis.

In view of these challenges, a number of innovative organizational experiments have been under way in many high-technology firms in Silicon Valley and elsewhere. Some pioneering moves have also been initiated by established corporations in the process of metamorphosis and transformation.[16]

BUILDING BLOCKS OF FLEXIBLE ORGANIZATIONAL DESIGNS

High-technology firms face significant organizational tensions in spite of their relative youth. Irrespective of their size or stage of development, they need to remain disciplined, lean, and focused, requiring minimal duplication of effort, stringent accountability, and effective control and coordination. However, a loose, hands-off management style is needed to manage expectant professionals, maintain a conducive environment for creative thinking, and provide the capability for rapid response to competitive and market developments. As depicted in Table 5-1, they need flexible organizational systems which can balance dialectical forces—facilitating creativity, innovation, and speed, while instilling co-ordination, focus and control, and the staying power to withstand periods of adversity.

The following comments capture the essence of some of the dialectical tensions facing these firms: "We want an environment that enhances individual creativity, but we do not want chaos . . . we want people involved in decisions that affect their work and we want teamwork, yet we want our employees to have a bias toward action . . . we want small groups of dedicated workers (decentralization) but such groups may feel aimless or may be charging in the wrong direction with hidden agendas . . . we want people to stretch to reach tough goals, so our real emphasis is on easily-measured short-term growth and profits—but we

TABLE 5-1   Organizational Dilemmas

Managing Opposing Tensions	
Control	*Autonomy*
Focus	Innovation
Global Products	Local Recipes
Less Duplication	Rapid Response
Time-to-Market	Future Products
Today's Performance	Long Term Vision

should also have time to develop our employees for the longer haul, to promote from within, to monitor the atmosphere for creativity."[17]

Similar tensions also seem to confront many established entities. Percy Barnevik, the CEO of ABB, described his firm's critical organizational challenge as dealing with three internal contradictions: "We want to be global and local, big and small, decentralized with centralized reporting."[18] The challenge facing British Petroleum is depicted in terms of a critical paradox: "How to reinforce its strengths as a corporation while allowing its constituent businesses much greater flexibility and speed of response."[19] Similarly, the modern "transnational" must simultaneously address the need for scale efficiency, local responsiveness, and continuous learning.[20]

A Multi-Polar Organization

The traditional model of the industrial enterprise has been one of an all-powerful center with various subsidiaries. The center has historically formulated the strategic direction, consolidated and integrated divisional plans, allocated resources, and monitored performance. For example, in the classic multi-divisional structure, senior corporate management—assisted by their staff—have set the long term direction while the divisions have implemented the plans.[21]

This model of the omnipotent center which functions as the enterprise's brain has been subjected to much pressure as business enterprises have had to think and act quickly, re-calibrating their strategies continuously in fast-moving conditions. Under these circumstances, the traditional approach has several drawbacks:

- Rapid change demands quick reactions and continuous re-calibration. Separating the brain (the center—which plans a response) from the muscles (the line units—which enact the response) can lead to slow response and result in information distortion through hierarchical filtering processes.

- The executives with the most up-to-date understanding of evolving market realities are typically in the trenches. They are thus best-positioned to strategize *and* execute the necessary actions in real time as new imperatives unfold.
- Line managers in knowledge-based companies have the professional expertise and the educational background to undertake much of the strategizing and analytical work; assisted by new technologies, they can minimize their reliance on corporate support groups.[22]

The emerging organizational system of high-technology firms is more akin to a "federation" or a "constellation" of business units that are typically interdependent, relying on one another for critical expertise and know-how. Moreover, they have a peer-to-peer relationship with the center. The center's role is to orchestrate the broad strategic vision, develop the shared organizational and administrative infrastructure, and create the cultural glue which can create synergies, and ensure unity of mission and purpose. However, these tasks are undertaken together *with* the line units, rather than for them. This sentiment is reflected in the following: "[The center's] mission is to support our business units in fulfilling their business goals, and perform the truly corporate services in an effective and cost efficient manner."[23]

Apple Computer is a case in point. Its main line units—although varying in size, scope, and style—have a peer-to-peer relationship with one another and with the center. The heads of the line units—Apple Products, Apple USA, Apple Europe, and Apple Pacific—are represented on its top management team together with the leaders of the corporate functions—finance, human resources, and legal and administrative services. Members of the different units collectively participate in setting and implementing the corporate direction; worldwide meetings (held twice a year) of the top 400 or so executives provide focused opportunities for discussing critical challenges; and the extensive movement of people between the units ensures that personal relationships are forged to enhance inter-unit cooperation.

Dualistic Systems

Many observers may have the impression that the organizational systems of high-technology companies are in a continuous state of flux; that formal structures—in the sense of clear reporting relationships, grouping of skills, and concise assignment of responsibility, authority, and accountability—do not exist in their organic setting. Such an impression, however, only reflects one dimension of the organizational reality. Many firms we observed were both *structured and yet chaotic*; they had evolved dualistic organizational systems, designed to strike a dynamic balance between stability on the one hand, and flexibility on the other.

The first component is a substrate of the formal structure which only periodically undergoes major transformation. This provides a formal mechanism for grouping skills, clustering activities, and assigning reporting relationships, as well as a base unit which gives many employees an anchor of stability.[24] However, due to inertial forces, these bedrock structures can not be changed as frequently as may be warranted by internal and external changes. Many firms compensate for the relative inflexibility of the bedrock structure by using overlays of temporary project teams and multi-functional groups whose members are drawn from various operating units. These enable a firm to focus on critical assignments without causing major disruptions.

A good case in point is the structural evolution of ROLM Corporation, a pioneering telecommunications company which was acquired by IBM in 1984. During its 15 years as an independent company, ROLM went through 4 major re-organizations of its bedrock structure, although it formed and disbanded many temporary groups and project teams. As depicted in Table 5-2, the first major structural change was initiated in 1973 (four years after its founding) when it entered the telecommunications business. This involved a fine-tuning of its functional structure to embrace the new venture. The second re-organization occurred in 1977 when 3 autonomous divisions were set up to focus on different businesses: mil-spec computers (its original business), telecommunications products, and a new venture (later discontinued) in the energy management field. The third re-organization (which was largely confined to the telecommunications business) was initiated in 1981 when a hybrid structure was created to consolidate its end-user sales and service organization and to focus on the new initiative in office systems. A further re-organization was completed in February 1984, prior to the IBM acquisition. It resulted in a partly functional superstructure and divisional substructures devised to ensure effective co-ordination of its telecommunications and office products.

TABLE 5-2   Organizational Evolution of ROLM Corporation: 1973–83

Year	Revenue (m$)	Business	Organization
1973	3.6 Million	Mil-Spec Computers New Venture: PBX	Functional
1977	30.0 Million	Mil-Spec Computers Digital PBX New Venture: Energy Management	3 Stand-Alone Divisions
1981	294.5 Million	Mil-Spec Computers PBX Systems New Venture: Office Systems	Hybrid: Partly Functional/ Partly Divisional
1983	502.6 Million	Mil-Spec Computers PBX Office System	Functional Superstructure; Divisional Sub-structure

In many of the observed firms, such fundamental re-organizations of the bedrock structure were typically undertaken in response to, or in anticipation of, metamorphic events—such as changes in the composition of top management teams, strategic re-orientations, shifting priorities, performance setbacks, and resource constraints. Temporary teams, on the other hand, were used for a wide range of activities—including new product development, strategic assessments, and the formation of management processes. For example, in early 1984 ROLM formed a five-person team in the System Development Group (the product development arm of its telecommunications business) to set up a company-wide business planning process. Team members were drawn from various product divisions, they made their recommendations within 6 months, and the teams were subsequently disbanded.

Such dualistic systems enable high-technology firms to deal with a widely felt tension: how to create a relatively stable organizational setting within whose boundaries people and resources can be flexibly deployed. Bedrock structures are the relatively stable base units. Temporary teams are the flexible, rapid deployment overlay. They enable the organization to pool together different individuals at short notice, put them to work on diverse projects, and disband them once their task has been accomplished.

Front-Line Orientation

Historically, organizational roles and departmental activities have been divided into staff and line positions. The first category comprise functions whose power and influence are based on advisory or monitoring roles, with "the right to advise, rather than the power to decide."[25] Typically, these groups have limited direct control over line operations, and hence over revenues and profits. Functions such as personnel, planning, and MIS, among others, have historically belonged to this category. By contrast, line functions, such as sales, manufacturing, or product development, have the "power to decide" with direct control over, and accountability for, revenues and profits. Critics have long argued that as a result, staff functions have been cushioned from the harsh realities of the "market."

This instrumental distinction between staff and line functions is becoming increasingly blurred, not just in high-tech companies, but also in many traditional organizations.[26] The impetus for change has largely come from competitive pressures to reduce costs. Many staff functions are becoming directly exposed to the "front-line" realities of their internal customers—funding their operations by selling their services to the line units.[27]

In many high-technology companies, support groups are also typically responsible for undertaking what would have traditionally been viewed as advisory assignments and are held directly accountable for the results. For example, an employee relations expert may deal with a disgruntled employee, and the training staff may actually design and deliver many courses. Other staff functions, such as strategic planning and business development, are more support-oriented, rather than control-oriented. These groups typically view their role as facilitators, consultants, and process managers, rather than as formulators of strategies and overseers of line activities.[28]

This front-line orientation has re-assigned power and influence to those in direct contact with the market and competitive realities. This trend is further reflected in the fact that CEOs of a number of technology firms have dual roles and are directly accountable for specific line operations. For example, John Sculley, Apple's Chairman and CEO, has also been partially responsible for the company's product development group. In a recent interview, he made the following observation:

> *"As I look back over the last eight and a half years and say, what things would I have done differently, the one that really stands out is that I should've gotten involved in product development a lot sooner than I did. To lead a high-technology company, you really have to lead it through the technology and through the products."*[29]

This orientation fuses the strategic and operational roles of senior executives—enabling them to re-calibrate strategies based on real-time information and realistic action plans.[30]

Cosmopolitan Mindset

Many technology firms become global very early in their development. For example, it is not unusual to find young companies—less than 10 years old—with manufacturing, research, and distribution facilities in the U.S., Europe, Japan, and the Pacific Rim. Moreover, many generate more than half of their sales outside the U.S., and have a large population of non-American employees.

Such a rapid process of globalization makes it necessary to develop a cosmopolitan mindset that incorporates different cultural assumptions and premises. This is a significant challenge since it requires balancing strong corporate values (which typically reflect the "home" culture) with a broad perspective (which accommodates the diverse viewpoints of global customers, employees, and competitors). Despite the inherent challenges, however, a pluralistic culture can provide considerable versatility by drawing on diverse perspectives, approaches, and solutions.

Apple Computer is a good case in point. Its executives have attempted to manage Apple not as an American entity, but as a global company: "we want to look and feel like a local company to our customers while successfully competing with worldwide corporations that rapidly leverage expertise and resources wherever they are located."[31] Apple strives to create a cosmopolitan organization—not with one heart rooted in U.S. culture, but with "multiple hearts which beat as one" reflecting the diversity of its markets and employees.[32] It has attempted to create a pluralistic organization and a cosmopolitan culture in a number of ways:

- Its top management team is composed of different nationalities. Until 1990, a French-born executive was in charge of worldwide product development, manufacturing and R&D. A German-born national is its current President and an Australian has been in charge of the Asia-Pacific group. The composition of this team sends a strong symbolic message to its employees, partners and customers, reinforcing the value of cultural diversity.
- Workforce diversity is an important part of Apple's human resource strategy. It is a key component of its recruiting plans, promotion policies, and management training and development programs.
- Apple is also focusing on other initiatives to further strengthen its global orientation. These include "dispersed expertise to leverage unique local talent, global dissemination of knowledge and skills partly through communication forums which bring together groups with similar interests, consistent treatment of global accounts with local look and feel, global account management information systems, integrated databases and networks, and global telecommunications facilities."[33]
- Simultaneous product launch in key global markets is another goal. For example, Claris Corporation, Apple's software subsidiary, has set out to develop the U.S. and international versions of its products at the same time, so they can be distributed in its global markets soon after their U.S. introduction.[34]

In summary, Apple's strong corporate culture provides a few bedrock values, which provide "sameness" and give cohesion to its global operations. However, each region can exercise discretion in evolving its structure and style to accommodate different market conditions and cultural values. Apple's genetic code permeates every unit, yet each has its own distinctive identity. In striking an effective balance, a key challenge is "figuring out what has to be the same so that everything else can be different."[35]

Capability-Based Organizations and Multi-Talented Employees

Andrew Grove, the President and CEO of Intel Corporation coined the expression: "Our assets have legs; they walk home every day."[36] Indeed, the core capability of high-technology companies is their know-how, which resides in people. The organization can thus be characterized as a montage of individual capabilities and informal networks and relationships, rather than a series of pre-determined roles and positions and formal hierarchical relationships.

The pivotal importance of informal networks in high-technology companies is due to the fact that the productivity of knowledge-based entities depend on employees' capabilities, commitments, motivations, and relationships. They can not be programmed around pre-determined roles and positions in a machine-like hierarchy. Moreover, continuous change typically renders institutionalized roles and positions somewhat obsolete. An individual's effectiveness in getting things done is based on results and credibility, perceived reputation, and network of relationships, rather than on formal authority, job descriptions, and position in the hierarchy. In this context, titles, seniority, spans of control, formal power, and hierarchical position are not necessarily significant determinants of individual success and organizational power.

Moreover, in contrast to the specialized orientation of traditional entities, many high-technology companies build versatility into their organizations by leveraging their employees in different capacities, depending on their situational needs. This is reflected in the following comments which were made by the founder of a medical electronics firm: "I want to recruit people who are absolute experts in a given area but who can also apply their talents to other areas; "A" class players in their field, but also "B" and "C" class players in other fields."[37] Effective employees have the flexibility and the confidence to leverage their knowledge and capabilities across different areas as and when conditions change and new needs arise.

Despite the inherent difficulties, many firms try to make their employees more versatile by putting them through different experiences and rotating them through various assignments. For example, the chief financial officer of one company took over the responsibility for building and managing its direct sales and service organization, despite the fact that he had no prior sales experience. The assignment made sense because he was both negotiating with and acquiring a number of its existing distributors—requiring an understanding of the company's strategy, coupled with financial acumen, and personal trust relationships forged over a number of years. The chief administrative officer of a network-server company was given the additional responsibility for co-ordinating its major accounts programs in Japan, despite the fact that he had no previous sales experience or familiarity with the Japanese market; in this case the critical requirement was the coordination of the different functional groups in addressing the client's needs. The executive in question was ideally positioned to do this because he continuously interacted with the various groups as part of his on-going administrative responsibilities.

Developing versatile employees by exposing them to different experiences is not new or unique to the high-tech sector. As early as the 1970s, Royal Dutch Shell used its corporate planning group as a vehicle for broadening its line managers' perspective and giving them a bird's eye or "helicopter" view of Shell's global operations.[38] Similarly, job rotation programs at companies such as IBM, Hewlett Packard, and many Japanese corporations have been a key component of their career planning systems for some time. What is different in the emerging high-tech sector is that employees need to possess a flexible mindset and the ability to adjust unexpectedly and quickly to the demands of a new assignment, without going through extensive training or being assigned the responsibility as part of a systematically planned career management program.[39]

Semi-Permeable Boundaries

Much has been written in recent years about the rise of strategic alliances and collaborative partnerships. The consensus seems to suggest that such alliances are a novel form of "hybrid" organizational arrangement, provide a mechanism for pooling complementary capabilities, addressing rapid product development cycles, reducing risks, and providing strategic flexibility.[40] Moreover, in recent years they have proliferated into various forms, and are continuously evolving.

High-technology companies have been at the forefront of initiating and managing many types of strategic partnerships. These vary in form, scope, and longevity. Many companies have forged their fundamental business proposition and organizational infrastructure around partnerships. Apple, for example, collaborates with third-party software developers, dealers, distributors and resellers, and sub-system and component suppliers.

While such "leverage" models of business partnership are at the extreme end of the alliance spectrum, others may have a more limited objective. They may be used for financing purposes—as is the case with many Japanese investments in new start-ups.[41] They may give the parties reciprocal access to geographic markets, or they may provide an effective way of pooling know-how and sharing risks in developing technologically advanced products. In many instances, they are an extension of the traditional supplier-customer relationships. Irrespective of their purpose, scope, or form, their continuous formation has broken down the solid walls which have historically separated the firm from its external stakeholders.

The emergence of these semi-permeable boundaries in the high-technology sector is organizationally apparent in a number of ways. Many firms have access to their partners' internal information systems through electronic mail networks. For example, Apple gives its partners—including software developers, consultants, dealers and resellers, and sub-system suppliers—access to its internal electronic mail system. This facilitates communication between the different groups and gives them timely information on new product releases, press announcements, and re-organizations, among other items.[42] Additionally, it is a common practice for engineers working on joint development projects to be assigned to a strategic partner. The employee in question becomes a temporary employee of the partner for a limited period of time—forging crucial relationships and gaining access to vital information about the partner's culture and modus operandi.[43]

In summary, the key organizational challenge facing many high-technology firms is balancing several opposing tensions: selling and servicing existing products while developing and bringing new ones on stream; remaining, disciplined, focused, and frugal, while continuously learning, experimenting, and re-calibrating; generating consensus, yet ensuring timely decisions; balancing individual contribution and teamwork; ensuring short-term profitability in the context of a long-term vision. The modern high-technology enterprise needs diverse capabilities and multi-faceted organizational arrangements to flexibly deal with these complex tensions. As depicted in Table 5-3, their organizational building blocks

TABLE 5-3   Organizational Attributes: A Comparison

Traditional Model	Emerging Model
Single Center	Multiple Centers
Self Contained	Steeples of Expertise
Independent Activities	Interdependent Units
Vertically Integrated	Multiple Alliances
Uniform Structure	Diverse Structures
Parochial Mindset	Cosmopolitan Mindset
Emphasis on Efficiency	Emphasis on Flexibility

have evolved in order to address these tensions, and to provide different forms of flexibility.

THE EMERGENCE OF A BI-MODAL ORGANIZATION

Many firms appear to have walked a tightrope between these tensions without having allowed any one imperative to dominate the strategic and organizational context. These attempts cannot be described in monolithic, unidimensional terms, as simple recipes and "either/or" solutions. Their organizational systems were by no means chaotic, but neither were they in total control. They were not frugal although a cost-conscious mentality pervaded their style. The management teams were not mavericks, yet an entrepreneurial zeal and anti-bureaucratic sentiments were frequently observed. They focused on generating short-term results but did not lose sight of their long-term mission. The resulting organizational systems can be best depicted as "bi-modal"—in that they could accommodate opposing tendencies and yet function as coherent and cohesive concerns. Signs of bi-modality were commonly observed in broaching three types of tension: Centralization versus decentralization, stability versus change, and uniformity versus diversity.

Centralization and Decentralization

The organizational system of many high-technology firms clearly transcends the centralization-decentralization spectrum.[44] On the one hand, it needs to remain loose, decentralized, and differentiated in order to provide the capability for creative initiatives and rapid responsiveness. On the other hand, tight centralized direction is needed to maintain strategic cohesion, manage interdependencies, and reduce the time lag between decision and action. This imperative is reflected in the following: "we like the idea of small, decentralized units . . . with focused accountability . . . but our products have to play together . . . our customers buy an integrated system . . . there is a major element of success that depends on co-ordination and close co-operation between the units."[45]

Centralizing tendencies can be observed in visible and involved leaders whose passion, vision, and charisma are critical in charting the direction, generating cohesion, defining the boundaries, and motivating the troops.[46] Moreover, top management teams are typically involved in new, risky projects during the formative stages and participate side-by-side with the troops in the development process. For example, a co-founder of ROLM was directly involved in the development of its office systems products during the early 1980s, even though he was an executive vice president and a member of ROLM's top management team.[47]

However, strong leadership and directed moves do not imply that leaders are the sole source of the corporate vision, or that strategies and decisions are imposed from the top. The scenario portrayed by individual contributors is one of a "great deal of autonomy," a "lot of room for initiatives," and "doing whatever it takes to get the job done." Indeed, those who are promoted and rewarded are typically champions of major initiatives and doers who have made things happen. Such levels of autonomy have historically been associated with decentralized structures.

The resulting organization can be best characterized as both centralized *and* decentralized. It is centralized in that top management teams are a critical force behind charting the strategic direction and defining the boundaries for individual and team initiatives. It is decentralized in that front-line personnel can exercise discretion in dealing with new imperatives as they arise—within broad, yet well-defined, strategic and cultural parameters.[48] The critical catalyst in creating this alignment is reliance on formal and informal bridging mechanisms which establish direct communication channels between the leaders and the doers. These include electronic-based communication, planning sessions and review meetings, informal opportunities for interaction, educational forums, and open access protocols.[49] Regular communication ensures that impending changes in market realities and strategic priorities can be quickly discussed, evaluated, and implemented.

Stability and Dynamism

Bi-modality is also manifest in the tradeoffs made between stability and change as reflected in the following remark: "we want to be flexible and respond to market changes without *creating chaos and confusion amongst our people.*"[50] Indeed, the priorities facing many high-technology firms are in a state of flux, resulting in continuous change and frequent re-calibrations. For example, one month the focus may be on launching a new product; another month it may shift over to volume manufacturing and procurement; and in the third month, product re-design, based on lead-users' feedback, may be on top of the business agenda.

Dynamism and change are accommodated through extensive reliance on project teams, micro re-organizations, and re-deployment of core employees in various capacities. Moreover, many high-technology firms seek to improve their flexibility by relying on temporary workers, specialist vendors, and consultants and contractors. Reliance on such a variable talent pool enables them to undertake different assignments without incurring the fixed cost and the long-term commitment expected by core employees.

However, constant change can also be threatening and de-motivating for individuals, and disruptive and unproductive for the organization. It is not surprising to find that many firms strive to create anchors of stability around which everything else can change. Some attempt to clarify and articulate a clear sense of purpose and a few overarching values which define the broad boundaries within which changes take shape.[51] For example, the mission of Conner Peripherals, a disk drive manufacturer and one of the fastest growing companies in U.S. corporate history, is described as follows: "Identify customers' needs sooner and fill them faster than the competition."[52] Moreover, their recruiting practices and orientation programs help set the employees' expectations and thereby ensure an effective fit between personal and organizational goals.

Uniformity and Diversity

There is a clear sense of corporate purpose and cultural identity associated with pioneering high-technology companies, yet their style professes to value diversity. Inculcating diversity enables these firms to become versatile, pool together different capabilities, and nurture the ability to address different contingencies.

Many high-technology companies attempt to become "diverse" by blending various management styles and cultural perspectives. For example, they may recruit inexperienced college graduates as well as experienced professionals with extensive track record. They also recruit people from different cultures and ethnic backgrounds to blend together different cognitive orientations. A young company in the network server business, for example, consciously sought to recruit a woman chief financial officer from a different cultural background in order to provide a role model for its women professionals and develop the capability base to deal with clients and partners from other cultures. In this case, after a period of extensive search, they recruited an Asian woman as their chief financial officer.

Composition of top management teams can also send an important symbolic message and further reinforce the importance of diversity. A well-known case is the complementarity between David Packard's business style and Bill Hewlett's technical orientation. Other famous examples include the late Noyce-Moore-Grove troika at Intel, and Oshman, Maxfield, and Chamberlain at ROLM. These teams represent unity through their shared values and overarching sense of purpose. Diversity is promoted in that they have complementary skills and management styles.

Recently, a number of high-technology firms have also set out to sensitize their employees to cultural diversity through in-house training and educational programs. A few companies have made strong commitments to internal training programs that prepare executives for global assignments and strive to build cultural awareness in all employees. The crucial value of diversity further highlights the importance of distinctive corporate values. These spell out a few boundary conditions within which everything else is free to operate. They define the limits and set the constraints for individual and team initiatives.

SUMMARY AND CONCLUSION

Developing flexible organizations is critical for business enterprises in the 1990s. Flexibility is a multi-dimensional concept—demanding agility and versatility; associated with change, innovation, and novelty; coupled with robustness and resilience, implying stability, sustainable advantage, and capabilities that may evolve over time.

A critical challenge facing many business entities is how to transform their traditional organizational systems and management practices in order to become more flexible. This task requires identifying and implementing those approaches, processes, and tools that can be used to manage a bimodal—rather than a monolithic—organization. This poses a major challenge because our existing organizational systems and managerial mindsets have evolved to address uni-dimensional imperatives, rather than the new, rampant multi-dimensional tensions.

Moreover, our expectations, norms of behavior, vocabularies, and frames of reference have evolved around the traditional themes of stability rather than change, uniformity rather than diversity, and optimality rather than flexibility. We need to forge new attitudes and behavior patterns by deploying educational programs, incentive systems, and communication protocols, among others, to support and reinforce the importance of flexibility, diversity, and dynamism. If the experience of the high-technology sector is indicative of broader trends, the 1990s is likely to be a decade of organizational experimentation and managerial innovation, and one likely to bring forth novel organizational systems and management approaches. This challenge requires focused attention, a readiness to experiment, and the willingness to share ideas and learn from different corporate experiences.

REFERENCES

1. The need for flexibility is discussed in a number of recent books. For example, see C. Handy, *The Age of Unreason* (Boston, MA: Harvard Business School Press, 1989); R.M. Kanter, *When Giants Learn to Dance* (New York, NY: Simon and Schuster, 1989); T. Peters, *Thriving on Chaos* (New York, NY: Harper and Row, 1987); R. Pascale, *Managing on the Edge* (New York, NY: Simon and Schuster, 1990).

2. These findings are derived, in part, from a study of 37 firms in the electronics sector, conducted during 1982–91. The firms varied in size, ranging from start-ups to multi-billion dollar corporations. Their businesses spanned several high technology industries—including computer hardware and software, networking and telecommunications, computer peripherals, semiconductors, and scientific instruments. Sources of

     data included structured and semi-structured interviews with a cross-section of senior executives and rank and file employees, analysis of internal documents, attendance at company meetings, and use of published data.

3. Speech given by Bill Joy, a co-founder of Sun Microsystems, at the Churchill Club, Palo Alto, California, 1990.

4. In an earlier article, it was argued that alignment between the apex and the core, or the generals and the troops, is critical in this context. See H. Bahrami and S. Evans "Stratocracy in High Technology Firms," *California Management Review* (Fall 1987).

5. Self-managing, multi-functional teams are considered to be the backbone of "fast cycle" companies. See J.L. Bower and T. Hout, "Fast Cycle Capability for Competitive Power," *Harvard Business Review* (November/December 1988). A "project orientation" enacted through "co-located, joint function teams" is viewed as the hallmark of innovative companies. See T. Peters, "Get Innovative or Get Dead," *California Management Review* (Fall 1990), p. 23. A recent British study concludes that in today's business environment career success often hinges on project management (and hence team management) skills. The business section in London's *Sunday Times,* March 11, 1990. Additionally, since the Hawthrone studies we have known that groups are a critical source of individual commitment, loyalty, and identity—essential ingredients for managing professional and expectant knowledge-workers. For an insightful perspective on the Hawthorne Studies, see F.J. Roethlisberger, *The Elusive Phenomena* (Boston, MA: Harvard University Press, 1977).

6. For example, general contractors in the construction industry have relied on their long-standing relationships with specialist sub-contractors. The textile sector has historically evolved around an intricate web of relationships between different specialists; and the automobile industry has traditionally benefited from the diverse capabilities of its subcontractors—each possessing a unique skill in a distinctive area. For further discussion see W. Powell, "Hybrid Organizational Arrangements," *California Management Review* (Fall 1987).

7. Ibid.

8. J.S. Evans. "Strategic Flexibility in Business," SRI Business Intelligence Program. Report #678, Menlo Park, California, December 1982.

9. As Kanter points out the broad implication is that "people's careers are more dependent on their own resources and less dependent on the fate of a particular company . . . no longer counting on the corporation to provide security and stature requires people to build those resources in themselves." See Kanter, op. cit., p. 357.

10. Speech given by K. Sullivan, Senior Vice President, Apple Computer, to the author's MBA class on Organizational Behavior at U.C. Berkeley, April 1991.

11. Miles and Snow characterize the firm of the future as a "network" in which "brokers" play significant roles as intermediaries. See R. Miles and C. Snow, "Organizations: New Concepts for New Forms," *California Management Review* (Spring 1986). Hedlund describes the emergence of "heterarchy" based on observations of Swedish multinationals. By way of contrast from their hierarchical predecessors, these firms are characterized by "diffusion of strategic roles, a wide range of governance modes, and holographic attributes." G. Hedlund, "The Hypermodern MNC—A Heterarchy?" *Human Resource Management Journal* (Spring 1986). Child discusses how information and communication technologies have enabled many firms to "externalize" internal activities to contractors, and yet retain a certain measure of operational

control—giving rise to novel organizational arrangements. See J. Child, "Information Technology and Response to Strategic Challenges," *California Management Review* (Fall 1987). Handy describes the firm of the future as resembling a "shamrock"—comprising partners, consultants and part-time workers, as well as full-time employees. See Handy, op.cit.

12. J.S. Evans, "Strategic Flexibility and High Technology Maneuvers: A Conceptual Framework," *Journal of Management Studies* (January 1991).

13. Ibid.

14. A. G. Hart, "Anticipations, Business Planning, and the Cycle," *Quarterly Journal of Economics* (February 1937), p. 272.

15. G.L.S. Shackle, *Expectations, Investment, and Income* (Oxford University Press, 1938).

16. Bell Atlantic and ABB are cases in point. See R. M. Kanter's interview with R. Smith of Bell Atlantic entitled "Championing Change," *Harvard Business Review* (January/February 1991), p. 26; and W. Taylor interview with P. Barnevik of ABB in "The Logic of a Global Business," *Harvard Business Review* (March/April 1991), p. 95.

17. Internal memorandum from the Executive Vice President of a $700 million high-technology firm on its business philosophy, May 26, 1981.

18. See Taylor, op. cit., p. 95.

19. On changes at B.P., see C. Lorenz, "A drama behind closed doors that paved the way for a corporate metamorphosis," *Financial Times,* March 13, 1990, p.13.

20. See C. Bartlett and S. Ghoshal, "Organizing for Worldwide Effectiveness," *California Management Review* (Fall 1988).

21. See A.D. Chandler, *Strategy and Structure* (Cambridge, MA: MIT Press, 1962) on the historical evolution of the multi-divisional structure.

22. J. Child, "New Technology and Developments in Management Organization," *Omega,* 12/3 (1984).

23. Source: internal board presentation at a software company. The firm employs about 100 professionals in roles which are classified as "corporate." These include "finance and administration" (corporate reporting, taxes, treasury, planning, investor relations, and internal audit), infrastructure support (facilities and safety, information systems, corporate purchasing, and risk management), legal services, human resources, and corporate communications.

24. See H. Bahrami and S. Evans "Emerging Organizational Regimes in High Technology Firms," *Human Resource Management Journal* (Spring 1989) for an account of the evolution of the formal structure in high technology firms.

25. H. Mintzberg, *Structure in Fives: Designing Effective Organizations* (Englewood Cliffs, NJ: Prentice Hall, 1983).

26. A good case in point is Bell Atlantic's "client-service" groups. During a recent reorientation process, many of its support functions have had to operate as line groups—enlisting the support of other units in order to continue their operations. In this case, the line units can either buy their required services from the support groups or from outside vendors; the only constraint is that they can not develop their own support functions. Reciprocally, the support units can also offer their services to outside clients, within certain competitive guidelines. In this way, the old staff entities have been transformed into line operations—with their own clients, revenues, profits, and direct ac-

countability to the user. If the activity can not be supported, it is disbanded, in direct response to market feedback. See Kanter, op. cit. The point was also discussed by Ray Smith, Bell Atlantic's Chairman and CEO, in a keynote speech given at a U.C. Berkeley Executive Program, Sturbridge, MA, October 1990.

27. For a detailed study of how the human resource function is being transformed along some of these dimensions, see The Conference Board, "The Changing Human Resource Function," Report number 950, New York, 1990.

28. This was the finding of a study conducted by the author; H. Bahrami, "Strategic Planning in Emerging and Established Firms: A Comparison," paper presented at the fifth Strategic Management Society Conference, Barcelona, Spain, 1985.

29. See R. Karlgaard, "Sculley Looks Ahead," *Upside* (October 1991), p. 101.

30. For more detail on how strategic decisions in high technology companies entail continuous re-calibration see H. Bahrami and S. Evans "Strategy Making in High-Technology Firms," *California Management Review* (Winter 1989); for a study on how effective executives in the microcomputer industry relied on real-time information to make decision, see K. Eisenhardt, "Speed and Strategic Choice," *California Management Review* (Spring 1990).

31. Internal presentation, Apple Computer, September 23, 1988.

32. Spindler, M. Speech given to Apple's worldwide sales force, March 1987.

33. Internal document on Apple's New Enterprise Project, 1988.

34. *San Jose Business Journal,* Special Report (March 1992), p. 14.

35. Personal Communication with executives at Apple Computer, 1990.

36. Indeed the phrase "people are our key asset" is often used not just in high-tech companies, but increasingly in traditional corporations. This is partly reflected in the recent focus on "human resources" as a critical function. See London's *Financial Times,* January 28, 1991, p. 14. Extensive reference to the importance of "networking" is another manifestation of this trend. In a recent article, Lorenz discusses the confusion surrounding the concept of the "networked" organization, especially concerning "official" and "unofficial" networking: "Official networks are certainly a praiseworthy advance over the bureaucracies they replace. But they are often little more than streamlined, well-run, and physically-dispersed committees . . . the real breakthrough is official blessing for all sorts of unofficial, informal networks . . . it is they, much more than the official variety, which will really help create the open and flexible learning organizations which most forward looking companies aspire to become." "Network Organizations," *Financial Times,* Management Page, April 3, 1991.

37. Personal Communication, W. New, M.D., August 1989.

38. Evans, op. cit.

39. It is commonplace to find employees assigned to new roles or seconded to other groups on a frequent and, at times, unplanned basis. For example, a key member of the engineering staff in a surveyed company was unexpectedly seconded for nine months to the manufacturing group because he was very knowledgeable about an outsourcing issue—a critical priority for the manufacturing group at the time.

40. See Powell, op. cit.; Evans, op. cit.; Kanter, op. cit.; B. Borys and D.B. Jemison, "Hybrid Organizations as Strategic Alliances," Working Paper 951r, Graduate School of Business, Stanford University, 1987; D. Mowery, *International Collaborative Ventures in Manufacturing* (Cambridge, MA: Ballinger, 1988); W. Ouchi and M. Bolton, "The

Logic of Joint Research and Development," *California Management Review* (Fall 1988); Y.L. Doz, "Technology Partnerships between Larger and Smaller Firms," *International Studies of Management and Organization,* 17/4 (1987).

41. See A. Besher, "Asian Investor Feast," *Upside,* (November/December 1989).

42. In order to differentiate between the information given to "outsiders" versus "employees," Apple has its "Hotlinks" electronic bulletin board which is only accessible by company employees.

43. See N. Rutter, "Kubota-San," *Upside,* (January/February 1990).

44. See Bahrami and Evans (1989), op. cit.

45. Interview with R. Maxfield, Executive Vice President and co-founder, ROLM Corporation, April 1985.

46. Well-known examples include ROLM and Ken Oshman, Digital Equipment and Ken Olson, Intel and Andrew Grove, Sun Microsystem and Scott McNeilly, Cypress Semiconductor and T.J. Rogers, Microsoft and Bill Gates, Software Publishing and Fred Gibbons, NeXT and Steve Jobs, ASK and Sandra Kurtzig, Electronic Arts and Trip Hawkins, Oracle and Larry Ellison, among others.

47. This contrasts with the practices observed in many traditional firms. As recent studies have shown, new activities in established entities are, by and large, initiated at the periphery of the firm [see Beer et al., "Why Change Programs Don't Produce Change," *Harvard Business Review* (November/December 1990)] or by lower level champions in an autonomous manner [see R.A. Burgelman and L.R. Sayles, *Inside Corporate Innovation* (New York, NY: Free Press, 1986)]. This makes sense since in established firms those on the periphery have much to gain and little to lose by embarking on presumably risky, new initiatives. By contrast, their senior colleagues would have typically advanced in the organization by playing according to the prevalent rules, without disturbing the status quo. In the absence of a major crisis, many are thus likely to support a major change either under crisis conditions, or when it has proved to be feasible and entails minimal risk to the organization.

48. New technologies have provided the means to transcend the centralization/decentralization spectrum, see J. Child, "New Technology and Developments in Management Organization," *Omega,* 12/3 (1984); and J. Child, "Information Technology and Response to Strategic Challenges," *California Management Review* (Fall 1987); G. Huber, "The Nature and Design of Post Industrial Organization," *Management Science,* 30 (1984); M.L. Markus and D. Robey, "Information Technology and Organizational Change," *Management Science,* 34 (1988); S. Zuboff, *In the Age of the Smart Machine* (New York, NY: Basic Books, 1988).

49. For further discussion, see Bahrami and Evans (1989), op.cit.

50. Personal Communication, Executive Vice President of a software company, prior to a major re-organization, March 1989.

51. For an assessment of the critical role of corporate culture in business organizations, see C. O'Reilly, "Corporations, Culture, and Commitment," *California Management Review* (Summer 1989).

52. "Managing at Conner," Internal Employee Orientation Handbook, Conner Peripherals, 1992.

The author would like to express sincere thanks to Glenn Carroll of the Haas School of Business, U.C. Berkeley, John Rollwagen of Cray Research, and Kevin Sullivan of Apple Computer for their helpful comments on earlier drafts of this article. The field research was made possible, in part, by the participation of many high-tech companies and their executives. Special thanks are due to Bob Maxfield, Ken Oshman, and Dennis Paboo-jian, formerly of ROLM Corporation, for sharing their insights and experiences.

6

The Organization
of Innovation

Tom Burns & G.M. Stalker

TECHNICAL PROGRESS AND SOCIAL CHANGE

In their most general form, the findings of this research can be put into two statements: Technical progress and organizational development are aspects of one and the same trend in human affairs; and the persons who work to make these processes actual are also their victims.

The connexion between progress in material technology and the emergence of new forms of social organization is familiar enough. But it has become submerged in the century-old controversy about the correct causal sequence of technical progress and social evolution. According to one view, widely held by American social scientists (see e.g.[4,5]), but stated in its most uncompromising form by Marx, technical progress underlies every kind of change in the social order: "Assume a particular state of development in the productive faculties of man and you will get a corresponding form of commerce and consumption. Assume particular degrees of development of production, commerce, and consumption, and you will have a corresponding form of social constitution, a corresponding organization of the family, of orders or of classes, in a word, a corresponding civil society."[6] The argument has an oddly up-to-date ring, not so much in terms of the interpretation of history as of the actualities of international politics. So convinced have we become of the dependence of the total social, political, and economic order on technical development that national output of scientific discoveries and rate of technological advance have begun to appear as an ultimate criterion of culture, and different political and social systems are compared as facilitators of this kind of achievement.

According to the other view, technical progress is the outcome of changes in the institutions of society, even simply, as Durkheim[7] argued, of population growth, which produces not only new needs but the improvements and expansions of knowledge and equipment necessary to satisfy them.

Like many another instance of the chicken-and-egg conundrum, the question which comes first conceals a false antithesis. A social technology, as witnessed in the growth of modern institutions, has been developed alongside technology in the material sense.

The clue lies in Tönnies' perception of the development of modern society as itself a technological process. The relationships and institutions he regarded as characteristic of the modern world are those which enable persons to manipulate others, individually and *en masse,* in the pursuit of their own ends. Thus other people take on more and more of the quality of a natural environment which man looks on as resources for him to consume and manipulate. In many important respects we treat "human beings like inanimate objects and tools."[8] It could almost be said that Tönnies regarded social change as one aspect of technical development; organizational techniques and devices for manipulating others were constantly invading the social order.

Progress in power technology, in agriculture, in engineering, in chemicals, and the rest have proceeded—quite inevitably and necessarily—alongside developments in working organizations and in communications, and alongside the elaboration of social and political controls, financial and other economic mechanisms.* Developments on each side have often been by way of adaptation to changes on the other side. Yet there remains the discrepancy, the obvious and awful gap between technical achievement and the constraint and fears which bear upon people in their day-to-day lives. Consciousness of the gap has sometimes, in recent years, found express on in opaque generalizations about man's control of nature out-running his social abilities.

The trouble about such statements is that they mask the realities to which they refer. What is true is that developments in the one have been forced through with just as little regard for ultimate consequences to human welfare as in the other. The advantages looked for, and won, by the progress of technology, both material and social, have been immediate or short-run. Very often, these rewards are of the kind which can benefit only individuals or interested minorities. The cost, in more destructive wars, in dust-bowls, in road accidents, on the one hand, and in slums and industrial servitude, emotional deprivation, loss of intellectual and economic independence on the other, only becomes apparent in the long run. It then manifests itself often enough as a price to be paid by others. Unforeseen long-term advantages have of course accrued too. The point is that technological development has typically occurred as a consequence of decisions made in the light of short-term views of the balance of advantage and cost to people in controlling positions.

All novelty involves some degree of risk. The vast majority of biological mutations are said to be harmful. When, as in human affairs, enormous numbers of

---

*Professor Jewkes has suggested that "Whilst no one would wish to deny that technology and science (in that order) have contributed much to the raising of standards of living in the last two centuries, there is a disposition in these days to exaggerate the contribution they have made and to underestimate that made by new social organisations and institutions."[9]

random possibilities are eliminated by rational choice, the chances of harm rather than good resulting are reduced, not eliminated. The harm consists in both cases in making the individual or organization less fit to survive in its environment than was its predecessor. Very often, the environment of the person or organization is itself changing, so that even to maintain the same degree of fitness for survival, people and institutions may have to change their ways. So the risks attendant upon change may have to be weighed against other risks arising from maintaining the same state of affairs.

This condition of ordinary human existence is made explicit and articulate in the institutions and procedures of industry. And in those sectors of industry in which the creation of innovations is a constant and important part of the total enterprise, the processes of change become visible in an obvious and dramatic way. Here too, the mutual, procreative impact of developments in material technology and social organization finds its clearest expression.

In one very important sense, the link between the two trends is a necessary interdependence. Invention, even more than science, is a social phenomenon; in quite matter-of-fact ways, it is a human activity which can only be fulfilled when certain social conditions obtain, when the inventor inhabits a milieu which prompts him to devote himself to a specific line of work with the promise of rewards—in money, power, or even a secure livelihood, in fame, or even self-esteem—and which will thereafter support him economically and intellectually. The notion of the hermit genius, spinning inventions out of his intellectual and psychic innards, is a nineteenth-century myth, useful then, as myths may always be, but dangerous, as myths always are, once its period of usefulness is past.

If, as Whitehead said, the greatest invention of the nineteenth century was the invention of the method of invention,[10] the task of the succeeding century has been to organize inventiveness. The difference is not in the nature of invention or of inventors, but in the manner in which the context of social institutions is organized for their support.

THE SOCIAL CONTEXT OF INVENTION

The review of the past institutional context of industrial innovation which follows is designed, therefore, to underline the importance of that context and to point out the ways in which it has significantly changed. It is not offered as a history, even in a very abridged form, of the relationship between science and industry during the last two hundred years, but rather as a sketch of the phases of change in institutions of some importance to society. It forms the background to the succeeding account of the attempt by industrial concerns to digest the thing they have swallowed.

During the middle years of the last century the electrical industry was established on the basis, largely, of supplying telegraph services. Within a few years the development of electric motors for tramways and stationary machinery led to very considerable expansion. As new applications multiplied, the need for heavier and more efficient generating plant and distribution equipment accelerated the process. By 1880 there was a flourishing, keenly competitive, electrical industry not only in Britain and in the United States, but also in Germany, France, and other European countries. It was an industry, moreover, in which the technological base was very recent—middle-aged men in the industry would be well aware of the first commercial applications—and in which new applications and design improvements followed each other extremely rapidly. Yet the two major innovations during the last twenty years of the century, incandescent electric lighting[11] and radio,[12] were the work of newcomers, of inventors and enterprises unconnected with the existing industry. No spectacular "discovery" lighted upon by an individual genius was really responsible; electric lamps and wireless transmission were "in the air" many years before the first commercial companies were floated.

Swan, a chemist, made experimental incandescent lamps in 1860 which employed the same high-resistance conductor, carbonized paper, as was used in the first commercial lamps marketed twenty years later. There were, by 1880, large industrial concerns manufacturing lighting and other electrical equipment; yet in the event it was Edison who, two years after becoming interested in the possibility, first developed the lamp and formed an independent concern to manufacture it.

Lodge, following upon Hertz's earlier experimental work, demonstrated wireless reception before the British Association in 1894, and two years earlier a physicist had written in the *Fortnightly Review* of the "possibility of telegraphy without wires, posts, cables, or any of our present costly appliances," adding "this is no mere dream of a visionary philosopher. All the requirements needed to bring it to within grasp of daily life are well within the possibilities of discovery, and are so reasonable and so clearly in the path of researches which are now being actively prosecuted in every capital of Europe that we may any day expect to hear that they have emerged from the realms of speculation to those of sober fact" (quoted[12]). Yet the development of this obviously profitable venture interested no commercial concerns for ten years.*

In the case of radio, it was the twenty-year-old Marconi who, on the basis of Hertz's work as described in an Italian journal, constructed home-made equipment which was sufficiently advanced after three years' work to communicate messages over eight miles and to bring the Marconi Company into being.

Anyone who has read accounts of technological advances, of inventions, during the nineteenth century will perceive this pattern of development as in many ways entirely typical. It is typical not only of the way in which invention then "happened," but, even more, of the way people thought of invention as happening at any time. Invention was seen as the product of genius, wayward, uncontrollable, often amateurish; or if not of genius, then of accident and sudden

---

*In America the pattern was oddly repetitive, for in the 1870's Graham Bell had tried to interest telegraph companies in the new, and rival, method of communication by telephone which he had invented; after unavailing efforts he founded the American Telephone and Telegraph Company. By the 1890's this company was the "most research-minded concern" in the industry. Yet it felt unconcerned about radio (apart from one brief and unsuccessful episode in 1906) until 1911, when the threat from wireless telegraphy was too strong to be any longer ignored.

inspiration. As such, it could not be planned for, organized as a part of the field of existing industry, the idea was intrinsically absurd. In nineteenth-century Britain the archetypal formula for the process of innovation was enshrined in the fantasy of Watt and the kettle.

The fitting of this latter myth to the key episode of the earlier technical revolution was itself characteristic. Of course, the myth of accident and inspiration did go some way towards accounting for the *nineteenth-century* facts. And the outstanding fact was the random distribution of scientific and technical information through the new journals, popular lectures, and societies. These diffusers, and the continued exploitation of major inventions by craftsmen, made it seem possible for any individual innovation to be produced by almost anybody, almost anywhere. Again, the disciplined attack on one difficulty after another, which is how the gap between the scientific idea and the ultimate product is bridged, was still intrinsic to the achievement, but the process was an individual, usually personal, enterprise. Often, as in the case of the electric lamp and radio, many individuals at great removes from each other were involved over a period of years in the development of a single invention.

Images and myths about the past had to fit these contemporary facts. So the boy Watt sat dreaming in front of a boiling kettle and later invented the steam engine. The essential condition of membership of a closely linked group of "applied scientists," as they would now be called, in the Universities of Glasgow and Edinburgh, the especial circumstance of friendship with Joseph Black, whose discovery of latent heat lay at the bottom of Watt's improvements to the Newcomen engine, the inclusion of the industrialist Roebuck in the circle of personal acquaintanceship—these, the really significant factors, were simply left out of popular account. They were social circumstances which were no longer appropriate to the progress of technology.

Coteries and Clubs

In the latter half of the eighteenth century the Scottish universities were centrally involved not only in the primal discoveries of the industrial revolution in chemistry and engineering but in the technical applications and commercial ventures which exploited them. The rapidity of technological development in so many fields which were being explored simultaneously in the laboratories of Edinburgh and Glasgow was the direct outcome of close personal association between persons with different expertises and different resources. But the association between people like Watt, Black, and Roebuck was founded not so much on their membership of a common profession or organization as on membership of a small, closely integrated society.[13] In the Scotland of the eighteenth century, for such men to be acquainted with each other was virtually inevitable.

Such circles of personal acquaintanceship served as a social medium for a further decade or so. By the beginning of the nineteenth century, fellow-students and friends sought to institutionalize their informal acquaintanceships. Clubs rather than learned societies, as the Lunar Society and the Royal Society of Edinburgh were, they and their off-spring and kindred in Manchester and Newcastle, and the archetype in London, included the persons responsible for scientific advance, technical invention and, to a large extent, industrial innovation.

"Towards the close of the last century," says Smiles in his life of Boulton and Watt,[14] "there were many little clubs or coteries of scientific and literary men established in the provinces, the like of which do not now exist—probably because the communication with the metropolis is so much easier, and because London more than ever absorbs the active intelligence of England, especially in the higher departments of science, art, and literature. The provincial coteries of which we speak were usually centres of the best and most intelligent society of their neighbourhoods and were for the most part distinguished by an active and liberal spirit of inquiry. Leading minds attracted others of like tastes and pursuits and social circles were formed which proved, in many instances, the source of great intellectual activity, as well as enjoyment. At Liverpool, Roscoe and Currie were the centres of one such group; at Warrington Aiken, Enfield, and Priestley of another; at Bristol Dr Beddoes and Humphrey Davy of a third; and at Norwich the Taylors and the Martineaus of a fourth. But perhaps the most distinguished of these provincial societies was that at Birmingham, of which Boulton and Watt were among the most prominent members.

"*The object of the proposed Society was to be at the same time friendly and scientific.* The members were to exchange views with each other on topics relating to literature, arts, and science; each contributing his quota of entertainment and instruction." (our italics.)

But the rate of expansion of science and technology was too rapid to be accommodated by adapting and multiplying the institutions of sociable intercourse, vigorous as they were in middle-class society at that time. The founding, in 1831, of the British Association, a self-conscious attempt to institute personal links between all scientists and technologists, may be regarded as marking the end of the period when a network of personal relationships on the necessary scale was feasible.

The Diffusion of Technical Information

What took the place of the circle of people who were at once friends, fellow scientists, and business partners, or the coterie whose common interests were at the same time scientific, technological, and financial? Instances of the kind quoted earlier, and the myth, still surviving today, of the lonely inventive genius, suggest that in the period roughly from 1825 to 1875—succeeding the great days of the provincial Societies—information about scientific discoveries became available to a wide variety of people. Personal communication was replaced by mass communication.

The change from speech and letters, involving small-scale contact of a peculiarly intimate and undisturbed kind, to print, by which leisurely and undisturbed communication is effected impersonally, randomly, and with large numbers of individuals, is an institutional change of a particularly potent kind; we are familiar with the part played by printing in accelerating the diffusion of information and ideas in the Renaissance and Reformation, and thus acting as a multiplier of their social impact. A similar function as accelerator and diffuser may be ascribed to the appearance of scientific journalism in the nineteenth century.

There are three phases of this latter-day diaspora, according to the kind of evidence which may be found from the catalogues of journals published by the British Museum. In 1800 there were less than ten scientific journals published in the British Isles. By 1900 there were over a hundred and thirty. The first quarter-century saw the appearance of new general scientific journals, but their numbers are fairly constant (about fifteen) from 1830 onwards. From 1825, the main growth is in specialized and technical journals; there were three in 1825 and over forty by 1860. From mid-century onwards the published transactions and journals of learned societies begin to grow rapidly in numbers, from a dozen in 1850 to about seventy in 1900.[15]

Not only did books and journals appear at an accelerating rate, but clubs and institutes spread the new learning to the utmost limits of literacy in industrial Britain. Attendance at lectures by eminent scientists became as obligatory in the manufacturing towns as was attendance at church and chapel in the country; interest in science, even to the point of patronizing individual scientific workers or building a private laboratory, became gentlemanly. In short, the institutional process which we know as technology—the linking of (a) knowledge of the laboratory demonstrations which established scientific hypotheses with (b) knowledge of manufacturing operations, and of these two with (c) knowledge of existing or presumptive demand for goods and services—this process was spread at random among a very large proportion of the literate population. The fact that it was so spread meant that innovations might appear almost anywhere, might be lighted upon by almost anyone.

The incoherence of the social institutions of technology at the time was reflected in the rudimentary social forms by which innovations were socialized. Technological changes occurred largely through the birth and death of organizations, the simplest form of institutional change. Capital was plentiful, liquid, and diffused, and was readily available for the exploitation of a new device or product. But the institutional build-up around the invention was normally rigid and was identified closely with the line of application and development originally conceived. New concerns had a fairly restricted expectation of life, even if they survived the highly lethal period of early infancy; "clogs to clogs in three generations" was a piece of proverbial wisdom current in the oldest factory area in the world. The new devices which arose to render the old ones obsolete were generally exploited by new concerns. As Elton Mayo has remarked, the small scale of business enterprises allowed this change to take place without too much dislocation of the social and economic order.[16]

Invention could, and did, make big fortunes in astonishingly short times. The supply of risk capital was relatively enormous. Technical limitations to large lot production were such that the build-up of production had to be slow, and the manufacture of a single device, progressively improved, could absorb all the energies and resources of its designer and backers over a period of years. In this milieu the economic, social, and psychological pressures were all against the organization of research as an industrial resource, and against instituting invention in a professional salaried occupation. The anecdote of Ferranti's weaning from the post he entered at Siemens when he left school reflects the ethos of technical innovation at that time. Ferranti, at the age of seventeen, had invented his first alternator. A meeting with another engineer, Alfred Thompson, led to an introduction to a London barrister:

> *"And you mean to tell me you're content to be at Siemens'," he said, "earning £1 a week! Good God!"*
>
> *Lawyers see life on the seamy side; small wonder then that they become suspicious of all men.*
>
> *"Ferranti," he said, "if you continue at a job like that, I'll tell you what will happen. As soon as they discover you've got an inventive ability they'll offer you £5 a week and proceed to rob your brains. You'll do the inventing and they'll collect the cash."*
>
> *This was rather bewildering, but it chimed in with certain thoughts that had arisen in Ferranti's own mind.*
>
> *"Perhaps I'd better ask for a rise," he suggested.*
>
> *"For God's sake, don't do anything of the sort," Francis Ince advised. "Just clear out. That's no place for you. You might stay there till your teeth fall out and never get a dog's chance to doing anything. There's only one thing for you to do. You must start right away on your own."*
>
> *Ferranti objected that he had no capital.*
>
> *"Leave that to me," said his new friend.*[17]

But even before Ferranti had his conversation with Ince, the situation was changing. The distribution of scientific information was rapidly becoming organized. The English provincial universities were founded in the second half of the nineteenth century; the major scientific and professional societies were created during the same period.

Professional Scientists and Technologists

By the end of the century, science was the province of groups of specialists working in and supported by universities or quasi-academic institutions. The unity of natural philosophy became separated into departments of chemistry, physics, geology, and later derivatives and hybrids. Information was organized in the form of textbooks and courses; traditions as to what was relevant and irrelevant were created under the authority of qualifying examinations. The intellectual segregation of scientific specialists was promoted by the way in which the new and reformed universities organized studies and teaching. Exchanges of the kind which had been characteristic of the earlier social milieux tended, outside the departmental enclave, to become attenuated and formalized in the meetings and journals of learned societies, where geologists produced papers for other geologists, physicists communed with physicists, and so on. By 1900 scientists were salaried professional men.

On the other hand, the situation of industrial technology was itself changing. When, before the middle of the century, the major scientific discoveries had been and could be the work of gifted amateurs and a few academic scientists, technically competent craftsmen like Maudslay, Nasmyth, and Whitworth had created the machine-tool industry. The engines and machines that were the showpieces of the 1851 Exhibition were largely the work of skilled mechanics and master men who had matched the opportunities presented all around them with the basic training of their apprenticeship, self-acquired mathematics, and a clear grasp of the principles of the new engineering. Yet even then, the development by improvement and new application was becoming a task beyond the capacity of men trained according to traditional craft methods. The outclassing of British products by European competitors at the 1867 Paris Exhibition made this quite explicit. The Royal Commission appointed thereafter to survey technical progress in a number of countries confirmed the impression that Britain had lost, or was losing, the technical lead established in the previous hundred years.

In Britain the answer to the problem was sought in improving and expanding the educational system. It is sought there now; it always is. One may remark at this point the different course followed in Germany. With social distinctions in many social, political, and economic fields more rigid and often more crippling (given the course then set for Western societies) than those prevailing in Britain, yet in one generation Germany overhauled and at many points outdistanced the technical advance of British industry. It was very puzzling.* Perhaps the clue to this sudden acceleration lies in the alliance between the new ethos of nationalism with science and technology, as the other presumptive heirs to the future; the cult of Reason in revolutionary France had set the fashion. The alliance was the orthodox basis of progressive ideas all over Europe, but the arrest of political liberalism in Germany, and its later asphyxiation, may have channelled aspirations and effort much more powerfully in the direction of scientific and technical achievement. Whatever the reason, there is little doubt that the rise of German industry was the consequence of the energy and enthusiasm with which academic scientists like Liebig and the members of the Berlin Physical Society preached their technical gospel and, in the case of the Siemens brothers, themselves created industrial empires.[19] Given this kind of liaison, the appropriate educational system followed.

---

*It still is. Sir Charles Snow, in his 1959 Rede Lecture, remarked "The curious thing was that in Germany, in the 1830's and 1840's, long before serious industrialization had started there, it was possible to get a good university education in applied science, better than anything England or the U.S. could offer for a couple of generations. I don't begin to understand this: it doesn't make social sense: but it was so."[18]

Without it, as in England, the educational system which was devised—in imitation, as it was thought—widened the breach between science and industry.

As the numbers of scientists rose with the foundation of the provincial universities and university colleges, another educational system was devised "to meet the needs of industry for technical training." Graduate scientists went for the most part[20] to teach in the schools and universities. For industry, there were the polytechnics and technical colleges, trade schools and evening institutes.

So with the founding of the provincial universities and university colleges, a parallel network of polytechnics, technical colleges, and evening institutes was created. A central examining body for technical subjects was provided in the City and Guilds Institute. By 1902, when local government authorities became largely responsible for all education below university level, the main structure of a separate educational system "to meet the needs of industry for technical training" was established and lasted for the first half of the present century.

The whole context of industrial innovation had changed. Before 1850 the worlds of science and industry, though separate, had not been distinct; the very existence, on such a large scale, of amateur scientific and technical enquiry demonstrates the ease of access to the world of science enjoyed by anyone with interests which might be satisfied by scientific information. By 1900 science and industry were distinct social systems, entered by different routes, and with very few institutional relationships by which people or information could pass between them. And by 1900, says Cardwell, "The new applied science industries had left this country, or else had never been started here. In the natural sciences it could hardly be doubted that the lead was Germany's, while in technology the enormous possibilities of the internal combustion engine, for example, were being developed by the French, the Germans, and the Americans. . . . Lockyer, writing in 1901, compared our position at the beginning of the new century with what it had been in 1801, at the outset of the railway age—now, the chief London electric railway was American."[20] (p. 147).

The New Technological System

Eventually, with a continuing need for the gap to be bridged, new social institutions have been developed. The gap became itself a new territory, explored, mapped, and eventually controlled by new specialists, the professional technologists, going by the name of applied scientists or industrial scientists.

Leaving out of account the prior development in Germany of a liaison initiated and purposefully maintained by the scientists themselves, the first successful institution set up to exploit this new territory was not only outside Great Britain, where the worst effects of the separation were experienced, but independent of both industry and established scientific institutions. Edison's Menlo Park Laboratory, employing a hundred workers, was established in 1870. But the entrepreneurial method followed contemporary practice: the concerns to manufacture the new devices were set up and financed as separate ventures.

This earliest model was not followed until the founding of the Department of Scientific and Industrial Research by the British Government in 1917. And until the years immediately before the first World War, very little had been done by industry, apart from chemicals,* to provide the link itself.

Ever since 1918 the development of industrial research in Britain has depended on Government action much more than in the United States. This may be attributed, as it usually is, to the unenterprising character of British industry in the fields of technical development, to the unwillingness of entrepreneurs to divert resources to development work as being too risky. Yet there were exceptions between 1900 and 1938, notably in chemicals, the industry which had learned from German methods and technological organizations, and enjoyed most stability; and the case is now altered.

It is in the situation of industry as it was in the first decades of the century rather than in such hazy ineluctables as national character that the explanation lies; for such over-caution, such reluctance to take the profit-making opportunities latent in new scientific discoveries, can be explained only by the ignorance of the run of industrialists about the utility of contemporary scientific activity, by the lack of effective means of communication between the two worlds.

By the end of the first World War the need for such communication was publicly acknowledged. Since industry itself was not supplying the intermediary technologists, the Government set up, in 1917, the Department of Scientific and Industrial Research. Between the wars also, the Government supply of intermediary resources increased very considerably with the need to assure the translation of new inventions with military applications into manufactured weapons. It was from these sources that most of the industrial research and development effort in contemporary Britain has grown.

In 1938 Bernal put the amount spent on industrial research, apart from Government expenditure, at £2,000,000, a figure which possibly includes expenditure on routine testing. From a survey carried out by D.S.I.R. in 1955, it was estimated that British firms spent £183 million on research and development during that year.[21]

The Report on Scientific and Engineering Manpower in Great Britain, 1956, put the total numbers of qualified scientists and engineers employed in industry on research and development as 22,000. There is no comparable pre-war figure, but if the figures of scientific staff employed by Defence Ministries and by the De-

---

*The chemical industry had long before this incorporated scientific laboratory work as part of the normal organization of the business concern, but apart from the notable association of Lawes and Gilbert in fertilizer production, the function of the laboratory seems to have been, what it still is in the smaller chemical concerns, to test the product, and control and refine the processes. As in other branches of industry in the nineteenth century, discovery was normally the starting-point of new concerns which exploited it, but firms did not set aside resources of capital and technically qualified people to search for further innovations. In Britain the change came at the end of the century with Brunner and Mond, with the United Alkali Company, and with Nobel, i.e., with the stabilization of the industrial concern.

partment of Scientific and Industrial Research are taken as a guide, the story is plain enough. Scientific staff were first employed in peacetime by the Army, Navy, and Air Force in the early 1920's. In 1935 the total number employed was less than 500. By 1939 there were 2,000, and by 1951, 15,000. D.S.I.R., which employed less than 300 salaried staff in its research establishments in 1920, had about 1,000 in 1938, & almost 3,500 by 1950.[22]

The work of producing innovations is now largely in the hands of salaried professionals employed in industrial firms, government establishments, or in institutions directly dependent on industry or government for funds.

Technologists (industrial scientists) are now normally people who have graduated in science at a university or a technical college and have thereafter served a period as junior members of a development or design team in an industrial, governmental, or other laboratory. The essential factor is not who employs them, but membership of the appropriate system of communication—electronics, biochemicals, fibres, nucleonics, metallurgy, aeronautics—through which flows information which may contribute to the development of any individual innovation. The comparative independence of technology from industry is reflected in the comparative independence of the technologist. The status of the technologist is a professional one, and there is fairly precise equivalence between ranks as well as salaries in the types of organizations employing technologists. They move freely, and would like to move much more freely, between posts in governmental, university, and industrial establishments. The career is not enclosed by the pressure either of "loyalty to the firm" or of "best prospects" within the individual firm.

For the individual firm the technologist is an alien element; he does not fit into the factory system in the same way as other functional specialists, since these are no more than bits of the general management-entrepreneurial function. The actual information held by the technologist, as well as his training and skill, has value outside the firm. This lies at the bottom of the differences in manners, behaviour, dress, and language which so clearly distinguish him from the other members of the firm which employs him.

THE ROLE OF INDUSTRIAL RESEARCH AND DEVELOPMENT

Yet technological progress has become of vital concern for the individual firm in many industries, and the increasing pace of innovation makes it inevitable that the firm provide more and more support for research and development as a condition of its own survival. This is not only because other sectors of industry have become "infected" by the work of government establishments, or even because industrialists have experienced the profitability of such work, and have overcome their inhibitions about scientific work. There is also a fundamental change in the institutional character of the industrial firm.

The most familiar aspect of this change is in scale, which is a function of alterations in the balance of production and of consumption within the economy. Mass markets have created, and in turn been created by, techniques of mass production; the use of such techniques has made possible certain economies by mere increase in the size of plant.

Secondly, concurrently with increase in scale, there has developed a separation between ownership and control, between the holding of shares and the control of the policy and activities of a company by management itself or by holders of a minority of shares.[23] This tendency is held to be as inherent in the structure of capitalist enterprise as is the tendency towards monopoly in the economy, arising as it does out of the division between the ownership and the use of property.[24] (p. 244)[25] (p. 15). During earlier periods of capitalism economic power resided with the owners of the property, i.e., the shareholders—although in law such owners merely possess documents which give them certain claims against the company, which formally has full ownership. During the present century, however, power has been passing more and more into the hands of the management, of the directors of enterprise. Shares are commonly dispersed among multitudes of small shareholders whose joint influence does not compare with that of a single compact minority interest. The technical and administrative complexities of modern large-scale enterprise have transformed the relationship between the shareholding owner and the manager of productive capacity.

Both these developments have affected the character of the industrial concern. Their influence on the internal organization has been considerable. Increased size has made necessary the division of the general task of management into a multiplicity of individual tasks, each of which has become the province of specialists—salesmen, cost accountants, works managers, designers, planners, secretaries trained in company law, personnel managers, production engineers. Greater administrative complexity, bigger size, and the development of the specialist skills called for have both aided and been promoted by the shift of control from owner to manager.

A significant fraction of resources in Britain have become concentrated and comparatively inelastic. Too much capital, and, more important, too many social commitments are involved in industrial concerns for change to occur through the elementary birth and death cycle usual a hundred years ago. Firms employing many thousands of people cannot close down without wrecking large areas of social organization. Such concerns must keep alive, and in order to keep alive they must become adaptive; change must occur within the organization and not through its extinction and replacement, if it is to occur at all.

Survival of the individual firm becomes a more significant criterion of economic activity the closer the approximation to monopolistic conditions. Keirstead introduces a lengthy exposition of actual pricing policies employed by a "giant multi-product corporation" as follows: When we define time concretely in terms of the processes of which it is constituted, we are obliged to ask whether the firm aims at a maximum temporal rate of profit . . . or whether it aims to obtain the largest estimated profit over some (indefinite) period of time. I am convinced that the latter notion is . . . more in accord with real facts of actual situations. . . . The maximization of profit at any moment may result in the appearance of competitors whose supplies would reduce price to the point where total net profits over a sufficient period would be reduced below what they might have been had a lower rate been accepted and the potential competitors kept out of the market."[26]

Directly one introduces time as a function of the profit-maximizing assumption, it is obvious that almost every consideration tends to become subordinate to survival. Directly, that is, the realities of industrial enterprise are organized in terms of the individual firm rather than of the individual entrepreneur, then almost any profit terms upon which the firm can survive become preferable to grosser profits on which it might possibly not survive. There is, in fact, no change in the logical basis, but merely in the way in which it works: (a) through individual mortals, (b) through corporations which are relatively potentially longer-lived. For an individual entrepreneur, profit-taking can be maximized for any period of time however short, since the rewards will certainly be a substantial help towards his own survival. Moreover, for the individual the random sector of circumstances affecting his strategies increases enormously with time. And he makes hay, therefore, when the sun shines, and a bird in the hand is worth two in the bush. For the corporation, randomness does not increase at anything like the same rate. And survival means only survival of the firm. The birds in the bush, which are tomorrow's or the next ten years' production, are just as important as that in the hand.

To sum up: two major changes have occurred in the social circumstances affecting the production of innovations. First, industrial concerns have increased in size: ever greater administrative complexity has brought a wide range of bureaucratic positions and careers into being; control has moved from owners to management. Their survival is therefore a matter of much more intense and widespread concern to themselves and to society; the chances of survival are improved if the technical innovations which might render its processes or products obsolete are developed within it and not by newcomers.

The other change has occurred in the form of institutional relationships and roles within which invention has been possible. The familiar and sociable relationships typical of the eighteenth century provided the ease of communication necessary for the major syntheses of ideas and requirements which introduced the early revolutionary inventions. The scale of scientific and industrial activity rapidly outgrew the social institutions within which the Industrial Revolution was generated; the syntheses which produced inventions and innovations tended to be random or opportunistic. Later in the nineteenth century, new institutional forms introduced barriers between science and industry, and between "pure" and "applied" science, as well as between departments of science. In the twentieth century the new and elaborate organization of professional scientists has been eventually matched by one of technical innovators into groups overlapping teaching and research institutions, Government departments and agencies, and industry.

Neither change is complete. Neither set of contrasts is clear. Few sectors of industry, outside chemicals, have fully accepted the changed situation. It was still possible, in the years between the wars, for a major innovation like the gas turbine to be developed in ways reminiscent of the classic days of nineteenth-century back-parlour invention. The jet engine's invention depended on an individual's persistence and enterprise, although the new massive organizations of government and industry were also involved.[27] On the other hand, the career of the most publicized inventor of the nineteenth century, Edison, reflects both the previous epoch, in the almost conscious exploitation of sociable contact with scientists and technologists, and the later, in the maintenance of development groups and the opening of professional careers in invention. Yet the process of change is now far enough advanced for the shape of the forms characteristic of the present system to be discernible.

REFERENCES

4. Ogburn, W. F. *Social Change*. New York: Viking Press, 1922.

5. Boulding, K. E. *The Organizational Revolution*. New York: Harper, 1953.

6. Marx, K. "Letter to P. V. Ennenkov," 1846. In: Karl Marx and Frederick Engels, *Selected Works,* Vol. II. London: Lawrence and Wishart, pp. 401–2.

7. Durkheim, E. *De la Division du travail social*. 1893. Trans.: *On the Division of Labour in Society,* by G. Simpson. Glencoe, Ill.: Free Press, 1954.

8. Tönnies, F.: *Gemeinschaft und Gesellschaft,* Leipzig, 1887. Trans.: *Fundamental Concepts of Sociology,* by C. P. Loomis. New York: American Book Company.

9. Jewkes, J. "How much Science." Presidential Address to British Association, Economic Section, 1959. *Economic Journal,* No. 277. March 1960, 70, p. 12.

10. Whitehead, A. N. *Science and the Modern World*. London: Cambridge Univ. Press 1926. (7th Impression, 1933, p. 120.)

11. Bright, A. A. *The Electric Lamp Industry: Technological Change and Economic Development from 1880 to 1947*. London: Macmillan, 1949.

12. Maclaurin, W. R. *Invention and Innovation in the Radio Industry.* New York: Macmillan, 1949.

13. Clow, A., and Clow, N. *The Chemical Revolution*. London: Batchworth, 1952 (pp. 593–4).

14. Smiles, S. *Life of Boulton and Watt*. London: Murray, 1865 (p. 367).

15. *British Museum Catalogue of Printed Books,* Vol. 36 (Periodicals: Enlarged Edn.), 1899.

16. Mayo, E. *The Social Problems of an Industrial Civilization*. London: Routledge, 1949 (p. 32).

17. Ferranti, G. Z. De, & Ince, R. *The Life and Letters of Sebastian Ziani de Ferranti*. London: Williams and Norgate, 1934 (pp. 51–2).

18. Snow, C. P. *The Two Cultures and the Scientific Revolution*. London: Cambridge University Press, 1959.

19. Bernal, J. D. *Science and Industry in the Nineteenth Century.* London: Routledge, 1954 (pp. 63–4).

20. Cardwell, D. S. L. *The Organization of Science in England.* London: Heinemann, 1957.

21. Department of Scientific and Industrial Research: *Estimates of Resources devoted to Scientific and Engineering Research and Development in British Manufacturing Industry,* 1955. H.M.S.O., 1958.

22. Treasury: *Civil Estimates,* 1918–51.

23. Berle, A. A., Jr., and Means, G. C. *The Modern Corporation and Private Property* London: Macmillan, 1932.

24. Friedmann, W. *Legal Theory.* London: Stevens, 1949 (p. 244).

25. Friedmann, W. *Law and Social Change in Contemporary Britain.* London: Stevens, 1951 (p. 15).

26. Keirstead, B. S. *The Theory of Economic Change.* London: Macmillan, 1948 (p. 254).

27. Whittle, H. *Jet.* London: Muller, 1954.

7

When a Thousand Flowers Bloom: Structural, Collective, and Social Conditions for Innovation in Organizations

Rosabeth Moss Kanter

"Let a thousand flowers bloom." This slogan, designed to awaken an entire nation to new ideas, offers an apt metaphor for innovation. Innovations, like flowers, start from tiny seeds and have to be nurtured carefully until they blossom; then their essence has to be carried elsewhere for the flowers to spread. And some conditions—soil, climate, fertilizer, the layout of the garden—produce larger and more abundant flowers.

Innovations can grow wild, springing up weed-like despite unfavorable circumstances, but they can also be cultivated, blossoming in greater abundance under favorable conditions. If we understand what makes innovations grow—the microprocess by which they unfold—we can see why some macro-conditions are better for their cultivation.

It is increasingly common among writers to emphasize the nonlinear, slightly chaotic, usually sloppy, sometimes random, and often up-and-down nature of innovation (Quinn, 1985). Taken to an extreme though, as some popular writers have done, it might be tempting to conclude that it is impossible to plan for innovation, manage it, or design an organization structure to support it. This extreme viewpoint holds individual variables like creativity and leadership to be more important than structural variables and, indeed, tends to see organizations in general as negative forces, with innovations generally occurring *despite* the organization, through accidents, lucky breaks, and bootlegged funds.

My own conclusion, after systematic comparative research (Kanter, 1983), in depth fieldwork, and literature review, is more moderate. Organizational con-

From *Research in Organizational Behavior*, Vol 10: 169–211. Copyright © 1988 JAI Press Inc. Reprinted with permission.

ditions—structure and social arrangements—can actively stimulate and produce innovation, as long as those conditions take into account the "organic," "natural," and even the "wild" side of innovation. Innovation is the creation and exploitation of new ideas. At its very root, the entrepreneurial process of innovation and change is at odds with the administrative process of ensuring repetitions of the past. The development of innovation requires a different set of practices and different modes of organization than the management of ongoing, established operations where the desire for or expectation of change is minimal. Stevenson and Gumpert (1985) have cast this management difference in terms of the contrast between the "promoter" type stance of the entrepreneur, driven by perception of opportunity, and the "trustee"-like stance of the administrator, driven to conserve resources already controlled (see also Hanan, 1976). Structures and practices that may work well for the perpetuation of the known tend to be at odds with innovation.

Innovation—whether technological or administrative, whether in products or processes or systems—tends to have four distinctive characteristics (Kanter, 1985).

1. *The innovation process is uncertain.* The source of innovation or the occurrence of opportunity to innovate may be unpredictable. The innovation goal may involve little or no precedent or experience base to use to make forecasts about results. Hoped-for timetables may prove unrealistic, and schedules may not match the true pace of progress. "Progress on a new innovation," Quinn (1979) wrote, "comes in spurts among unforeseen delays and setbacks . . . in the essential chaos of development." Furthermore, anticipated costs may be overrun and ultimate results are highly uncertain. Indeed, analysts have variously estimated that it takes an average of 10 to 12 years before the return on investment of new ventures equals that of mature businesses (Biggadike, 1979); 7 to 15 years from invention to financial success (Quinn, 1979); and 3 to 25 years between invention and commercial production (Quinn, 1985).

2. *The innovation process is knowledge-intensive.* The innovation process generates new knowledge intensively, relying on individual human intelligence and creativity and involving "interactive learning" (Quinn, 1985). New experiences are accumulated at a fast pace; the learning curve is steep. The knowledge that resides in the participants in the innovation effort is not yet codified or codifiable for transfer to others. Efforts are very vulnerable to turnover because of the loss of this knowledge and experience. There need to be close linkages and fast communication between all those involved, at every point in the process, or the knowledge erodes.

3. *The innovation process is controversial.* Innovations always involve competition with alternative course of action. The pursuit of the air-cooled engine at Honda Motor, for example, drew time and resources away from improving the water-cooled engine. Furthermore, sometimes the very existence of a potential innovation poses a threat to vested interests—whether the interest is that of a salesperson receiving high commis-

sions on current products, or of the advocates of a competing direction. (Fast, 1979, for example, argues that "political" problems are the primary cause for the failure of corporate New Venture Departments.)

4. *The innovation process crosses boundaries.* An innovation process is rarely if ever contained solely within one unit. First, there is evidence that many of the best ideas are interdisciplinary or interfunctional in origin— as connoted by the root meaning of entrepreneurship as the development of "new combinations"—or they benefit from broader perspective and information from outside of the area primarily responsible for the innovation. Second, regardless of the origin of innovations, they inevitably send out ripples and reverberations to other organization units, whose behavior may be required to change in light of the needs of innovations, or whose cooperation is necessary if an innovation is to be fully developed or exploited. Or there may be the need to generate unexpected innovations in another domain in order to support the primary product, like the need to design a new motor to make the first Apple computer viable.

If innovation is *uncertain, fragile, political,* and *imperialistic* (reaching out to embrace other territories), then it is most likely to flourish where conditions allow flexibility, quick action and intensive care, coalition formation, and connectedness. It is most likely to grow in organizations that have integrative structures and cultures emphasizing diversity, multiple structural linkages both inside and outside the organization, intersecting territories, collective pride and faith in people's talents, collaboration, and teamwork. The organizations producing more innovation have more complex structures that link people in multiple ways and encourage them to "do what needs to be done" within strategically guided limits, rather than confining themselves to the letter of their job. Such organizations are also better connected with key external resources and operate in a favorable institutional environment.

Not all *kinds* of innovation appear everywhere in equal proportions of course. Product innovations are more likely in new entrant organizations and process innovations in established ones. Product innovations are more common in earlier stages of a product's history; process innovations in later stages (Abernathy & Utterback, 1978). Technological innovations are more frequent when resources are abundant; administrative innovations when resources are scarce (Kimberly, 1981). Evolutionary innovations (modest, incremental changes) are more likely in organizations that are more formalized and "centralized"; more revolutionary innovations in organizations that are more complex and "decentralized" (Cohn & Turyn, 1984). But in general, the overall rate of innovation across types should be associated with the circumstances I have outlined.

Some of these structural and social conditions are more important at some points in the innovation process than at others. Like the flowers whose cultivation requires knowledge of its growth pattern, so does the understanding of innovation benefit from examining structural and social facilitators as they wax and wane with the innovation development process. This requires a dynamic model, a combination of a "variance" model of the factors influencing innovation and a "process" model showing how innovation unfolds (Mohr, 1978).

Recent research examining sets of innovations as they unfold over time (Schroeder, Van de Ven, Scudder, & Polley 1986; Van de Ven, 1986) has discredited the usual process models of innovation that posit discrete stages through which an innovation idea progresses. I agree that stage models do not always adequately capture the give-and-take of innovation, and they risk artificially segmenting the process. But I propose that the structural and social conditions for innovation can be understood best if the innovation process is divided into its major tasks.

There are four major innovation tasks, which correspond roughly (but nowhere near exactly) to the logic of the innovation process as it unfolds over time and to empirical data about the history of specific innovations. These tasks are: (a) *idea generation* and activation of the drivers of the innovation (the "entrepreneurs" or "innovators"); (b) *coalition building* and acquisition of the power necessary to move the idea into reality; (c) *idea realization* and innovation production, turning the idea into a model—a product or plan or prototype that can be used; (d) *transfer* or diffusion, the spreading of the model—the commercialization of the product, the adoption of the idea.

While sometimes occurring in sequence, these tasks also overlap. But by understanding the nature of each task, we can see more easily why certain properties of organizations are related to the success of innovation. This, in turn, contributes to our knowledge of the relationship between structure and behavior, between macro-context and micro-process.

IDEA GENERATION AND INNOVATION ACTIVATION

Innovation begins with the activation of some person or persons to sense or seize a new opportunity. Variously called "corporate entrepreneurs" (Kanter, 1983), "intrapreneurs," "idea generators," or "idea champions" (Galbraith, 1982), such individuals are able to initiate a process of departing from the organization's established routines or systems.

Innovation is triggered by recognition of a new opportunity. Once the opportunity is "appreciated," as Van de Ven (1986) put it, someone needs to supply the energy necessary to raise the idea over the threshold of consciousness, much as Schon (1971) described the emergence of new public policies as a result of being pushed into awareness. The first key problem in the management of innovation, then, is how to get people to pay attention—how to trigger the action thresholds of individuals to appreciate and pay attention to new ideas, needs, and opportunities.

Drucker (1985) has argued that the opportunities that give rise to innovation lie in incongruities and discontinuities—things that do not fit expected patterns or that provide indications that trends may be changing. But unless we are to assume these are purely individual cognitive abilities, it is important to look at the structural conditions that facilitate the ability to see new opportunities.

Close Connection with Need Sources

Opportunity exists because need exists, so it is not surprising that close customer or user contact is an important innovation activator. An often cited national study found that over three-fourths of a set of 500 important industrial innovations owed their origins to user suggestions and even user invention; only one-fifth originated in technical ideas looking for a home (Marquis & Myers, 1969). Users had originated 81% of the innovations in scientific instruments in another study, and 60% of those in process machinery (von Hippel, 1981).

Effective innovation thus derives from active awareness of changing user needs and sometime from direct user demands or solutions. Therefore, structural arrangements and social patterns that facilitate contact across boundaries, between potential innovators and their "market," help produce more innovation. Potential innovators benefit from being linked directly to the market, to gain a fuller personal appreciation for what users need, as well as from being connected with those functions inside the organization that manage the interface with the outside. Quinn (1985) found that high innovation companies in the United States, Japan, and Europe were characterized by a strong market orientation at the top of the company and mechanisms to ensure interaction between technical and marketing people at lower levels. At Sony, for example, new technical hires were assigned to weeks of retail selling as part of their orientation. In the prosperous years for People Express Airlines, the incentive system was designed to ensure that all executives spend at least some time each year flying as crew on their planes.

Van de Ven (1986) hypothesized that direct personal confrontations with problem sources are needed to reach the threshold of concern and appreciation required to motivate people to act. Perhaps this is why it has been observed that well-managed companies search out and focus on their most demanding customers, not the ones who are easily satisfied. Similarly, successful examples of innovations offered by managers in high technology firms tended to involve radical redefinition of the product or service as a result of encounters with the "real world" of customers or users—direct, first-hand experience of their need (Delbecq & Mills, 1985).

Raytheon's New Products Center demonstrates this principle in action. The center services a series of consumer products divisions, and also it has two levels of "users" and need sources: its internal divisional customers and the ultimate external consumer. Center practices involve frequent visits and tours to all of these need sources. Technical staff routinely attend trade shows, tour manufacturing facilities, and browse at retail outlets, striking up conversations with consumers.

Extra-organizational ties with users can be formalized, to ensure continuing close connection. Many computer and software companies have formed user groups, which allow them to gather ideas for new products and product improvements. Some manufacturing application laboratories solicit proposals from their customers for things they might work on (von Hippel, 1981).

These principles apply to internal administrative or organizational innovations as well as technological or product innovations. I propose, based on field observations, that those staff groups successful at creating innovations are the ones with the closest connections with the needs in the field; Honeywell's corporate human resources staff, for example, has created "councils" of key executives to ensure the continuing relevance of its offerings to the changing needs of users.

In general, then, innovation activation benefits from structural or social connections between those with the technical base (potential innovators) and those with the need (potential users). Indeed, one research group found that a higher proportion of new products failed for "commercial" reasons (misreading the need) rather than technical ones, indicating a poor interface between developers and users (Mansfield, Rapoport, Schnee, Wagner, & Hamburger, 1981).

"Kaleidoscopic Thinking": Cross Fertilization

Awareness of need is one element; ability to construct new ways to address the need is a second. I have come to refer to the creativity involved in activating innovation as "kaleidoscopic thinking" (Kanter, 1986).

The kaleidoscope is an apt metaphor for the creative process, because the kaleidoscope allows people to shake reality into a new pattern. In a kaleidoscope a set of fragments form a pattern. But the pattern is not locked into place. If the kaleidoscope is shaken or twisted, or the angle of perspective is changed, the same fragments form an entirely new pattern. Often, creativity consists of rearranging already existing pieces to create a new possibility. For example, Malcolm McLean did this about 30 years ago when he developed the concept for Sea-Land, the first company to offer containerized shipping. Before Sea-Land, shipping was a tedious matter of packing and unpacking crates in order to move objects from one form of transportation to another. McLean's innovation was simple: move the whole container.

Contact with those who see the world differently is a logical prerequisite to seeing it differently ourselves. "Cosmopolitan" rather than "local" orientations—seeing more of the world—has been identified by many researchers as a factor in high rates of innovation (Rogers & Shoemaker, 1971). So the more innovative organizational units who face outward, as well as inward, taking in more of the world around them, and taking better advantage of "boundary spanners" to bring them intelligence about the world beyond (Robertson & Wind, 1983; Tushman, 1977). High-performing research and development (R&D) project groups have far greater communication with organizational colleagues outside the group than low-performing teams (Allen, 1984); sometimes this communication occurs in two steps, mediated by certain communication "stars" who then transmit it to the rest of the group (Tushman, 1979).

One classic set of studies of research scientists found that the most productive and creative ones were those who had more contacts *outside* their fields, who spent more time with others who did not share their values or beliefs (Pelz & Andrews, 1966). At the same time, the dangers of closing off were also clear. It took only 3 years for a heterogeneous group of interdisciplinary scientists who worked together every day to become homogeneous in perspective and approach to problems. Sociologists have used the terms "occupational psychosis" and "trained incapacity" to describe the tendency for those who concentrate on only one area and interact only with those who are similar in outlook to become less able over time to learn new things.

The "twists" on reality causing creativity may derive from uncomfortable situations where basic beliefs are challenged and alternatives suggested. It is not surprising, then, that the patterns in most large, established bureaucracies inhibit rather than activate innovation. Once people enter a field, they spend most of their time (especially their discretionary time) with other people just like them who share their beliefs and assumptions. At the top, leaders are increasingly insulated from jarring experiences or unpleasant occurrences that cause them to confront their assumptions about the world, and they spend an increasing portion of their time with people exactly like themselves. And if corporate culture encourages an orthodoxy of beliefs and a nonconfrontational stance, then idea generation is further discouraged.

Cross-fertilization of ideas instead comes from cross-disciplinary contact. Creativity often springs up at the boundaries of specialties and disciplines, rather than squarely in the middle. It is often a matter of combining two formerly separate ideas—wafers and ice cream making the world's first ice cream cone. A large oil company considers one of its greatest innovations the development of a new, highly useful chemical compound that was created because researchers from two distinct fields collaborated. Ocean Spray staged a comeback for cranberry juice because a marketing executive spent time learning about packaging; the company was the first in its industry to put juice in paper bottles. Some organizations actively facilitate cross-disciplinary exchange through product fairs or cross-division "show and tell" meetings or cross-functional teams that visit customers together (Tushman & Nadler, 1986).

But when departments of specialties are segmented and prevented from contact, when career paths confine people to one function or discipline for long periods of time, and when communication between fields is difficult or excessively formal, creativity is stifled. Huge buildings consisting of all those in one field, physically separated from people in another field, make contact impossible.

Under that kind of circumstance, outsiders may be better able to see the big picture and take a new angle on the pattern, because they are not yet aware of all the details the "experts" see that inevitably confirm the view that no change is possible. People too close to a situation often become hopeless about change, blind to the possibilities.

Thus, a great deal of important industrial innovation comes from what Schon (1967) called "innovation by invasion": a new player enters the game, bringing a new method or technique. For example, half of all major innovations in pharmaceuticals from 1935 to 1962 were based on discoveries made outside the firm that later exploited them (Mansfield et al., 1981). It was Apple that first successfully commercialized the personal computer; IBM was a latecomer—and it is hard to imagine more outsiderlike amateurs than Steve Jobs and Steve Wozniak. Similarly, in my study of leading companies, newly appointed managers who came from a different field by an unusual career route—in a word, outsiders—were somewhat more likely to innovate than those who rose by orthodox means (Kanter, 1983).

In general, then, contact with those who take new angles on problems facilitates innovation.

Structural Integration: Intersecting Territories

Activation of innovation is encouraged by structural integration across fields—by intersecting territories. Researchers have long observed that "communication integration" (closer interpersonal contact or connectedness via interpersonal communication channels in an organization) is positively related to the innovation rate (Rogers & Shoemaker, 1971; Tushman & Nadler, 1986). Isolation of individuals and units tends to reduce innovation at the idea generation stage by limiting awareness of opportunity, alternative approaches, and the perspective of those functions who need to contribute other "parts" to make the innovation add up to a "whole." (Van de Ven, 1986, considered the management of part-whole relationships one of the four critical innovation tasks.) These who are isolated, in short, are less attuned to alternatives than those who are well-connected.

"Matrix" organization structures (Davis & Lawrence, 1977) are highly integrative, and it is not accidental that they were first developed to aid technological innovation—the large-scale development projects in the aerospace industry—and are found more frequently in rapidly changing, highly innovating organizations (Kanter, 1983). Matrix organizations, in which mid-level employees report to both a project boss and a functional boss, force integration and cross-area communication by requiring managers from two or more functions to collaborate in reaching a decision or taking some action. This is frequently characterized as a "dotted line" relationship for those in one department to another department, signifying a working relationship but not always direct authority.

By requiring extensive cross-functional consultation, the matrix diffuses authority among a group of managers. In many instances, this opportunity can be used in a positive manner by particularly entrepreneurial managers who are able to envision alternatives and assume responsibility for pursuing them—alternatives that cut across territories.

In general, measures of complexity and diversity in an organization are positively related to initial development of innovations (though they are sometimes negatively related to eventual acceptance of the same innovation by the rest of the organization). Diversity gives the individual more latitude for discovery, but may make it difficult later to get agreement on which many proposals or demonstration projects should be implemented on a wider scale. Similarly, innovation is aided by low formalization at the initiation stage, when freedom to pursue untried possibilities is required.

Therefore, to produce innovation, more complexity is essential: more relationships, more sources of information, more angles on the problem, more ways to pull in human and material resources, more freedom to walk around and across the organization (also see Burns & Stalker, 1968; Mintzberg, 1981). One does not need a formal matrix structure to do this. Indeed, it is the general characteristics of an integrative structure that make a difference in terms of encouraging innovation: looser boundaries, crosscutting access, flexible assignments, open communication, and use of multidisciplinary project teams. So specifying multiple links between managers in a formal sense (through showing more than one solid-line or dotted-line reporting relationship on an organization chart) is merely a way of acknowledging the interdependencies that complex products and innovative projects require.

Dividing the organization into smaller units based on a common end use goal but not around function or specialty also aids activation of innovation by producing structural integration at micro-level. When it comes to innovation, "small is beautiful," and flexible is even better (see Quinn, 1985). Or at least small is beautiful as long as the small unit includes all functions or disciplines and forces contact across them. Cross-fertilization across disciplines and a focus on users is built into the structure.

The idea of dividing into smaller but complete business units has been appealing to organizations seeking continual innovation. In smaller business units it is possible to maintain much closer working relationships across functions than in larger ones—one of the reasons for Hewlett-Packard's classic growth strategy of dividing divisions into 2 when they reached more than 2,000 people or $100,000,000 in sales. Even where economies of scale push for larger units, the cross-functional project or product team within a single facility (captured in such ideas as the factory-within-a-factory) helps keep the communication and the connection alive.

Broad Jobs

Idea generation is also aided when jobs are defined broadly rather than narrowly, when people have a range of skills to use and tasks to perform to give them a view of the whole organization, and when assignments focus on results to be achieved rather than rules or procedures to be followed. This, in turn, gives people the mandate to solve problems, to respond creatively to new conditions, to note changed requirements around them, or to improve practices, rather than mindlessly following procedures derived from the past.

Furthermore, when broader definitions of jobs permit task domains to overlap rather than divide cleanly, people are encouraged to gain the perspective of others with whom they must now interact and therefore to take more responsibility for the total task rather than simply their own small piece of it. This leads to the broader perspectives that help stimulate innovation.

In areas that benefit from more enterprise and problem solving on the part of job holders, broader jobs seem to work better. This is the principle behind work systems that give employees responsibility for a major piece of a production process and allow them to make decisions about how and when to divide up the tasks. Pay-for-skill systems similarly encourage broader perspectives by rewarding people for learning more jobs (Tosi & Tosi, 1986).

Does this argument conflict with the numerous findings that adoption of innovation is more likely in organizations with more specialists and professionals? (E.g., Hage and Aiken's [1967] conclusion that the rate of innovation is higher when there are occupational specialties, each with a greater degree of professionalism.) No, because while specialized knowledge is an asset, confinement to a limited area and minimal contact with other professionals inhibits the ability for experts to use their knowledge in the service of change.

Potential innovators can become interested in a particular issue that develops into an innovation for several reasons. The initial impetus for innovation activation can stem from (a) an obligation of his or her position (March & Olsen, 1979); (b) a direct order; (c) a stimulus from the environment or "galvanizing event" (Child, 1972; Kanter, 1983); (d) self-motivated, entrepreneurial behavior; (e) organizational rewards and payoffs; or (f) accidental conditions (Perrow, 1981).

While much of the literature emphasizes the random, spontaneous, or deviant aspects of idea generating, some research has found that the nature of job assignments can be an activating force—either directly, because the assignment requires a new solution, or indirectly by allowing a scanning process to occur beyond what is programmed into the position. Job assignments (new ones or simply those understood as part of the job) stimulated a high proportion (51%) of the innovations in one study (Kanter, 1983). Managers did not necessarily have to think up projects by themselves to begin acting as organizational entrepreneurs; their enterprise came from accepting the responsibility and finding a way to build something new while carrying out an assigned task.

What is important is not whether there is an assignment, but its nature: broad in scope, involving change, and leaving the means unspecified, up to the doer. In my study, a manager's *formal* job description often bore only a vague or general relationship to the kinds of innovative things the manager accomplished (Kanter, 1983). Indeed, the more jobs are "formalized," with duties finely specified and "codified," the less innovation is produced in the organization. An emphasis on the "numbers" (a quantitative versus a qualitative thrust in jobs) and on efficiency also depresses the amount of innovation. "Low formalization," on the other hand, is associated with more innovativeness (Hage & Aiken, 1967).

Broad assignments are generally characteristics of staff managers in problem solving or bridging positions who have a general change mandate to "invent something" or "improve something." The innovation-producing companies are often marked by a large proportion of problem solvers in operating departments who float freely without a "home" in the hierarchy and thus must argue for a budget of find a constituency to please. The incentive to enterprise is the *lack* of defined tasks (Kanter, 1983). Thus, organizational slack (Galbraith, 1982) and stack in assignments enables the activation of innovation.

The more routinized and rules-bound a job is, the more it is likely to focus its performers on a few already-known variables and to inhibit attention to new factors. Starbuck (1983) argued that highly programmed jobs are like superstitious learning, recreating actions that may have little to do with previous success or future success. Overly elaborate and finely detailed structures and systems make organizational participants unable to notice shifts in their environment and the need for innovation, especially if they are required to send "exceptions" somewhere else for processing.

Where jobs are narrowly and rigidly defined, people have little incentive to engage in either "spontaneous" innovation (self-generated, problem-solving attempts with those in neighboring tasks) or to join together across job categories for larger top-directed innovation efforts—especially if differences in job classification also confer differential status or privilege. Companies even lose basic efficiency as some tasks remain undone while waiting for the person with the "right" job classification to become available—even though others in another classification may have the skills and the time. And people tend to actively avoid doing any more work than the minimum, falling back on the familiar excuse. "That's not *my* job"—a refrain whose frequent repetition is a good sign of a troubled company.

Organizational Expectations for Innovation

Even if people are *able* to generate new ideas in the innovation activation stage, they must also feel confident that their attempts at innovation will be well received. The signals they receive about the *expectations* for innovation play a role in activating or inhibiting innovation.

One way organizations signal an expectation for innovation is by allocating funds specifically for it. In one study comparing innovation successes with failures, it was found that the failures were handicapped by a lack of resources anywhere other than in already committed operating budgets, while the successes benefitted from the existence of special innovation funds (Delbecq & Mills, 1985). Despite all the heroic glamour of associating innovation with "bootlegging" funds spent on the sly, it is clearly easier to innovate when funds exist for this purpose.

Since innovations generally require resources beyond those identified in operating budgets (Kanter, 1983) for reasons that are logical—the exact nature and timing of innovation is often unpredictable—the existence of multiple sources of loosely committed funds at local levels makes it easier for potential innovators to find the money, the staff, the materials, or the space to proceed with an entrepreneurial idea. Because no one area has a monopoly on resources, there is little incentive to hoard them as a weapon; instead, a resource holder can have more influence by being one of those to *fund* an innovative accomplishment than by being a nay sayer. Thus, managers at one computer company could go "tin-cupping" to the heads of the various product lines in their facility who had big budgets, collecting a promise of a little bit of funding from many people (Kanter, 1983). This process reduced the risk on the part of all "donors" at the same time that it helped maintain the "donee's" independence.

Sheer availability of resources helps, of course. Research shows that richer and more successful organizations innovate more than poorer and less successful ones, especially in technology areas (Kimberly & Evanisko, 1979; Kimberly, 1981; Zaltman, Duncan, & Holbek, 1973).

There are a variety of ways that high innovation companies make resources accessible locally or give middle-level people alternatives to tap when seeking money or materials for projects. One is to have formal mechanisms for distributing funds outside the hierarchy. 3M has put in place "innovation banks" to make "venture capital" available internally for development projects. Honeywell divisions have top-management steering committees guiding their organizational-change activities. The original steering committee solicited proposals quarterly from any employee for the formation of a problem-solving task team; the teams may receive a small working budget as needed. Also, "decentralization" keeps operating units small and ensures that they have the resources with which to act, and thus makes it more likely that managers can find the extra they need for an innovation locally.

Of course, some innovations, particularly organization ones, can be handled without money at all. Instead, the most common resource requirement in one study was staff time (Kanter, 1983). This was also decentralized in the form of "slack" and local control: people locally available with uncommitted time, or with time that they could decide to withdraw from other endeavors to be attached to an appealing project. Because mid-level personnel, professionals, and staff experts had more control over the use of their time in the more frequently innovating companies, it was easier to find people to assist in a project, or to mobilize subordinates for a particular activity without needing constant clearances from higher-level, nonlocal bosses.

A second general source of expectations for innovation lies in whether the organization's culture pushes "tradition" or "change." Innovators and innovative organizations generally come from the most modern, "up-to-date" areas rather than traditional ones with preservationist tendencies, and they are generally the higher-prestige "opinion leaders" that others seek to emulate (Rogers & Shoemaker, 1971; Hage & Dewar, 1973). But opinion leaders are innovative only if their organizations' norms favor change; this is why the values of the leaders are so important. Most people seek to be culturally appropriate, even the people leading the pack. There is thus more impetus to seek change when this is considered desirable by the company.

Pride in company, coupled with knowing that innovation is mainstream rather than countercultural, helps to stimulate innovation (and occurs as a *result* of innovation as well). A feeling that people inside the company are competent leaders, that the company has been successful because of its people, supports this. For instance, of the companies in one study, Polaroid Corporation knew that it is the technological leader in its field; Hewlett-Packard prided itself on its people-centered corporate philosophy, the H-P way, as well as on its reputation for quality, important in its retention of customers (Kanter, 1983).

Such cultures of pride stand out in sharp distinction to the cultures of inferiority that lead less innovating companies to rely on outsiders for all the new ideas, rather than on their own people.

Success breeds success. Where there is a "culture of pride," based on high performance in the past, people's feeling of confidence in themselves and others goes up. They are more likely to take risks and also to get positive responses when they request cooperation from others. Mutual respect makes teamwork easier. High performance may *cause* group cohesion and liking for workmates as well as result from it (Staw, 1975); pride in the capacity and ability of others makes teamwork possible. In an extension of the "Pygmalion Effect" to the corporation, supervisors who hold high expectations of subordinate's abilities (based on independent evaluations) may enhance that person's productivity (Wortman & Linsenmeier, 1977).

Thus, organizations with "cultures of pride" in the company's achievements and in the achievements and abilities of individuals will find themselves more innovative. This is why formal awards and public recognition make a difference—sometimes less for the person receiving them (who has, after all, *finished* an achievement) than for the observers in the same company, who see that the things they might contribute will be noticed, applauded, and remembered.

It is a self-reinforcing upward cycle—*performance stimulating pride stimulating performance*—and is especially important for innovation. Change requires a leap of faith, and faith is so much more plausible on a foundation of successful prior experiences.

Finally, feeling valued and secure helps people relax enough to be creative, as Amabile's (1983) experiments on the conditions facilitating creative problem solving indicate. Groups were asked to solve problems in one of two conditions, and the creativity of their solutions was rated. In condition I, they were paid for their participation before they began to work. In condition II, which tended to resemble the corporate norm, they were paid on a contingency basis, depending on how well their group performed. In which condition were groups more creative? The first, the one that can be called a high security/high value condition. Knowing that they were already paid, members could relax, and they could assume that they were with a set of talented people. Without the tension that worry about paycheck might have caused, they could free themselves to be much more creative. Furthermore, they "rose to the occasion": because expectations for innovation were set by advance pay, they innovated.

Integration versus Isolation

Overall, I argue that the generation of new ideas that activates innovation is facilitated by organizational complexity: diversity and breadth of experience, including experts who have a great deal of contact with experts in other fields; links to users; and outsiders, openness to the environment; and integration across fields via intersecting territories, multiple communication links, and smaller interdisciplinary business units. Conversely, isolation, or what can be termed "segmental-ism" (Kanter, 1983), inhibits this critical first phase of innovation.

It is important to explain an apparent contradiction in the literature here. Some analysts appear to argue that innovation does indeed require isolation, a special organization separated from the rest and dedicated to innovation. For example, Galbraith (1982) argued that innovation requires an organization specifically designed for that purpose, with a structure, processes, rewards, and people combined in a special way; he also made clear that his focus was on "good ideas that do not quite fit into the organization's current mold." But note that the "good idea" already *exists,* and the special organization is designed to focus on developing and elaborating it without distraction *once it has been identified.* Thus, isolation of the innovator group appears appropriate *later in the process,* when project ideas have been formulated.

To generate ideas in the first place, a great deal of diverse outreach is involved. R&D units that remain isolated are less creative than those that maintain close integration in the search of exploration stage. Recall the example of the Raytheon new products department, a unit with an unusually strong track record of creative outputs. It is indeed physically isolated from the rest of the organization to allow it to work on projects undistracted. But to generate ideas and activate innovation in the first place, department members immerse themselves in the world outside the lab, wandering around the organization, seeking problems to work on from their dense network of ties in other units, attending professional conferences in scientific fields other than their own, going to trade shows to view the exhibits, etc.

COALITION BUILDING

Once a specific project idea has taken shape, it must be sold—a necessity even when the innovator was initially been handed the area as an assignment. It must be sold because the initial assignment, though bearing some legitimacy, may contain no promises about the availability of resources or support required to do something of greater magnitude than routine activities (Kanter, 1982; 1983). Thus, the second task of the innovation process involves coalition building, acquiring power by selling the project to potential allies.

Overwhelmingly, studies of innovation show the importance of backers and supporters, sponsors and friends in high places, to the success of innovation (Quinn, 1979; Maidique, 1980). Galbraith (1982) distinguished the roles of "sponsor"—those who discover and fund the increasingly disruptive and expensive development and testing efforts that shape an innovation—and "orchestrator"—managers of the politics surrounding a new idea. Observing that sponsors were usually middle managers and orchestrators were higher level executives, he argued that these informal roles could be formalized, with sponsors given resources earmarked for innovation, and orchestrators allocating time to protecting innovations-in-progress.

While most studies emphasize single roles (the "champion," the "sponsor"), detailed accounts of the history of innovations reveals the importance of a whole coalition, embryonic and informal or assembled and formal (Summers, 1986). Van de Ven (1986), in a similar vein, focuses not on a single sponsor but on the importance of transactions or "deals" in the innovation process, and he sees the management of the innovation process as managing increasing bundles of transactions over time. Indeed, he and his colleagues found, in a comparative study of seven very different large scale innovations in different sectors, that "much more than sponsorship" was involved; higher management, one or two levels removed from the innovation was directly involved in making major decisions about the project and often "ran interference" for it as well as securing necessary resources (Schroeder et al., 1986). Furthermore, a comparison of over 115 innovations found in the successful ones a set of allies, often peers from other areas as well as more senior managers, behind successful innovations, ranging from the "stakeholders" who would be affected if the project was implemented to the "power sources" who contributed the tools to ensure that implementation (Kanter, 1983).

Thus, it is more appropriate to conceptualize the second major innovation task as coalition building, a broader notion that ties in more of the organization, rather than as seeking sponsorship, a narrower concept. In general, the success of an innovation is highly dependent on the amount and kind of power behind it. In contrast, innovation failures are characterized by ambivalent support; inadequate resources during the initial fragile stages of development; constant efforts to "sell" and "justify"; and personalized infighting over resources (Delbecq & Mills, 1985).

Thus, the effectiveness of the political activity the innovation entrepreneur engages in, coupled with structural conditions conducive to power acquisition and coalition building, may largely account for whether an idea ever moves into the later phase of innovation production. Social and political factors, such as the quality of the coalition building, may account for as much or more than technical factors, such as the quality of the idea, in determining the fate of innovation.

Research shows that there are some kinds of ideas that are inherently better able to attract support. The most salable projects are likely to be *trialable* (can be demonstrated on a pilot basis—see especially Delbecq & Mills, 1985); *reversible* (allowing the organization to go back to pre-project status if they do not work); *divisible* (can be done in steps of phases); consistent with sunk costs (build on prior resource commitments); concrete (tangible, discrete); *familiar or compatible* (consistent with a successful past experience and compatible to existing practices); *congruent* (fit the organization's direction); and have *publicity value* (visibility potential if they work) (Kimberly, 1981; Zaltman et al., 1973). When these features are not present, as they are unlikely to be in more "radical" innovations, then projects are likely to move ahead if they are either *marginal* (appear off-to-the-sidelines so they can slip in unnoticed) or *idiosyncratic* (can be accepted by a few people with power without requiring much additional support) (Zaltman et al., 1973; Kanter, 1983).

The features of successful ideas have more to do with the likelihood of gathering political support than with the likelihood of the idea to produce results. In general, the relative economic advantage of a new idea, as perceived by members of an organization, is only weakly related to its rate of adoption (Rogers & Shoemaker, 1971). Instead, "political" variables may play a larger role, especially the acquisition of "power tools" to move the idea forward.

Power Tools

Organizational power tools consist of supplies of three "basic commodities" that can be invested in action: *information* (data, technical knowledge, political intelligence, expertise); *resources* (funds, materials, space, time); and *support* (endorsement, backing, approval, legitimacy) (Kanter, 1983).

To use an economic strategy, it is as though there were three kinds of "markets" in which the people initiating innovation must compete: a "knowledge market" or "marketplace of ideas" for information; an "economic market" for resources; and a "political market" for support or legitimacy. Each of the "markets" is shaped in different ways by conditions in the environment (e.g., critical contingencies, resource scarcity; Pennings & Goodman, 1977; Pfeffer & Salancik, 1977), and by organizational structure and rules (e.g., how openly information is exchanged, how freely executives render support). And each gives the person a different kind of "capital" to invest in a "new venture" (also see Pfeffer & Salancik, 1977).

We can hardly speak of "market" at all, of course, where the formal hierarchy fully defines the allocation of all three commodities, for example, when money and staff time are availably *only* through a predetermined budget and specified assignments, when information flows *only* through identified communication channels, and when legitimacy is availably *only* through the formal authority vested in specific areas with no support available for stepping beyond official mandates. In organizations where there is really no market for exchanging or rearranging resources and data, for acquiring support to do something outside the formal structure, because it is tightly controlled either by the hierarchy or by a few people with "monopoly" power, then little innovative behavior is likely. Indeed, when people feel "powerless" through structural locations that limit them access to the tools, they become more controlling and conservative (Kanter, 1977; Kanter & Stein, 1979).

While some portion of the power innovators need may be already attached to their positions and available for investing in an innovation, the rest must be sought through allies. Thus, the organization's structure determines the amount and availability of power via both the distribution of power tools and the ease with which coalitions can be formed. Access to external and internal sources of power increases an innovation entrepreneur's chances of successfully creating an innovation.

Coalition Structure

Which parties are potential coalition members? Principally those on whom the innovator may be dependent—where there is interdependency affecting the fate of the idea. The concept of organizational interdependency has both a technological (Thompson, 1967) and a political (Pfeffer, 1981) component.

First, people often form interdependent relationships because of mutual task dependence. For example, a manager in a finance department may require financial information on operations costs from a production manager, who in turn receives back the financial information in some evaluated or analyzed form and uses it to assess production efficiency. The timeliness and quality of the information provided by each manager affects the other's work.

Second, interdependencies may be political in nature, since organizations are tools for "multiple stakeholders" (Kanter, 1980); managers identify and seek out others with complementary and sometimes competing interests for the purpose of trading resources, demands, etc. (March, 1962; Cyert & March, 1963). Networks of interdependent members also form where people are joined by a variety of links through which goods, services, information, affect and influence flow (Tichy & Fombrun, 1979; also see Kaplan & Mazique, 1983).

In short, there are many types of interdependent relationships: *hierarchical* (Weber, 1978; Schilit & Locke, 1982); *lateral* (Thompson, 1967; Burns & Stalker, 1968); *oblique* (Kaplan & Maidique, 1983). In addition, people also work in the midst of multiple constituencies that are defined by common political or organizational interests and include persons outside the formal boundaries of the organization (Pennings & Goodman, 1977; Connolly, Conlon, & Deutsch, 1980). Constituencies may form around task, issues, attempts to create change or block change, or salient values.

The size of the coalition is affected by how many territories the innovation crosses. The broader the ramifications of the issues involved in the proposed innovation and the greater the attendant uncertainties, the larger the coalition of supporters needs to be if the idea for innovation is to result in product action (Thompson, 1967).

Mobilizing a few potential members into an active, visible coalition also mirrors a classic dilemma in organization theory, that of finding the appropriate mix of inducements to obtain the desired contributions and work behavior from employees (Barnard, 1938). The inducements an innovator can offer to participate in a coalition include a variety of payments, such as financial incentives, resources, information, policy promises, learning experience, personal development, or emotional satisfaction (March, 1962; Riker, 1962; Gamson, 1968). The exchange of inducements for coalition participation can also extend across both vertical and lateral levels of an organization (e.g., Dalton, 1959; Blau, 1963).

Mobilizing coalition members through exchange assumes that "commodities" are available for trade, and that the organizer had some control over their distribution (managers we interviewed often referred to this process as one of "horse trading"). Such commodities used to mobilize coalition members can also serve as the basis of organizational power; e.g., resources, slack, information, and political support (Mechanic, 1962; Kanter, 1977).

Access to these commodities depends to a large degree on their distribution within the firm; their munificence increases the ability to draw people into coalition that can work on an innovation.

Because corporate entrepreneurs often have to pull in what they need for their innovation from other departments or areas, from peers over whom they have no authority and who have the choice about whether or not to ante up their knowledge, support, or resources, to invest in and help the innovator, their work is facilitated by integrative devises that aid network formation and collaboration across areas; open communication; frequent mobility, including lateral career moves; extensive use of formal team mechanisms; and complex ties permitting crosscutting access.

Communication Density

Innovation flourishes where "communication integration" is high (Rogers & Shoemaker, 1971). Open communication patterns make it easier to identify and contact potential coalition members and to tap their expertise.

Examples of "open communication" systems from innovating companies stress access across segments. "Open door" policies mean that all levels can, theoretically, have access to anyone to ask questions, even to criticize. At several high innovation companies examined in one study, there were policies barring *closed* meetings. In others, the emphasis was on immediate face-to-face verbal (not written) communications (Kanter, 1983), unlike "mechanistic," low innovation organizations where written communications prevail (Burns & Stalker, 1968). Such open communication norms acknowledge the extent of interdependence—that people in all areas need information from each other.

"Openness" at such organizations is reflected in physical arrangements as well. There may be a few "private" offices, and those that do exist are not very private. One manager had a "real" office enclosed by chest-high panels with opaque glass, but people dropped by casually, hung over the walls, talked about anything, and looked over his desk when he was not there. In general, people walk around freely and talk to each other; meetings and other work are easily interrupted, and it is hard to define "private" space. They often go to the library or conference room to "hide" to get things done, especially on "sensitive" matters like budgets (Kanter, 1983).

Open communication serves a very important function for the potential innovator. Information and ideas flow freely and were accessible; technical data and alternative points of view can be gathered with greater case than in companies without these norms and systems. And thus both the "creative" and the "political" sides of innovation are facilitated.

Network Density

Coalition formation in the interest of innovation is also aided by conditions that facilitate dense ties through networks. Circulation of people is a first network-facilitating condition. Mobility across jobs means that people rather than formal mechanisms are the principle carriers of information, the principal integrative links between parts of the system. Communication networks are facilitated (see Thurman, 1979–1980), and people can draw on first-hand knowledge of each other in seeking support. Knowledge about the operations of neighboring functions is often conveyed through the movements of people into and out of the jobs in those functions. As a set of managers or professionals disperse, they take with them to different parts of the organization their "intelligence," as well as the potential for the members to draw on each other for support in a variety of new roles. In just a few moves, a group that has worked together is spread around, and each member now has a close colleague in any part of the organization to call on for information or backing.

A second network-forming device is more explicit: the frequent use of integrative team mechanisms at middle and upper levels. These both encourage the immediate exchange of support and information and create contacts to be drawn on in the future. The organizational chart with its hierarchy of reporting relationships and accountabilities reflects only one reality in innovating organizations; the "other structure," not generally shown on the charts, is an overlay of flexible, ad hoc problem-solving teams, task forces, joint planning groups, and information-spreading councils.

It is common at innovating, entrepreneurial companies to make the assignments with the most critical change implications to teams across areas rather than to individuals or segmented units for example, at one company a team of mixed functional managers created a five-year production and marketing plan for a new product. This was a model of the method that top management endorsed for carrying out major tasks and projects. At a computer company, the establishment of formal interdepartmental or cross-functional committees was a common way managers sought to improve the performance of their own unit (Kanter, 1983).

The legitimacy of crosscutting access promotes the circulation of all three of the power tools: resources, information, and support. This allows innovators to go across formal lines and levels in the organization to find what they needed—vertically, horizontally, or diagonally—without feeling that they are violating protocol. They can skip a level or two without penalty. This is essential if there is to be hands-on involvement of managers up several levels, as Schroeder et al. (1986) found characteristic of large-scale innovations.

Matrix designs, though not essential for crosscutting access, can be helpful in legitimizing it, for the organization chart shows a number of links from each position to others. There is no "one boss" to be angered if a subordinate manager goes over his head or around to another area; it is taken for granted that people move across the organization in many directions; and there are alternative sources of power. Similarly, formal cross-area and cross-hierarchy teams may provide the occasion and the legitimacy for reaching across the organization chart for direct access (Kanter, 1983).

IDEA REALIZATION AND INNOVATION PRODUCTION

The third task of the innovation process involves assembling a working team to "complete" the idea by turning it into a concrete and tangible object (physical or intellectual) that can be transferred to others. The idea becomes a reality; a prototype or model of the innovation is produced that can be touched or experienced, that can now be diffused, mass-produced, turned to productive use, or institutionalized.

There are a number of critical organizational issues related to the ability to move a innovation through this phase. These issues join with social psychological (intragroup) variables to account for the performance of the group responsible for producing the innovation model.

Physical Separation

While structural isolation is a liability for idea generation or innovation activation, it is an asset for idea completion or innovative production.

Differentiated innovation units, separated from ongoing operations in both a physical and an organizational sense, are not necessary to *stimulate* or activate innovation (a task for which isolation is counter-productive), but they do appear helpful for ensuring that the working out of the innovation, the production of the initial model, actually occurs. Lockheed's term, "skunkworks," (taken from a Peanuts cartoon) has been used to refer to the special setting where innovation teams can create new things without distractions.

Galbraith (1982) has argued for the importance of "reservations"—organizational units, such as R&D groups, totally devoted to creating new ideas for future businesses—havens for "safe learning" managed by a full-time sponsor. Reservations can be internal or external, permanent or temporary. Galbraith found that some innovations, including the new electronics product he studied, were perfected at a remote site before being discovered by management; thus "the odds [for innovation] are better if early efforts to perfect and test new 'crazy' ideas are differentiated—that is, separated—from the function of the operating organization" (Galbraith, 1982).

High innovation companies in the United States, Europe, and Japan have flatter organizations, smaller operating divisions, and smaller project teams (Quinn, 1985). Small teams of engineers, technicians, designers, and model makers are placed together in "skunkworks," with no intervening organizational or physical barriers to developing the idea to prototype stage. Even in Japanese organizations supposedly known for elaborate (and slow) consensus-building processes, innovation projects are given autonomy, and top managers often work directly on projects with young engineers, including the founder of Honda himself. This approach eliminates bureaucracy, allows fast and unfettered communication, enables rapid turnaround time for experiments, and instills a high level of group loyalty and identity by maximizing communication and commitment among team members.

Boundary Management

If small, separate units aid idea model production, then boundary management is a particular problem. The team must continue to procure information and resources and return output to the rest the organization (Gladstein & Caldwell, 1984), but without becoming so outwardly focused that ability to do the job is jeopardized.

Success in building the innovation may be a function of how well external relations are handled as much as the technical feasibility of the idea. On the one hand, those who are prone to interfere must be kept from distracting the focus of the working team; on the other hand, the stakeholders, coalition members, and others whose support will be required at the transfer phase must be communicated with and involved, to ensure their support. The group must both buffer itself against too much input from its environment (Thompson, 1967) as well as manage the demand for what it is producing so that it has an appropriate level-of exchange with the world around it—not too much, and not too little.

While many analysts have argued that "gatekeeping" is an important function in the management of innovation. Gladstein and Caldwell (1984) have gone further by identifying four boundary management roles in the new product teams they studied, roles that can all be played by one person or distributed throughout the group:

- Scouts, bringing in information or resources needed by the groups;
- Ambassadors, carrying out items that the group wants to transmit to others;
- Sentries, controlling the transactions that occur at the boundaries, deciding how much can come in;
- Guards, controlling how much goes out of the group.

Whereas scouts and ambassadors keep extra group relationships smooth and get the group its needed supplies, sentries and guards buffer the group from outside interference. But note that all of these roles may be played by one person or just a few people, allowing the rest of the group to work on tasks without paying any attention to the world outside the project team. In the much publicized case of the building of a new computer at Data General, the project manager and his two aides handled all of the boundary tasks, allowing the team members to focus on completing the project in what proved to be record time (Kidder, 1981).

Boundary management is important not merely to get the working group what it needs and save it from unnecessary interference but also to handle any subtle threats to the continued existence of the innovation project. In one study, it was striking how little *overt* opposition is encountered by entrepreneurial managers—perhaps because their success at coalition building determines whether a project starts at all. Opposition or resistance seemed to take a more passive form instead: criticism of specific details of the plan, foot-dragging, low response to requests, unavailability, or arguments for preferential allocation of scarce time and resources to other pet projects. Early opposition was likely to take the form of skepticism and therefore reluctance to commit time or resources. Later opposition was likely to take the form of direct challenge to specific details of the plan that is unfolding (Kanter, 1983).

The nature of the opposition becomes clearer at the idea production points in the innovation process for several reasons. First, the very act of contacting others in the course of realizing an idea may mobilize what would otherwise have been latent or unorganized opposition. Most people will not spend their fund of political capital by overtly opposing a new idea right away, especially if it has the support of someone who is powerful, because it may never "get off the ground." Political capital would have been depleted unnecessarily. It is when it looks as though the project might actually happen that the critics begin to surface, generally arguing at the project's most vulnerable point that it has had enough time to prove itself; time to move on to something else (usually the critic' own pet project) (Kanter, 1983).

At the same time, many new ventures or innovation projects tend to be relatively invisible in the beginning, occurring in hidden corners of the organization or not significant enough to warrant their rivals' or competitors' attention. But as the effort gets closer and closer to results, it becomes more of a threat, and rivals begin to take action to crush it. At Apple, for example, a start up company by an employee was passively tolerated by chairman Jobs, but when it looked like that group might actually have a rival technology, he threatened suit, saying that it had been developed on Apple time and Apple owned it (Moritz, 1984).

My research identified a number of tactics that innovators used to disarm opponents: *waiting it out* (when the entrepreneur has no tools with which to directly counter the opposition); *wearing them down* (continuing to repeat the same arguments and not giving ground); *appealing to larger principles* (tying the innovation to an unassailable value or person); *inviting them in* (finding a way that opponents could share the "spoils" of the innovation); *sending emissaries to smooth the way and plead the case* (picking diplomats on the project team to periodically visit critics and present them with information); *displaying support* (asking sponsors for a visible demonstration of backing); *reducing the stakes* (deescalating the number of losses or changes implied by the innovation); and *warning the critics* (letting them know they would be challenged at an important meeting—with top management, for example). Note that many of these are more likely to succeed when the innovation group has a strong coalition backing it. The effectiveness of interpersonal processes depends on structural conditions.

Because of the controversy that surrounds many innovations, it is important for the working team to continue to send information outward. For example, when the project nears completion and there are things to see, they may begin to bring important people in to view the activities. Successful innovators have been observed to "manage the press," working to create favorable and up-to-date impressions in the minds of peers and key supporters (Kanter, 1983). Similarly, Friedlander and Scott (1981) found that activities of change teams were given more legitimation and were more likely to be implemented when there was a great deal of communication with top management, including two-way dialogue about particular project ideas.

Continuity

Structural and social conditions within the innovation team also make a difference in success. Because "interactive learning" (Quinn, 1985) is so critical to innovation, innovation projects are particularly vulnerable to turnover. Continuity of personnel, up to some limits (Katz, 1982), is an innovation-supporting condition.

There are sometimes good reasons, from the project's standpoint, for people to leave: inadequate performance, interpersonal tensions, the wrong skills. But every loss-and-replacement can jeopardize the success of the innovation process, in three different ways:

1. Each person leaving removes knowledge from the pool, that has not yet been routinized or systematized. In a sense, everyone leaving an innovation project does indeed take "secrets" with them—private knowledge they may have gained that has not yet been shared with the rest of the team because of the intensity with which everyone is gathering knowledge.
2. Each person entering deflects the energies and attention of the others from knowledge development to education—to try to duplicate the experience base of current staff and avoid reinventing the wheel. But telling about it is not only time consuming; it is indeed no substitute for having been there.
3. Each person entering in a key position may wish to change course in order to exercise his or her own power, thereby failing to take advantage of accumulated knowledge. So every new boss is indeed a new beginning.

Turnover in key positions outside the project team can also create problems, though not necessarily as severe: The division is reorganized, for example, and the new management does not "understand" the venture. The coalition is disrupted and needs to be rebuilt. An organization can easily undermine an innovation without "officially" stopping it simply by reorganizing and changing its reporting relationships.

In one case, the problems of turnover are illustrated. A senior executive of a major instruments manufacturing company was recalling one of the company's venture failures—a new product start-up in one of the divisions. He knew this project well, because he had been the venture manager for the first 6 months. "I think about this often," he said, "because if I had stayed I think I could have made it work." Six months into the project, he was offered a promotion up several levels, from managing 15 people in the start-up to managing 6,000 in an established division. The career implications were clear: take it now or lose his place in line. The rewards were also clear: "The corporation was set up to reward the person running a stable $200 million business more than someone growing a business from zero to $10 million to $200 million, which is much, much harder." Even so, he remembered, "I wanted a week to think about it; I felt torn." Eventually he took the promotion. The start-up team understood the corporate career message, but they still felt abandoned. And the new manager sent in to replace him simply did not have "the feel" for what it would take to get his business going. Even more than loss of leadership, it was loss of experience that hurt this project.

Ironically, creating *change* requires *stability*—continuity of people especially during the information-rich, knowledge-intensive development stage. But established corporations often exacerbate the vulnerabilities of their new ventures and innovation efforts by the instability they encourage in and around them. Lock-step career systems that tie rewards to promotions, thus requiring job changes in order to "advance," or that put more value on the "safer" jobs in already-established businesses, encourage people to abandon development efforts before their knowledge has been "captured." Thus, organizational structures and cultures that allow *continuity* on innovation teams by facilitating unusual or "off-line" career paths, allocating human resources on a project basis rather than a time basis, and rewarding completion are helpful ingredients for successful innovation production.

Continuity is also supported where strong commitment is generated, so that people *want* to stay and *want* to contribute. Three kinds of commitment mechanisms are relevant to innovation efforts:

- Conditions encouraging a rational calculation of the benefits of continuing participation;
- Those encouraging strong social and emotional ties with the group;
- And those encouraging a strong belief in the fundamental values or purposes of the efforts (Kanter, 1972).

Structural and social facilitators of commitment to innovation teams would thus include these kinds of things, among others: A sense of "investment" might be produced by a financial stake in outcomes which grows with time spent, as AT&T's new venture teams have. A sense of "communion" might come from clear group identity and sense of specialness through team names, rituals, and celebrations like those in Data General's new computer development group (Kidder, 1981). A sense of strong values might come from reminders of the connection to user needs. At the same time, where there is also physical isolation of the team and very long working hours, energies have to focus inward, and the lure of competing ties is diminished. (See the discussion of "renunciation" in Kanter, 1972.)

It is important to note, however, that if too much time goes by before innovation completion, then team loyalty and stability can become a liability instead of an asset. Katz (1982) found that the "ideal" longevity of R&D teams is between 2 and 5 years. It takes 2 years to begin to work well together, but after 5 years the group becomes stale.

Flexibility

Flexibility is another requirement for idea realization. It is quite common for innovations to fail to proceed as planned but instead to encounter unexpected roadblocks or obstacles that require replanning and redirection if the innovation is ever to be produced. Cost overruns and missed deadlines are common, due to the inherent high uncertainty of the development process. For example, in one pharmaceutical company the ratio of actual to expected cost of new products was 2.11; the ratio of actual to expected time was 2.95 (Mansfield et al., 1981).

Numerous cases in numerous fields illustrate the unpredictable nature of innovation, and therefore the need for flexibility in order to persist with a project. For example:

- GTE's Telemessenger would not show returns fast enough because, like most innovation, the product employed technology so unknown in the marketplace that prospective customers were not receptive to it, and several rounds of replanning were necessary to get the right configuration. Even assumptions about the scope of the test market had to be changed in the light of experience. What the team had originally imagined was a local test had to be rethought when the product was reconceived (successfully) as an aid to communication across the time zones, thus necessitating a national test. This change in tactics paid off. Though only 6 units were sold after a local mailing of 60,000 letters, 200 were sold at one crack to a multi-national company immediately after the test went national (Powell, 1985).
- The historic town of Alexandria, Virginia, now has an important factory redevelopment project on its waterfront, a project that seemed simple and straightforward when it was first voted on 10 years earlier but required several changes of direction midstream. But the city-owned Alexandria Torpedo Factory and Art Center almost didn't happen. Among a number of unexpected obstacles that nearly killed the project and required additional entrepreneurial effort to resolve was the fact that it threatened a small building used by a public school rowing program. Without the flexibility to make changes in order to persist with the project, the city

would never have seen the results: a rise in the value of its property from $4 million to $31 million.

Thus, as Quinn (1985) found across three countries, multiple approaches, flexibility, and quickness are required for innovation because of the advance of new ideas through random and often highly intuitive insights and because of the discovery of unanticipated problems. Project teams need to work unencumbered by formal plans, committees, board approvals, and other "bureaucratic delays" that might act as constraint against the change of direction.

Furthermore, innovations often engender secondary innovations, a number of other changes made in order to support the central change (Kanter, 1983). As necessary, new arrangements might be introduced in conjunction with the core tasks. Methods and structure might be reviewed and when it seems that a project is bogging down because everything possible has been done and no more results are on the horizon, then a change of structure or approach, or a subsidiary project to remove roadblocks, can result in a redoubling of efforts and a renewed attack on the problem. This is why Van de Ven (1986), among others, argued for the lack of utility of distinctions between technical and organizational innovations; in practice, one often entails the other. Indeed, restructuring of the organization often occurs during the innovation process, including joint ventures, changes in organizational responsibilities, use of new teams, and altered control systems (Schroeder et al., 1986).

Flexibility is an organizational rather than a purely individual variable. Those organizations that permit replanning, give the working team sufficient operating autonomy, and measure success or allocate rewards for results rather than adherence to plan are likely to have higher rates of innovation production. Because of the inherent uncertainty of innovation, advance forecasts about time or resource requirements are likely to be inaccurate; it is difficult to budget or to forecast when lacking an experience base by definition, in the case of a new idea. The GTE Telemessenger was almost aborted when the project manager's first market test failed, because he had not brought in the results he promised, and he went through several rounds of argument to get an original "15 days to fix it" extended to 2 months (Powell, 1985). Requiring commitment to a predetermined course of action interferes with the flexibility needed for innovation.

Balancing Autonomy and Accountability

Some analysts argue that innovation production occurs better when the working team is left completely alone, freed from all bureaucratic procedural demands and allowed total concentration, total focus on its work. But there is a middle ground between the extreme of so many reporting requirements that the team spends more of its time preparing reports than doing the work, and the other extreme of no controls or measures until the end.

If some innovation projects fail because they are *overly constrained* by the need to follow bureaucratic rules and seek constant approvals, others may equally fail because they are *overfunded and undermanaged* by top leaders, which can remove the incentive to produce results efficiently. Indeed, Bailyn (1985) learned from her studies of R&D labs that many engineers were subject to overly constraining operational controls while permitted too much "strategic autonomy" to set their own research goals—just the opposite of the combination needed for success.

This can be a particular problem in large new ventures. In one case in a leading corporation, top management generously funded a new project development effort and then left it alone, assuming that they had done the right thing by providing abundant resources. Because they were so rich, the team wasted money on dead-ends and intriguing but unnecessary flourishes and failed to replan when early results were disappointing. The team did not need to justify their actions to anyone, and the project eventually failed. This is one reason why Stevenson and Gumpert (1985) argued that successful entrepreneurship involves *multi-stage commitments*—smaller amounts of money at more frequent intervals.

The ideal structural context surrounding an innovation project, then, should offer procedural autonomy coupled with multiple milestones that must be reached in order for the project to continue. These milestone points represent the major interface with organizational decision makers and perhaps coalition members. They also help maintain team members' own commitment by giving them targets to shoot for and occasions to celebrate.

TRANSFER AND DIFFUSION

The culmination of innovation production is transfer to those who will exploit the innovation or embed it in ongoing organizational practice. Transfer needs to be handled effectively, if new products are to be successfully commercialized or new organizational practices or techniques to be successfully diffused. Isolated in its development, the innovation must again be connected with the actors and activities that will allow it to be actually used.

Social arrangements, from organization structures to patterns of practice, again make the principal difference, even more than the technical virtues of the innovation (Rogers & Shoemaker, 1971).

Strategic Alignment and Structural Linkages

Whereas creation and development—production of the innovation model— can occur with few resources, little visibility, modest coalitions, and the isolated activity of relatively small teams, *use* of the innovation is a different matter. If creation is an *intensive* process; diffusion is an *extensive* process. Use requires many other people, activities, patterns and structures to change to incorporate the innovation.

Thus, a first condition for effective transfer is minimal new change requirements because the innovation is aligned with strategy or direction and linked to the other parts of the structure, so that adjustments and changes have already been made in *anticipation* of the innovation.

It is not surprising that innovations are more successfully transferred, commercialized, or diffused where the organization or market is already receptive to the idea and prepared for its use. This is almost tautological. Where there is stronger organizational commitment in the development process, signified by funding, visibility, coalition support, and so forth, there are more "side bets" placed on the idea (that is, staking of reputations in the outcome) as well as greater "sunk costs." Thus, there will be more pressures to use the innovation in more ways and make it more central to the organization's strategy. Organizational arrangements will already have begun to bend in anticipation of the successful development, often through the negotiations among departments, the "logical incrementalism" through which new strategies are adopted (Quinn, 1980).

On the other hand, those innovations that begin life as random deviance, or unofficial bootlegging in a hidden corner of the organization, or the idiosyncratic dream of a tolerated-but-marginal actor, have a harder time getting adopted regardless of their virtues. Other actors, other departments have already made their plans without taking the possible availability of an innovation into account. Therefore, structures and practices have already been established that would have to be rearranged. These structural constraints to diffusion or transfer may be matched by political constraints: controversy over the innovation or refusal to use it by those uninvolved in its development. The latter is the common NIH (not invented here) problem: this problem particularly plagues organizational innovations (Kanter, 1983; Walton, 1975).

It has long been a cliche in the innovation literature (primarily because most scholars cite the same handful of studies) that diffusion or adoption of an innovation, once developed, is aided by formalization and centralization in the organization, by a concentration of power and a set of employees accustomed to following orders. The *opposite* structural features, then, from those that are conducive to a free flow of many new ideas are held to be necessary for ensuring the rapid acceptance of any one.

Recent evidence, however, makes this a much more contingent proposition (Kimberly, 1980). Cohn and Turyn (1984), in a quantitative comparison of innovations in the domestic footwear industry, found that formalization and centralization were associated with adoption of *evolutionary* innovations but *not* with *revolutionary* ones.

A concentrated source of power is needed to *impose* the innovation on the organization or move it quickly through preexisting formal channels whenever the innovation has *not already been appropriately linked* to the units to which it will be transferred. Indeed, strong central authority can be argued to be just a functional alternative to strong direct links between an innovation project and those to whom its product is handed-off.

If an innovation development project is structurally well-integrated as it comes to completion, rather than segmented and isolated from the rest of the organization (Kanter, 1983), then it does not require the power of centralized authority to ensure its effective transfer. Other units have readied themselves to receive the innovation. Indeed, the hand-off or diffusion process is more difficult in organizations where interdepartmental rivalries and lack of integration cause friction when anything comes from a sister unit; then only "orders" from central authority are attended to. Perhaps this is why evidence indicates that successful new ventures in large corporations are more likely to be the ones sponsored by operating line executives rather than by corporate executives (Hobson & Morrison, 1983); the line-sponsored ventures are already closely connected with implementors.

Of course, effective transfer also requires a strategic decision that this innovation should get resources allocated to it, resources necessary to exploit its potential. For product and technical process innovations, and even for some organizational innovations, the greatest financial requirements *begin* after the model has been developed. Thus, the nature of the strategic decision process and how top management is linked to the innovation project is another critical structural element in an innovation's success or failure (Burgelman, 1984).

At the transfer point, when resources to exploit the innovation are allocated, visible and well-connected projects already aligned with the organization's strategic objectives are likely to fare better. In turn, the degree of investment the project gets, as it is moved into commercialization, routine production, or institutionalization affects its prospects for success as an ongoing product or practice. "Thinking small" and not providing adequate investment is often identified as a reason for new venture failures (Drucker, 1985). Research on the first 4 years of operation of 117 corporate ventures in established markets in manufacturing found that the businesses above the median in success began with capacity that could meet twice the current total market demands, whereas those below the median began with a capacity that could meet only 6% of the current total market demands. Furthermore, the "winning" ventures initially set higher market share objectives, had R&D spending levels twice those of the other ventures in the first 2 years and marketing expenditures about 1.5 those of the other ventures in the same period (Hobson & Morrison, 1983).

Interface Structures: Active Agents and Communication Channels

The transfer or diffusion issue should be conceptualized as a continuum. At one extreme there is perfect identity between the developers and the ultimate users, so that the innovators are essentially producing the innovation for themselves, to their own specifications, with foreknowledge that they will be using whatever it is that they make. Organizations can come close to replicating this condition in customized development work for specific clients already internally committed to use, in which client representatives actually sit on the development team. In this case, transfer or diffusion is nonproblematic; it is an inevitable part of successful development.

At the other extreme, there is little or no connection between developers and those to whom the innovation could potentially be transferred, nor is there an established transfer process. There is high uncertainty (an information issue) and controversy (a political issue) about what the next step is to get anyone to use the innovation, who should take it, and whether there are identifiable customers for the idea, whether anyone does or should want the innovation.

A variety of interface or bridging structures can reduce both the uncertainty and the controversy, thus making it more likely that successful transfer will occur.

One method for diffusing new ideas is to establish a group whose formal responsibility is to move new ideas into active use (Engel, Kollate, & Blackwell, 1981). Members serve as active agents of diffusion, managing the process by which the realized idea is transferred to those who can use it. Part of their mandate is to gather the information to make systematic the process of getting the innovation to users.

Inside organizations, such bridging structures might take the form of product managers, whose job is to manage the successful entry of a new product into the marketplace, drawing on every function in the organization that might contribute, from continuing work on the design to the manufacturing process to the sales effort. Or, in the case of organizational or work innovations, the bridging structure might be a transition team or "parallel organization" (Stein & Kanter, 1980) that concentrates on the change process as a management task in and of itself.

Agents of diffusion may also exist outside the organization. Indeed, it can be argued that external agents are even more important in diffusion than champions inside the organization, for they add real or imagined legitimacy to the idea, why Rogers and Shoemaker (1971) found contact with consultants such an important part of the diffusion of innovation. What is important is not only the cloak of respectability in which the external party clothes the innovation, but also the communication service provided. Thus, Walton (1987) found that the diffusion of work innovations in shipping in eight countries was aided by formal organizations set up to study and write about those innovations. They served as a necessary communication channel to transfer innovations to other users.

How well organized the environment is for the transfer of ideas can account for how rapidly a particular innovation is diffused. By "organized" I mean the case with which those with common interests can find each other, and therefore how easily connections can be made between innovations and users. Thus, the existence of conferences, meetings, and special interest associations should all be valuable in diffusing innovations, even product innovations, which have to be brought to the attention of specific groups. Again, this can occur within as well as outside a particular organization. 3M and Honeywell both organize a large number of internal conferences and "idea fairs" to connect ideas with those who can use it or help take it the next step.

Trade associations, professionals and societies, and specialist consulting organizations are among those serving this purpose more broadly. The Food Marketing Institute, trade association for grocers and supermarkets, was largely responsible for facilitating the spread of universal price codes on packages from manufacturers and hence the spread of scanners in stores.

The Institutional Environment

The last issue in transfer and diffusion is a receptive and social and legal environment. The institutional environment, I propose, is so often taken for granted in the study of innovation that it tends to be visible mostly when it impedes. But the institutional environment is one of the most important factors distinguishing between eight nations in their overall record of diffusion of work innovations in shipping (Walton, 1987). Among the specific elements making a difference are patterns of labor organization and government policy and regulations. In the United States, for example, where innovation diffusion has been low, a series of fragmented labor unions bargaining independently with shipowners, with no vehicles for industry-wide collaboration by either party, accounted in part for the low diffusion rate.

The role of government in influencing innovation transfer can be a strong one. Hollomon and colleagues (1981) identified specific ways in which government policies and programs directly affect innovation adoption patterns:

- Assessment of new and existing specific technologies
- Direct regulation of the research or development of new products and processes
- Direct regulation of the production, marketing, and use of new or existing products
- Programs to encourage the development and utilization of technology in and for the private goods and services sector
- Government support of technology for public services for consumers
- Policies to affect industry structure that may affect the development and use of innovation
- Policies affecting supply and demand of human resources having an impact on technological change
- Economic policies with unintended or indirect effect on technological innovation
- Policies affecting international trade and investment
- Policies intended to create shifts in consumer demand
- Policies responding to worker demand having impact on technological change.

Whether innovations are ultimately spread and used, then, may be a matter of societal as well as industry organization. This level of analysis is not common in the innovation literature, but it demands more attention, particularly with respect to innovations that themselves have organizational consequences. Unfortunately, much of the literature is shortsighted in still looking for determinants of adoption of innovations in individual attitudes or intraorganizational structures.

But as organizations themselves bump up against the institutional limits to innovation diffusion, then the issues become clearer. For example, if the use of technological innovations has implications for job security, then the institutional patterns of labor relations in the industry may be among the most important determinants of an organization's ability to use such innovations. Several major companies are now attempting to reshape the broader institutional context in order to create conditions for more rapid diffusion of innovation within their borders. General Motors, is a notable example, planning the new Saturn subsidiary jointly with the United Auto Workers Union, using a series of joint committees. Pacific Telesis is also reshaping relations with its principal unions through local common interest forums of company officers and union presidents that define many workplace policies together. But even if the unions concur, the current labor law framework may be a significant impediment; Pacific Telesis has already faced one legal challenge to institutional restructuring.

Innovation, and the spread of innovation, is also a function of industry conditions and the support an organization can draw from its larger community, as research by Ruttan and Hayami (1984) and Trist (1981) shows. The more dependent an organization is on others (Pfeffer & Salancik, 1977), the more likely that it will be shaped or constrained in its internal innovation by those portions of the environment which dominate it. But the opposite also holds. Some environments represent "fertile fields" that provide more of the surrounding conditions conducive to innovation.

"Fertile fields" include these kinds of features, associated with entrepreneurship in the form of start-ups as well as innovation in established organizations:

- Close proximity and ample communication between innovators and users
- A more highly skilled, professionalized, cosmopolitan workforce
- A flow of new technical ideas from R&D centers
- A more complex, heterogeneous environment that encourages innovation as an uncertainty-reduction strategy (Kimberly, 1981)
- Channels of communication for exchange of innovation ideas
- Competition from entrepreneurial new companies, in turn benefiting from the availability of venture capital
- More interorganization interdependence and integration (Pierce and Delbecq, 1977)
- Public encouragement of new ideas as social goods.

This brings us full circle, for many of these same conditions help activate the innovation process as well as diffuse the models later.

The ultimate set of social structural factors supporting innovation, then, comes from the nature of the environment in which an organization operates as well as its connections to various key units in that environment. Although an innovation model may be produced in one organization independently and in isolation, it takes the actions of many for the innovation to diffuse.

It is appropriate to look beyond the borders of one organization for the determinants of innovation. Indeed, some innovations can start life as the joint product of more than one organization, through joint ventures, cooperative research efforts, and strategic alliances. The reputed Japanese "edge" in technology diffusion is said to come precisely from an institutional context allowing and encouraging such interorganizational cooperation in the same industry—a strategy still largely limited by U.S. antitrust laws. Furthermore, sometimes organizations unwittingly cooperate in innovation. For example, the failure of innovation in one organization can be the trigger for the creation of a new organization designed solely to develop that same innovation, the entrepreneurial process that has led to spinoffs from larger companies that reject innovations developed and exploited successfully by start-up companies. And the contribution of some organizations to innovation is to generate new organizations (e.g., Wiewel and Hunter, 1985).

CONCLUSION

I have tried to connect the major tasks in the innovation process to those structural arrangements and social patterns that facilitate each. Innovation consists of a set of processes carried out at the micro-level, by individuals and groups of individuals; and these micro-processes are in turn stimulated, facilitated, and enhanced—or the opposite—by a set of macro-structural conditions. Overall, the common organizational threads behind innovation are breadth of reach, flexibility of action, and above all, integration between those with pieces to contribute, whether inside or outside a single organization.

Undeniably, innovation stems from individual talent and creativity. But whether or not individual skills are activated, exercised, supported, and channelled into the production of a new model that can be used, is a function of the organizational and interorganizational context. Throughout, I have marshalled evidence to show the importance of integration to the innovation process, close structural connections between potential innovators and users, between functions and departments, between the innovation project and the units or organizations that will move the model into production and use. I have also shown that the integrative organizational model helpful for innovation extends beyond the borders of a single organization. Innovation benefits from interorganizational ties and organization-environment linkages as well as from internal integration.

Making a thousand flowers bloom is not a fully random or accidental process, unless we are satisfied with spindly, fragile wildflowers. Instead, the flowers of innovation can be cultivated and encouraged to multiply in the gardens of organizations designed on the integrative model, organizations where the growth rhythm of innovation is well understood.

ACKNOWLEDGMENT

The highly competent assistance of David V. Summers and Paul Myers is gratefully acknowledged.

Funding was provided by the Division of Research of the Harvard Business School, whose generosity is appreciated.

REFERENCES

Abernathy, W.J., & Utterback, J.M. (1978). Patterns of industrial innovation. *Technology Review, 80* (June/July) 41–47.

Allen, T.J. (1984). *Managing the flow of technology: Technology transfer and the dissemination of technological information within the R&D organization.* Cambridge, MA: MIT Press.

Amabile, T.M. (1983). *The social psychology of creativity.* New York: Springer-Verlag.

Axelrod, R. (1970). *Conflict of interest.* Chicago: Marham.

Bacharach, S.B., & Lawler, E.J. (1960). *Power and politics in organizations.* San Francisco: Jossey-Bass.

Bailyn, L. (1985). Autonomy in the industrial R&D lab. *Human Resource Management,* 24 129–146.

Baldridge, J.V., & Burnham, R.A. (1975). Organizational innovation: individual, organizational, and environmental impacts. *Administrative Science Quarterly,* 20 165–176.

Barnard, C.I. (1938). *The functions of the executive.* Cambridge, MA: Harvard University Press.

Bendix, R. (1956). *Work and authority in industry.* Berkeley, CA: The University of California Press.

Biggadike, R. (1979). The risky business of diversification. *Harvard Business Review, 57* (May–June), 103–111.

Blau, P.M. (1963). *The dynamics of bureaucracy* (2nd ed.). Chicago: The University of Chicago Press.

Block, Z. (1982). Can corporate venturing succeed? *The Journal of Business Strategy, 3* (Fall), 21–33.

Block, Z. (1983). Some major issues in internal corporate venturing. In J.A. Hornaday, J.A. Timmons, & Karl H. Vesper (Eds.). *Frontiers of entrepreneurial research* (pp. 382–389). Wellesley, MA: Babson College Center for Entrepreneurial Studies.

Boissevain, J. (1971). Second thoughts on quasi-groups, categories, and coalitions. *Man. 6,* 468–472.

Brittain, J.W., & Freeman, J.H. (1980). Organizational proliferation and entity development in selection. In J.R. Kimberly & R.H. Miles (Eds.). *The organizational life cycle* (pp. 291–341). San Francisco: Jossey-Bass.

Burgelman, R.A. (1984). Managing the internal corporate venturing process. *Sloan Management Review, 25* (Winter), 33–48.

Burns, T., & Stalker, G.M. (1968). *The management of innovation* (2nd ed.). London: Tavistock.

Carroll, J. (1967). A note on departmental autonomy and innovation in medical school. *Journal of Business, 40* 531–534.

Child, J. (1972). Organizational structure, environment and performance: The role of strategic choice. *Sociology, 6,* 1–22.

Cohn, S.F., & Turyn, R.M. (1984). Organizational structure, decision-making procedures, and the adoption of innovations. *IEEE Transactions on Engineering Management, EM31* (November), 154–161.

Connolly, T., Conlon, E., & Deutsch, S. (1980). Organizational effectiveness: A multiple-constituency approach. *Academy of Management Review, 5,* 211–217.

Cyert, R.M., & March, J.G. (1963). *A behavioral theory of the firm.* Englewood Cliffs, NJ: Prentice-Hall.

Dalton, M. (1959). *Men who manage.* New York: John Wiley & Sons.

Davis, S.M., & Lawrence, P.R. (1977). *Matrix,* Reading, MA: Addison-Wesley.

Dean, R.C. (1974). The temporal mismatch—innovation's pace versus management's time horizons. *Research Management, 19* (May), 12–15.

Delbecq, A.L., & Mills, P.K. (1985). Managerial practices that enhance innovation. *Organizational Dynamics, 14* (Summer), 24–34.

Drucker, P.F. (1985). *Innovation and entrepreneurship—Practice and principles.* New York: Harper & Row.

Engel, J.F., Kollat, D.T., & Blackwell, R.D. (1981). Diffusion of innovations. In R.R. Rothberg (Ed.). *Corporate strategy and product innovation* (pp. 472–481). New York: Free Press.

Fast, N.D. (1979). The future of industrial new venture departments. *Industrial Marketing Management, 8* (November), 264–273.

Friedlander, F., & Scott, B. (1981). The use of task groups and task forces in organizational change. In C. Cooper & R. Payne (Eds.), *Groups at work* (pp. 191–217). New York: John Wiley & Sons.

Galbraith, J. (1982). Designing the innovating organization. *Organizational Dynamics, 10* (Summer). 5–25.

Gamson, W.A. (1961). A theory of coalition formation. *American Sociological Review, 26,* 373–382.

Gamson, W.A. (1968). Coalition formation. *International Encyclopedia of the Social Sciences* (pp. 529–534). New York: The Macmillan Co. and The Free Press.

George, R., & MacMillan, I.C. (1984). Corporate venturing—ventue management challenges. Working Paper, New York University.

Gladstein, D., & Caldwell, D. (1985). Boundary management in new product teams. In *Academy of Management Proceedings* (pp. 161–165).

Hage, J., & Aiken, M. (1967). Program change and organizational properties: A comparative analysis. *American Journal of Sociology, 72,* 503–579.

Hage, J., & Dewar, R. (1973). Elite values vs. organizational structure in predicting innovation. *Administrative Science Quarterly, 18* 279–290.

Hanan, M. (1976). Venturing corporations: Think small to stay strong. *Harvard Business Review, 54* (May–June), 139–148.

Hobson, E.L., & Morrison, R.M. (1983). How do corporate start-up ventures fare? In J.A. Hornaday, J.A. Timmons, & Karl, H. Vesper (Eds.), *Frontiers of entrepreneurial re-*

search (pp. 390–410). Wellesley, MA: Babson College Center for Entrepreneurial Studies.

Hollomon, J.H. (1981). Government and the innovation process. In R.R. Rothberg (Ed.). *Corporate strategy and product innovation* (pp. 46–59). New York: Free Press.

Kanter, R.M. (1972). *Commitment and community.* Cambridge, MA: Harvard University Press.

Kanter, R.M. (1977). *Men and women in the corporation.* New York: Basic Books.

Kanter, R.M. (1980). *Power and change in and by organizations: Setting intellectual directions for organizational analysis.* Paper presented at American Sociological Association Annual Meeting.

Kanter, R.M. (1982). The middle manager as innovator. *Harvard Business Review, 61* (July–August). 95–105.

Kanter, R.M. (1983). *The change masters.* New York: Simon & Schuster.

Kanter, R.M. (1984). Innovation: Our only hope for times ahead? *Sloan Management Review, 25* (Summer), 51–55.

Kanter, R.M. (1985). Supporting innovation and venture development in established corporations. *Journal of Business Venturing, 1* (Winter), 47–60.

Kanter, R.M. (1986). Creating the creative environment. *Management Review, 75* (February), 11–12.

Kanter, R.M., & Stein, B.A. (Eds.) (1979). *Life in organizations.* New York: Basic Books.

Kaplan, R.E., & Mazque, M. (1983). *Trade routes: The manager's network of relationships* (Technical Report No. 22). Greensboro, NC: Center for Creative Leadership.

Katz, R. (1982). Project communication and performance: An investigation into the effects of group longevity. *Administrative Science Quarterly, 27, 81–104.*

Kidder, T. (1981). *The soul of a new machine.* Boston: Atlantic Little, Brown.

Kimberly, J.R. (1980). Initiation, innovation, and institutionalization in the creation process. In J.R. Kimberly & R.H. Miles (Eds.). *The organizational life cycle* (18–43). San Francisco: Jossey-Bass.

Kimberly, J.R. (1981). Managerial innovations. In W.H. Starbuck (Ed.). *Handbook of organizational design* (Vol. 1. pp. 84–104). New York: Oxford University Press.

Kimberly, J.R., & Evanisko, M.J. (1979). *Organizational innovation.* Working paper A27. School of Organization and Management, Yale University.

Kohn, M. (1971). Bureaucratic man: A portrait and an interpretation. *American Sociological Review, 38 461–474.*

Lawrence, P.R., & Lorsch, J.W. (1967). *Organization and environment.* Boston: Graduate School of Business Administration, Harvard University.

MacMillan, I.C., Block, Z., & Subba Narsimha, P.N. (1986). Corporate venturing: Alternatives, obstacles encountered, and experience effects. *Journal of Business Venturing, 1* (Spring), 177–191.

Maidique, M.A. (1980). Entrepreneurs, champions, and technological innovation. *Sloan Management Review, 21* (Winter), 59–76.

Mansfield, E., Rapoport, J., Schnee, J., Wagner, S., & Hamburger, N. (1981). Research and innovation in the modern corporation. In R.R. Rothberg (Ed.), *Corporate strategy and product innovation* (pp. 416–427). New York: Free Press.

March, J.G. (1962). The business firm as a political coalition. *The Journal of Politics, 24,* 662–678.

March, J.G., & Olsen, J.P. (1976). *Ambiguity and choice in organizations.* Bergen, Norway: Universitetsforlanget.

Marquis, D.G., & Myers, S. (1969). *Successful industrial innovations.* Washington, DC: National Science Foundation.

Martilla, J.A. (1971). Word-of-mouth communication in the industrial adoption process. *Journal of Marketing Research, 8,* 173–178.

Mechanic, D. (1962). Sources of power of lower participants in complex organizations. *Administrative Science Quarterly, 7,* 347–364.

Mintzberg, H. (1981). Organizational design: Fashion or fit? *Harvard Business Review, 59* (Jan.–Feb.). 103–116.

Mintzberg, H. (1983). *Power in and around organizations.* Englewood Cliffs, NJ: Prentice-Hall.

Mohr, L.B. (1978). *Explaining organizational behavior.* San Francisco: Jossey-Bass.

Moritz, M. (1984). *The little kingdom: The private story of Apple Computer.* New York: Morrow.

Murnighan, J.K. (1978). Models of coalition behavior: Game theoretic, social psychological, and political perspectives. *Psychological Bulletin, 85,* 1130–1153.

Nelson, R.R. (Ed.) (1962). *The rate and direction of inventive activity.* Princeton, NJ: Princeton University Press.

Normann, R. (1971). Organizational innovativeness: Product variation and reorientation. *Administrative Science Quarterly, 16,* 203–215.

O'Toole, J. (1983). Declining innovation: The failure of success. *Human Resource Planning, 6,* 125–141.

Pelz, D., & Andrews, F. (1966). *Scientists in organizations.* New York: John Wiley & Sons.

Pennings, J.M., & Goodman, P.S. (1977). Toward a workable framework. In P.S. Goodman, J.M. Pennings & Associates. *New perspectives in organizational effectiveness* (pp. 146–184). San Francisco: Jossey-Bass.

Perrow, C. (1981). *Normal accidents.* New York: Basic Books.

Pfeffer, J. (1981). *Power in organizations.* Boston: Pitman.

Pfeffer, J., & Salancik, G.R. (1977). Organization design: The case for a coalition model of organizations. *Organizational Dynamics, 6* (Autumn), 15–29.

Pfeffer, J., & Salancik, G.R. (1978). *The external control of organizations.* New York: Harper & Row.

Pierce, J.L., & Delbecq, A.L. (1977). Organization structure, individual attitudes and innovation. *Academy of Management Review, 2,* 27–37.

Pondy, L.R. (1980). Organizational conflict: Concepts and models. In H.J. Leavitt, et al. (Eds.). *Readings in Managerial Psychology* (pp. 473–492). Chicago: The University of Chicago Press.

Powell, J. (1985). Bootstrap entrepreneurs at GTE TeleMessenger. *GTE Together.* Winter.

Quinn, J.B. (1979). Technological innovation, entrepreneurship and strategy. *Sloan Management Review, 20* (Spring), 19–30.

Quinn, J.B. (1980). *Strategies for change. Logical incrementalism.* Homewood. IL: Irwin.

Quinn, J.B. (1985). Managing innovation: Controlled chaos. *Harvard Business Review, 63* (May–June), 73–84.

Riker, W.H. (1962). *The theory of political coalitions.* New Haven: Yale University Press.

Roberts, E.B. (1980). New ventures for corporate growth. *Harvard Business Review, 58* (July–August), 134–142.

Robertson, T., & Wind, Y. (1983). Organizational cosmopolitanism and innovation. *Academy of Management Journal, 26,* 332–338.

Rogers, E.M., & Shoemaker, F.F. (1971). *Communication of innovations: A cross-cultural approach* (2nd ed.). New York: The Free Press.

Rothberg, R.R. (Ed.) (1981). *Corporate strategy and product innovation.* New York: Free Press.

Ruttan, V.W., & Hayami, Y. (1984). Toward a theory of induced institutional innovation. *Journal of Development Studies, 20,* 203–223.

Salancik, G.R., & Pfeffer, J. (1977) Who gets power—and how they hold on to it. *Organizational Dynamics, 5* (Winter), 2–21.

Sapolsky, H. (1967). Organizational structure and innovation. *Journal of Business, 40,* 497–510.

Schilit, W.K., & Locke, E.A. (1982). A study of upward influence in organizations. *Administrative Science Quarterly, 27,* 304–316.

Schon, D. (1967). *Technology and change.* New York: Delacorte.

Schon, D. (1971). *Beyond the stable state.* New York: Norton.

Schroeder, R., Van de Ven, A. Scudder, G., & Polley, D. (1986). Observations leading to a process model of innovation. Discussion Paper No. 48, Strategic Management Research Center, University of Minnesota.

Shubik, M. (1982). *Game theory in the social sciences: Concepts and solutions.* Cambridge, MA: The MIT Press.

Starbuck, W.H. (1983). Organizations as action generators. *American Sociological Review, 48,* 91–115.

Staw, B.M. (1975). Attribution of the 'causes' of performance: A general alternative interpretation of cross-sectional research on organizations. *Organizational Behavior and Human Performance, 13,* 414–432.

Stein, B.A., & Kanter, R.M. (1980). Building the parallel organization: Toward mechanisms for permanent quality of work life. *Journal of Applied Behavioral Science, 16,* 371–388.

Stevenson, H., & Gumpert, D. (1985). The heart of entrepreneurship. *Harvard Business Review, 64* (March–April), 84–94.

Stumpe, W.R. (1979). What the research manager should know about new product psychology. *Research Management, 22* (March), 13–17.

Summers, D.V. (1986). Organizing in middle management: A politico-structural model of coalition formation in complex organizations. Ph.D. dissertation. Department of Sociology, Yale University.

Thompson, J.P. (1967). *Organizations in action.* New York: McGraw-Hill.

Thurman, B. (1979–1980). In the office: Networks and coalitions. *Social Networks, 2,* 47–63.

Tichy, N., & Fombrun, C. (1979). Network analysis in organizational settings. *Human Relations, 32,* 923–965.

Tosi, H., & Tosi, L. (1986). What managers need to know about knowledge-based pay. *Organizational Dynamics, 14* (Winter), 52–64.

Trist, E. (1981). The evolution of sociotechnical systems as a conceptual framework and as an action research program. In A. Van de Ven & W. Joyce (Eds.). *Perspective on organization design and behavior* (pp. 19–75). New York: John Wiley & Sons.

Tushman, M. (1977). Special boundary roles in the innovation process. *Administrative Science Quarterly, 22,* 587–605.

Tushman, M. (1979). Work characteristics and subunit communication structure: A contingency analysis. *Administrative Science Quarterly, 24,* 82–98.

Tushman, M., & Moore, W.L. (Eds.) (1982). *Readings in the management of innovation.* Marshfield, MA: Pitman.

Tushman, M., & Nadler, D. (1986). Organizing for innovation. *California Management Review, 28* (Spring), 74–92.

Van de Ven, A.H. (1986). Central problems in the management of innovation. *Management Science, 32,* 590–607.

Vesper, K.H. (1984). Three faces of corporate entrepreneurship: A pilot study. Working Paper, University of Washington.

Von Hippel, E. (1977). Successful and failing internal corporate ventures: An empirical analysis. *Industrial Marketing Management, 6,* 163–174.

Von Hippel, E. (1982). Get new products from customers. *Harvard Business Review, 60* (March–April), 117–122.

Von Hippel, E. (1981). Users as innovators. In R.R. Rothberg (Ed.), *Corporate strategy and product innovation* (pp. 239–251). New York: Free Press.

Walton, R. (1975). The diffusion of New York structures: Explaining why success didn't take. *Organizational Dynamics, 4* (Winter), 3–21.

Walton, R. (1987). *Innovating to compete.* San Francisco: Jossey-Bass.

Weber, M. (1978). Guenther Ross and Claus Wittich, (Trans.) *Economy and society* (Vol. 2). Berkeley, CA: The University of California Press.

Weick, K.E. (1976). Educational organizations as loosely coupled systems. *Administrative Science Quarterly, 21,* 1–19.

Weick, K.E. (1979). *The social psychology of organizing* (2nd ed.). Reading, MA: Addison-Wesley.

Wiewel, W., & Hunter, A. (1985). The interorganizational network as a resource: A comparative case study on organizational genesis. *Administrative Science Quarterly, 30,* 482–497.

Wortman, C.B., & Linsenmeier, J.A.W. (1977). Interpersonal attraction and techniques of ingratiation in organizational settings. In B.M. Staw & G. Salancik (Eds.), *New Directions in Organizational Behavior* (pp. 133–178) Chicago: St. Clair Press.

Yin, R.K. (1977). Production efficiency versus bureaucratic self-interest: Two innovative processes? *Policy Sciences, 8,* 381–399.

Zagare, F.C. (1984). *Game theory concepts and applications.* Beverly Hills, CA: Sage.

Zaltman, G., Duncan, R., & Holbeck, J. (1973). *Innovations and organization.* New York: John Wiley & Sons.

8

Knowledge Links

Joseph Badaracco

Managers are playing with fire when their company does not own and control its crucial resources, core capabilities, and key technologies. But what about the knowledge, resources, and skills that play supporting roles? As embedded knowledge and specialized capabilities are created in a growing number of companies and other organizations around the world, firms often find it too costly and cumbersome to develop, on their own, all the knowledge and capabilities they need or want to have available. In the words of IBM president, Jack Kuehler, "It's a dangerous thing to think we know everything."[1]

In response, many firms are creating knowledge links—alliances that give them access to the skills and capabilities of other organizations and sometimes enable them to work with other organizations to create new capabilities. Knowledge links can be tactical or strategic. A single knowledge link can help a company build new skills in a limited area of its operations. This is a tactical effort. In contrast, when a company creates a multitude of knowledge links with customers, suppliers, labor organizations, universities, and other organizations, and when these alliances strengthen each other and support the company's long-term objectives, then knowledge links are genuinely strategic.

This is how GM and IBM have sought to use many of their knowledge links during the 1980s. Their new knowledge-intensive relationships have played important supporting roles in each company's effort to renew and reshape its core capabilities and to change the competitive rules of the game in its favor. Such major strategic efforts are usually accompanied by changes in organizational structure, and this has been the case both IBM and GM. They are now structured more like city-states and less like citadels, because of their growing reliance on knowledge-rich alliances. Like city-states, each firm has at its core a dense network of relationships defined by ownership, control, and social bonds. It is no longer easy to define what is inside and outside the two companies. Instead, each firm is linked to other organizations through a multitude of arrangements in which control and ownership are shared, social bonds blurred, classical contracting compromised, and embedded knowledge is transferred, renewed, and created.

GM and IBM, like many other American firms, would be creating far fewer knowledge links today if it were not for the economic threats posed by competitors in Japan and elsewhere. By the 1980s, many of these foreign competitors had combined knowledge they had secured from the United States with their indigenous capabilities and were vying for the lead in worldwide technology and product contests. Sometimes, they held the lead. In the mid-1980s, for example, Toyota and other Japanese auto companies were pioneers in introducing powerful multivalve engines. At the same time, Japanese and U.S. car makers were racing each other to develop small, fuel-efficient, low-cost two-stroke engines and "active suspension systems" that electronically sensed road conditions and adjusted a car's ride. In computers, Fujitsu sold mainframes that ran faster than comparably priced IBM machines. (In the 1970s, a single American firm, Cray Research, had dominated the supercomputer field.) By the late 1980s, breakthroughs were taking place at Fujitsu, Hitachi, and NEC, as well as at small, startup firms in the United States such as Sequent and Thinking Machines. These products were the progeny of highly refined and specialized capabilities. Companies and countries were competing to develop, not just the latest products, but the capabilities to develop, refine, and sometimes revolutionize these products year after year.

American firms often create product links in response to such developments, thereby quickly securing products that other companies already have. Knowledge links do more. They are, in effect, a higher step in an evolutionary chain of alliances. Like product links, their forebears, they usually produce products or services, and they can also help to reduce risks, cut costs, increase speed to market, and so forth. But knowledge links also help the partners learn and sometimes create new capabilities. In fact, this is often a prerequisite for the alliance's success: without acquiring new knowledge, many partnerships could not produce the products or services that its parent organizations want.

CHARACTERISTICS OF KNOWLEDGE LINKS

The first distinguishing trait of knowledge links is that learning and creating knowledge is a central objective of the alliance. Knowledge links can help one company learn specialized capabilities from another; they can help a company combine its special capabilities with those of another organization to create new embedded knowledge; and they can enable one company to help another organization build up its skills and capabilities in ways that will benefit both companies later on.

Second, knowledge links are more intimate than product links. In order for two organizations to learn, create, or strengthen specialized capabilities, personnel from each must work together closely. This would not be the case if the companies were trying to transfer migratory knowledge: then they could simply exchange cash for a book of blueprints or a set of formulas. When companies seek to learn embedded knowledge from each other, their relationship resembles that of a master and an apprentice, which Michael Polanyi describes in this way:

> *You follow your master because you trust his manner of doing things even when you cannot analyze and account in detail for its effectiveness. By watching the master and emulating his efforts in the presence of his example, the apprentice learns unconsciously, picks up the rules of the art, including those which are not explicitly known to the master himself. These hidden rules can be assimilated only by a person who surrenders himself uncritically to the imitation of another.[2]*

The third distinctive feature of knowledge links is the extraordinarily wide range of partners with which these links can be formed. Product links are usually formed with competitors or potential competitors. GM, as we have seen, turned to four Asian car companies to help it fill the small car gap in its product line. Knowledge links, in contrast, can be formed with virtually any other organization—as long as it has a specialized capability to contribute to the partnership. Through knowledge links, buyers and suppliers can share expertise on manufacturing processes and work together to improve both the buyer's product and the components the supplier provides. Through knowledge links, university laboratories and companies share and create knowledge. Knowledge links can also include participatory, cooperative relations between companies and their workers and labor unions. Through these, managers learn from workers how to make higher-quality products and how to do so more cheaply and efficiently. At the same time, company-union alliances often involve extensive training programs, so that workers become "multiskilled": instead of performing simple, repetitive tasks, workers develop, as individuals and as teams, the broader range of capabilities that a company needs.

Finally, knowledge links differ from product links because of their greater strategic potential. Product links help one company catch up, buy time, defend itself, or recapture its investment in fixed costs by selling the product quickly and in high volume through partners around the world. Knowledge links can help a firm extend or modify one of its basic capabilities, and a constellation of knowledge links can contribute to a larger strategic effort to renew core capabilities or create new ones.

Knowledge links and product links differ more sharply in theory than in practice. Both are members of the same organizational species, corporate alliances, and both blur traditional firm boundaries through shared ownership and control, linked social systems, and departures from classical, arm's-length contracting. The two kinds of alliances often differ from each other in degree, not in kind. Just as the evolution of life has proceeded through trial-and-error adaptation to varied circumstances, so alliances have produced a spectrum of hybrids in response to the needs of companies. At one end are nearly pure cases of product links, where learning is much less important than access to a product or wider distribution for an existing product. At the other end, the parties seek to learn or create new capabilities as well as to develop a new product. Many alliances fall into the middle ranges of this spectrum.

The GM-Suzuki alliance and IBM's early PC alliances fall nearer the end of the spectrum defined by pure product links. In these alliances, learning played a small role. Neither company sought to learn new capabilities or to achieve a product breakthrough. To be sure, the parties did need to learn enough about each other to coordinate activities, and Suzuki needed to learn from GM about its product specifications and U.S. regulations. Suzuki also received some engineering assistance from GM. But the main aim of the alliance was not for GM to learn from Suzuki, nor for Suzuki to learn GM. GM needed a product quickly, and Suzuki wanted financing for a subcompact it had designed and access to distribution in the United States without the cost and risk of creating its own dealer network. This alliance, in its early phases, was a nearly pure case of a product link.

The GM-Daewoo alliance involved more learning than the GM-Suzuki deal, but mainly for Daewoo, which learned about many aspects of automobile manufacture. While GM learned more about the Korean market, its principal aim was to secure another source of low-cost small cars, and it was not creating a new product. GM provided Daewoo with existing GM technology and a vehicle from its Adam Opel subsidiary that GM was already making and selling in West Germany. In doing so, GM did not develop new knowledge or capabilities. The Daewoo alliance, for GM, was a product link; for Daewoo, a knowledge link.

NUMMI was a more complex hybrid. It was, in part, a product link, providing GM with access to a large number of very high-quality small cars. The product was not new (it was a car Toyota was already making and selling in Japan), but NUMMI helped both companies learn and create new capabilities. It helped Toyota learn about managing U.S. workers, suppliers, and trucking firms, and about dealing with the UAW and state and local governments. GM gained the opportunity to learn firsthand about the Toyota production system—its collaborative approach to worker and supplier relations, its just-in-time inventory management, and its highly efficient plant management. Most important, both companies were jointly creating new knowledge and capabilities, each experimenting with a United States-Japanese way of managing an auto plant.

Further along the spectrum was the alliance announced in early 1990 by IBM and Siemens, the West German electronics giant. In this case, the partners planned to pool existing skills and to acquire new ones in the design, manufacture, and testing of computer chips, in order to develop chips two generations more sophisticated than any on the market. To be sure, IBM brought greater technological prowess to the alliance, and, like a product link, the partnership would manufacture a product and reduce the partners' financial risks (designing an advanced microchip and building a plant were expected to cost over $1 billion). But the creation of new capabilities played a vital role in the partnership and in this way it differed dramatically from the GM-Suzuki or IBM PC alliances.

EXTENDING CAPABILITIES THROUGH ALLIANCES

When go-it-alone strategies, classic market transactions, or mergers and acquisitions seem unable to meet a company's needs, knowledge links can help a company gain access to the capabilities of other organizations or work with them to create new capabilities. One of GM's knowledge links, the GMFanuc Robotics Corporation (GMF), demonstrates how a knowledge link can help two companies turn the challenges of embedded knowledge into opportunities for each firm to extend and broaden its capabilities.[3]

In 1982, GM and Fanuc, the Japanese controls and robotics company, each invested $5 million to create GMF. Its charter was to design, market, service, and develop applications for factory automation robots. Technology would flow to and from GMF's parents, without royalties or licenses. GMF expected to move far beyond "duck-drinking-water" robots that perform the same simple task at the same spot on the same product time and time again. Future robots would have sensory functions; they would use television cameras and laser beams or extend sensitive probes to locate objects, reducing the need for manufacturers to develop ways of aligning objects for robot processing. Clearly, GMF was a knowledge link between GM and Fanuc.*

Fanuc was the personal handiwork of Dr. Sieuemon Inaba, its founder and chief executive. In 1955, Fujitsu, the Japanese electronics and computer company, placed him in charge of a team of 500 engineers whose mission was to develop a factory automation business. Under Inaba's leadership, Fanuc became the world's leader in computerized numerical controls—electronic boxes that control the movement of machine tools such as lathes and milling machines. Fanuc was an ultra-workaholic company: 14-hour workdays were ordinary for managers and researchers. Inaba ran Fanuc with military precision. In fact, Fanuc and GM formed their venture within three months of their first contact. Although this pace of decision making was almost unheard of at GM, it was quite natural for Fanuc, where Inaba had installed a clock in the product development lab that ran at 10 times normal speed.

GM executives gave several reasons for joining forces with Fanuc. First, as the largest U.S. user of robots, GM bought about a third of all robots sold in the United States. These, along with tens of thousands of computers and numerical control units, were part of GM's high-tech manufacturing strategy. Second, GM was dissatisfied with some of its own robot vendors. Third, GM had developed an expertise in robotics and wanted to find a way to convert this knowledge into products and sell it. Fourth, GM was afraid it might lose some of its robotics personnel and technology to other robotics companies. Inaba joined with GM because he wanted to build Fanuc's robotics business. In particular, he felt limited by Japanese robot technology. He believed that U.S. and European firms were ahead of the Japanese in developing intelligent robots with visual functions, robots capable of walking around factory floors and offices on their own feet, and robots connected with CAD/CAM systems.

---

*As is often the case, GMF served many of the purposes of a product link. The company, which would set up its headquarters and manufacturing facilities in Michigan, would have the exclusive right to sell robots made in Japan by Fanuc throughout North and South America, Australia, and New Zealand. In this way, GMF would help Fanuc increase its volume of operations and thereby make additional contributions to its fixed costs.

GMF development efforts were coordinated by meetings held four times a year and involving senior executives from GMF and Fanuc. Teams of engineers from Fanuc, GMF, and GM conducted individual projects. Some projects concentrated on hardware, aiming at developing smaller, more economical, and more specialized units. Others focused on programming and communications language. Perhaps the most extensive effort was the development of Karel, a programming language that linked GMF robots, vision systems, and other devices to both GMF and non-GMF products.

In creating GMF, its parents avoided the difficulties of trying to work together through a series of arm's-length market relationships. They were able to collaborate even though a merger of the two companies was impossible. Neither company had to rely wholly on its own resources for further development in robotics. They concentrated only on the particular projects that interested both parties. Their radically different company cultures could be kept largely separate and intact, while the project-driven interactions could be carefully monitored and managed. And, above all, key researchers and engineers from both companies could work together, day by day, in order to learn from each other, create adaptations of the technology and expertise that each had developed alone, and in so doing strengthen their capabilities and those of their partners.

The GMF example is instructive but somewhat limited. It does display two of the principal characteristics of knowledge links. GMF helped both partners broaden certain skills and capabilities, and it also created intimate working relationships among personnel from the parent organizations. GMF does not, however, display the two other characteristics of knowledge links. One is the way a company can use a multitude of knowledge links as part of an effort to transform its core capabilities. The other is the variety of knowledge partners from which a firm can choose.

TRANSFORMING CAPABILITIES THROUGH ALLIANCES

To understand these last two characteristics, it is necessary to take a strategic view of the many alliances GM and IBM created in the 1980s. Examining the risks, rationales, and structures of individual alliances is not enough. Such an approach results in scrupulous analysis of trees but little understanding of forests. It fails to answer a crucial question: how do all of a company's alliances relate to each other and how do they support and renew a firm's core capabilities? An answer requires an analysis of a company's strategy, its other alliances, changes in its core operations, and trends in its industry.

Viewed cumulatively rather than one at a time, the knowledge links created by GM and IBM in the 1980s were genuinely strategic. They were not simply product links, aimed at filling gaps in a product line or helping to cover fixed costs. Nor were they simply efforts to add a handful of new capabilities to the repertories of these two giants. Instead, IBM used a myriad of knowledge links as part of a larger effort to transform its traditional core capability of making and selling mainframe computers. GM began to use knowledge links with its suppliers, its workers and their union, and its dealers, as part of a bold, perilous effort to dramatically alter its capabilities for designing and manufacturing cars. IBM, in short, was trying to transform its products; GM, its operations.

The strategies of both firms were also preemptive: they aimed to change the terms of competition in their industries and tilt the playing field in their favor.[4] The 1990s will indicate whether GM and IBM succeed in their daring efforts; meanwhile, Niccolo Machiavelli's observation is pertinent to both firms: "There is nothing more difficult to plan, more doubtful of success, nor more dangerous to manage than the creation of a new order of things."[5]

IBM's Knowledge Links

Since the mid-1950s, IBM's core capability has been financing, designing, manufacturing, and selling mainframe computers. For most of this time, mainframes dominated the computer industry, and IBM dominated the mainframe business. As a result, it became one of the most profitable companies in the history of commerce. By the 1980s, however, the computer industry began to shift course dramatically and IBM's environment became less stable and more hostile.

Above all, IBM had to respond to the radical changes in the computer industry, which were driven by trends toward ever-cheaper computer power and toward larger, better-integrated networks. Kojii Kobayashi, the chairman of NEC, a major Japanese computer firm, described these developments by distinguishing between "point" and "space." Point represents the mainframe-dominated era in which all computerized data flowed to and from a single centralized machine. Space represents a future era in which networks of powerful local machines distribute data-processing capability throughout a company, a country, or the world. The shift from point to space gives a radically different answer to the question "What is a computer?" The old answer was: a solitary central-processing unit. The new answer: a computer is a network.

These developments gave rise to a surge of new entrants in the computer industry. They aggressively attacked the developing areas of the industry as well as its traditional market segments, including IBM's inner sanctum, the mainframe business. Moreover, entrants were not the only aggressors. Established computer companies, long accustomed to following in IBM's wake, were reinvigorated and emboldened by the prospect of competing against the giant on a new playing field with a new set of rules. Hundreds of companies were developing new capabilities that IBM might or would need to serve its customers. These capabilities took four basic forms: designing high-powered, customized computers for special tasks; using intimate knowledge of a customer's particular needs to write software for the customer; bringing state-of-the-art technology to market quickly in a rapidly changing and intensely competitive business; and using familiarity with customer requirements to design customized computer networks.

The transition from point to space reinforced old threats to IBM and created new ones. Computer buyers wanted to build networks using compatible hardware and software from a variety of suppliers. In computer jargon, they preferred open architecture to the proprietary systems of a single supplier. Almost every major computer company was offering customers an open architecture based on Unix, the operating system software that Bell Laboratories had developed in the early 1970s.[6] By 1987, AT&T had licensed Unix to 225 computer firms, including the two largest Japanese computer makers, Hitachi and Fujitsu, which both sold mainframes that ran Unix. For small specialized computer manufacturers trying to compete in niches against IBM or DEC, Unix offered a way to provide products that were compatible with and connected to a wide range of different computer systems. Some industry estimates suggested that nearly 25% of all computers in the world, as measured by dollar value, would use Unix by the end of 1991.[7]

In essence, Unix was accelerating the trend toward building ever more powerful minicomputers, workstations, and microcomputers and toward linking these machines in a vast communications network. It threatened to create an alternative computer standard to IBM's proprietary operating systems. A specter haunting IBM was the prospect of a loose, worldwide alliance of Unix-based manufacturers, including IBM's most daunting Japanese competitors as well as the growing number of Unix customers.

In response to this threat and to the growth of new capabilities throughout the industry, IBM created scores of knowledge links. Through them it hoped to secure access to and build new skills and, ultimately, to transform its basic capabilities. IBM fought the battle to survive and prosper on two principal fronts: in the United States, its largest market, and in Japan, where it could counterattack its Japanese adversaries in their home market.

In telecommunications, for example, IBM Japan created a series of collaborative endeavors with NTT, the Japanese telecommunications monopoly, which the government was gradually deregulating in the 1980s. The two companies worked together to develop hardware, software, and organizational capabilities in large-scale computer networks. IBM Japan also formed alliances with Mitsubishi, Japan's largest trading company, to create a joint satellite communications service in Japan and to design and sell equipment for information network services. As a trading company, Mitsubishi wanted to combine IBM's technological know-how with its own expertise in managing a global network of trading operations and customer relationships.[8]

Starting in the mid-1970s, IBM USA formed a series of alliances in the telecommunications business. One of its partners was MCI Communications. MCI was AT&T's major U.S. competitor in long-distance telephone services, and its market share was expected to climb from 10% in 1987 to nearly 14% by 1991. Through the deal, MCI gained credibility, customers, and access to a communications network that IBM was developing, while IBM strengthened its position in telecommunications by becoming a major shareholder in the industry's most important independent company. IBM and MCI engineers and managers collaborated on large communications projects for the government and for firms creating private networks. In the late 1980s, MCI decided to buy back IBM's 16% stake, but industry analysts expected the two companies to continue working closely together because of their complementary skills in computer equipment and communications lines.[9]

In the 1980s, IBM also formed an alliance with Rolm, one of the world's leading manufacturers of private branch exchanges (PBXs), which are, in effect, computers that switch telephone calls and data. IBM hoped that Rolm would provide it with capabilities to route data and voice communications within an information network. Rolm, on the other hand, hoped to benefit from the cash the IBM deal provided, from IBM's corporate relationships, and from IBM's capabilities and overseas marketing. The IBM-Rolm alliance was ultimately unsuccessful; IBM soon bought all of Rolm's shares and made it a subsidiary, and later IBM placed Rolm's operations in an alliance with Siemens. Despite the turbulence and frustrations, the alliances with Rolm and, later, with Siemens were a part of IBM's worldwide effort to build up its capabilities in telecommunications.

To develop applications software and other capabilities, IBM created scores of cooperative alliances. In Japan, it formed Nissan Systems Development with Nissan Motor to create applications software for basic research, product development, and manufacturing, particularly in automotive electronics. The Mitsubishi Bank and IBM Japan embarked on a joint venture to develop and sell software for Japanese banks. With Nippon Kokan, the second largest Japanese steel maker, IBM jointly developed an artificial intelligence system for planning steelmaking schedules. IBM Japan also worked with many of its newly created dealerships, such as liquor wholesalers and heating oil distributors, to develop specialized software that could be sold to them and to other companies in their businesses.[10]

In the United States, in the late 1980s, IBM USA created more than a dozen alliances—usually through minority equity investments—with companies that had expert capabilities in particular areas of software design. These included firms specializing in molecular simulation, image processing, insurance company transactions, management of large commercial projects, and software used to design software. Other new partners, such as a producer of signal converters for fiber optics communications, made hardware that would help IBM build customized networks. IBM's alliances also included a joint venture with Stephen Chen, one of the world's leading supercomputer designers; the creation and partial financing of Sematech, a consortium of U.S. semiconductor manufacturers; and an R&D partnership with Motorola to improve semiconductor manufacturing. Through these partnerships, IBM secured access to capabilities developed by firms that competed, in effect, in niches within niches. The firms relied upon specialized areas of expertise that IBM lacked and did not intend to develop on its own, but that it needed to provide to some of its customers. Through the Sematech, Motorola, and supercomputer alliances, it aimed to strengthen its partners and work with them to create new capabilities.

Through this constellation of knowledge links, IBM was slowly transforming itself from a supplier of mainframe hardware into an international computer and telecommunications firm that could provide global companies, as well as smaller firms, with companywide networks for transmitting and processing voice, data, and images.[11] In essence, IBM was changing itself to adapt to and capitalize on the transition from point to space. Its scores of knowledge links were part of its effort to become efficiently global and, simultaneously, intensively local and responsive. IBM could offer a company with worldwide operations, such as

Nomura Securities or Ford Motor, customized hardware and software that linked all their desks, offices, machines, and factories around the world. IBM's national subsidiaries, like IBM Japan, could also rely upon their partners to offer the local offices of Nomura or Ford customized applications software and computer networks.

GM's Knowledge Links

Viewed one at a time, many of GM's alliances, like GMF Robotics, served to extend particular capabilities. Cumulatively, however, they also contributed to most dramatic strategic changes at GM in the past half-century. Like IBM, GM has used a multitude of new alliances as part of a strategy of transformation. The alliances have given GM access to capabilities and pools of expertise that it needs, but that it chose not to invent or reverse engineer or develop on its own. GM's vast array of new alliances can appear confusing at first glance. Fortunately, a single effort—the Saturn project—can introduce GM's new boundary arrangements and can provide a helicopter view of GM's effort to transform itself. Saturn and Saturn-like changes throughout GM also represent GM's bid to recapture leadership in the world automobile industry and to hold it well into the twenty-first century. In particular, GM threw down the gauntlet to Toyota, challenging it to venture forth from its redoubt in Toyota City and confront GM in North America, in a battle to be fought with capital and advanced technology.

The basic facts about the Saturn subsidiary, GM's sixth car division, are straightforward. In 1983, GM announced that it would spend $3.5 billion to create a compact car called Saturn, the first new GM nameplate since the introduction of Chevrolet in 1918. The Saturn plant, a new facility to be located in Spring Hill, Tennessee, would employ 6,000 workers and produce 500,000 cars a year, beginning in 1989. Because it would manufacture all the major car parts, the plant would include extensive foundry, machining, engine, and transmission assembly facilities, as well as metal stamping and final assembly operations. Parts and components imported from Japan would account for less than 1% of the cost of the Saturn, a dramatic shift from GM's reliance on car and parts suppliers in its portfolio of Asian alliances. In 1986, GM scaled down plans for Saturn because of capital constraints, halving its budget to about $1.7 billion. Its initial capacity would be 240,000 cars per year, and the first cars would be launched in the fall of 1990. In the early 1990s, GM would start a second construction phase to double Saturn's capacity.

What this brief overview does not make clear is that the Saturn project was hardly an ordinary car operation.[12] It was designed on a "clean sheet of paper" basis, so that its personnel could design, engineer, manufacture, distribute, and sell cars in pathbreaking ways. GM chairman Roger Smith announced:

> GM believes that what it is doing is potentially significant to anyone who operates a plant in any industry, anywhere in the United States, because the

leading-edge technologies that Saturn represents could affect every one of them. And the improvements that flow naturally from Saturn could ultimately dwarf past accomplishments and establish U.S. industry, once again, as the leader in a new age of almost cosmic industrial achievement.[13]

Martin Weitzman, a labor relations expert and economics professor at MIT, said that "if Saturn succeeds, you can legitimately call it revolutionary."[14] *Business Week* described Saturn as a "bid to do nothing short of revolutionizing automobile manufacturing."[15] Saturn would draw on technology and skills from within GM, from EDS and Hughes Aircraft (GM's major high-tech acquisitions of the 1980s), from the many partnerships already described in this chapter, and from a new set of knowledge links with the UAW, with suppliers, and with dealers.

The alliances with the last three groups were a vital part of the transformation GM sought to achieve. For the UAW, Saturn represented a new era of collaboration. The project marked the first time in GM history that the UAW had participated in GM corporate planning. In the words of president Owen Beiber, the union would be a "full partner" in all of Saturn's decision making, and "no decision could be reached without its approval."[16] Saturn would be run by a strategic action council, consisting of the project's president and staff and the top UAW advisers. A "manufacturing action council," also including UAW representatives, would oversee the day-to-day operations, and work units—teams of 6 to 15 workers led by a UAW "councilor"—would perform manufacturing and assembly tasks.

Saturn sought to go beyond even NUMMI in encouraging participatory labor relations. GM had many motives for pursuing this new relationship, but a crucial one involved knowledge and capabilities. Toyota's approach to labor relations succeeds, in part, because it motivates workers to develop thousands of ideas about ways of improving automobile manufacturing and design. It thus makes practical use of the knowledge and experience of the workers who make the cars and their components. Toyota's approach also provides workers with incentives and opportunities to communicate what they know to the rest of the organization.

Moreover, Toyota-style manufacturing builds embedded knowledge at the individual and team levels. Its workers are cross-trained in a variety of skills. Hence, they can detect flaws in each other's work, suggest ways they can work together more effectively, and gradually develop higher levels of skill through experience and training. (At one GM plant, 30 cross-trained workers reduced warranty costs on suspension systems by 400% in a mere two years.) Finally, cross-training helped workers handle the increasingly complex, often computerized equipment on the factory floor. Saturn executives wanted every member of the organization to contribute steadily and vigorously to the creation and dissemination of knowledge. Saturn would succeed if the new partnership between GM, the UAW, and its workers could create a powerful information-sharing team. This approach departed radically from traditional, arm's-length, adversarial management-union relationships in the auto industry, and it sought to halt the decades-long trend toward deskilling automobile manufacturing and "dumbing down" the tasks it required of workers.

For similar reasons, at Saturn and at many other GM facilities, GM was seeking to create new collaborative relationships with its suppliers. In the past, GM had handled most of its suppliers by—in the words of one of its purchasing executives—"handing them our list of requirements and asking for a sealed bid." In effect, GM had practiced classical, arm's-length, market contracting. Many supplier relationships had been renewed on a year-to-year basis, and GM had often switched suppliers to secure lower prices. At Saturn, in contrast, supplier relations would be far more intimate and collaborative. One reason was the just-in-time system that Saturn was implementing. JIT requires deliveries on an hourly rather than a weekly or monthly basis and hence calls for close communication and coordination with suppliers. GM's managers said that Saturn would establish long-term relationships with suppliers that would meet its time and quality demands, rather than shop around each year for the lowest-cost supplier. Moreover, suppliers could achieve "preferred supplier" status. That meant GM would work with them on product development, soliciting ideas and assisting them with designs and component production. Like GM's relationship with the UAW, this effort enlisted suppliers in the creation and dissemination of new knowledge. Through close collaboration, GM and its suppliers would work to develop proprietary technology that would give GM distinctive advantages and to find ways to enable GM to use the technology quickly and efficiently. GM needed these advances badly, in part to recover from the cost-cutting and parts standardization efforts that had led to look-alike cars some analysts nicknamed "Oldsbuicadillacs."

GM developed its capabilities in data processing through a wide network of knowledge links with its computer and computer-related suppliers. Together, they worked to create what GM called its Manufacturing Automation Protocol (MAP). In the past, GM's computer suppliers had provided proprietary systems and hardware that could not communicate with each other or could do so only through complex, expensive interface devices. MAP asked the vendors to integrate their islands of computing and to help GM create a common communication network based on a nonproprietary language—the equivalent of asking hundreds of locomotive manufacturers to alter their products so they could all run on the same gauge track. To develop MAP, GM engaged in ongoing technical discussions with committees representing scores of hardware and software suppliers, ranging from giants like IBM and DEC to small hardware and software shops. These discussions are expected to last well into the 1990s, as the committees develop a succession of communication standards, each moving a step closer to full compatibility.

GM also made minority equity investments in small, high-tech companies—such as Automatix, View Engineering, Diffracto, and Robotic Vision Systems—that provided opportunities for its engineers to work with and learn from their counterparts about advanced automation technology and also gave GM and its partners the opportunity to collaborate in designing products for the auto industry. For example, in 1988, GM and Teknowledge announced that they had developed an expert system—an artificial intelligence software program that simulates the judgments of experts in a particular field—that would troubleshoot various types of machine tools, metal-cutting systems, and assembly machines. It could detect problems stemming from conditions such as bearing wear, unbalanced parts, and misalignment. At MIT's Media Lab, a multidisciplinary research center studying communications and computer technology, GM joined with the U.S. Defense Department on projects studying holography and human-machine interfaces.[17]

Finally, Saturn's planners wanted its distribution system to break down the arm's-length, highly contractual, often adversarial relations between GM and its dealers. Hence, Saturn would have its own franchise system and dealer organization. Most important, however, the franchise agreements stated specifically that the dealers were to be "partners" in Saturn's operations. They would be involved in decisions not only about dealerships but also about product planning. As with suppliers and workers, GM sought to shift to a new relationship in which it could learn from and work more closely with its dealerships.

CONCLUSION

This overview of the strategies of GM and IBM shows how they have used knowledge links to meet the challenges of embedded knowledge. At the simplest level, these alliances served as organizational devices to help them avoid the difficulties of trying to gain access to or create embedded knowledge through the traditional methods of market relationships, acquisitions, or going-it-alone. But knowledge links can make broader contributions. They can help a company extend its expertise in one or more directions. And, if a company is willing to act as boldly as GM and IBM have, they can contribute to a strategy through which it may be able to transform its core capabilities and perhaps even change the terms of competition in its industry.

How likely IBM and GM are to succeed in this transformation is far from certain. IBM's fortunes will depend on its success at reducing costs and increasing its speed to market, on the strength of whatever Unix coalition emerges, on the progress of IBM's Japanese competitors, and on government regulation of telecommunications in many countries around the world. But IBM has built on a solid foundation: the communications networks that it has already created for some of the largest companies in the world; its dominant, highly profitable mainframe business; the prospect that many smaller companies, and even some government agencies, will accept its dominance in global networks; and its efforts through a vast range of strategic alliances to learn skills and capabilities that it did not have and make them available to customers throughout the world.

GM faced other difficulties. It began creating a large constellation of knowledge links at the same time as it was trying to transform its internal operations. The company spent much of the 1980s implementing and refining the most massive reorganization in 50 years. During the decade, GM also acquired Hughes Aircraft, the world's leading defense electronics firm, and Electronic Data Services, the world's leading systems integration firm, in order to secure technology and skills that it hoped would radically change its approach to auto making. GM paid a steep price for these simultaneous changes. Costs rose at a time when the intensively competitive U.S. market was limiting price increases. As a result, in 1988 and 1989, GM earned negligible profits on its North American auto operations. Worse, its GM-10 cars—a new series of more stylish, higher-quality, mid-sized cars—reached market late, well after Ford's Taurus and Sable had made deep inroads in GM's market position.

The difficulties encountered by IBM and GM in the late 1980s could easily lead to skepticism about the value of knowledge links. This reaction, however, would be wrong. Many of the most powerful and competitive Japanese companies, such as Toyota and Matsushita, rely heavily upon knowledge links with suppliers and labor unions. During its renaissance in the 1980s, Ford Motor relied on alliances in Japan and Korea, on much closer and more cooperative ties with suppliers, and on a new partnership with workers and the UAW. Michael Porter's recent study of countries with internationally competitive industries concluded that a nation's successful firms are often linked together in "clusters." Within these, an assortment of mechanisms—various forms of knowledge links—promote the flow of knowledge among a wide range of organizations.[18]

In the cases of GM and IBM, efforts to look more closely at individual alliances and to trace their effects are riddled with difficulty. Many GM and IBM alliances are quite recent, so final judgments must wait several years. Moreover, both companies are in the midst of what may prove to be historic transformations—or perhaps declines—and they are changing in response to many factors, not just to alliances. Consider the cases in which productivity, absenteeism, and quality measures indicate than GM has created a successful, collaborative relationship with the UAW—at Saturn, for example, or at the Chevrolet plant that makes Corsicas and Berrettas. How much credit goes to what GM learned from its alliance with Toyota, how much to internal efforts beginning with the Quality of Work Life program in the early 1970s, and how much to the shift toward more cooperative industrial relations underway in many American companies? To the extent that GM has failed to change its labor relations quickly enough, how much of its tardiness comes from not knowing how managers can help their organization learn new capabilities from an alliance, and how much from the traditional adversarial relationship between GM and its workers? Even ostensibly precise quantitative measures fail to tell much of a story. For example, GM's sales of cars made with its Asian allies have fallen short of initial targets. Why? Because of the alliances themselves, the wrong choice of partners, or the mid-1950s market shift toward larger cars? Or was it because Pontiac dealers earned higher margins for selling large cars like Bonnevilles and Grand Prix's rather than the subcompact LeMans's made by the Daewoo alliance?

Moreover, the question of comparison makes assessments of alliances even more difficult. Alliances are often criticized as unstable because many of them last only several years. But compared to what? Are partnerships less stable, in general, than organizational arrangements inside firms? In the 1980s, General Electric created roughly 100 strategic alliances; some prospered, others failed, and many needed redesign during their lives. But in the same period, General Electric reorganized itself dramatically, reduced total employment by 100,000, and bought and sold scores of businesses. GM and IBM both overhauled their internal operations and organization in the 1980s, and then made a multitude of corrections and refinements. During this period of organizational earthquakes and aftershocks inside GE, GM, and IBM, were the core operations of the companies less turbulent than their alliances?

Even if some of the alliances created by U.S. companies in recent years have proved difficult to manage, it does not follow that companies should avoid them. Historical comparison is also important. Early in this century, American firms spent decades adopting, refining, and learning to manage the multidivisional form of organization that Du Pont, Sears, GM, and a few other companies had invented. In contrast, the U.S. experiment with alliances has been brief. From the perspective of a twenty-first century historian, product and knowledge links may represent only the initial phases of a decades-long effort to find new and more flexible forms of organization suited to knowledge-driven, global markets.

While it is difficult to foresee and assess the ultimate effects of these changes, one conclusion is quite firm: the pace and magnitude of the changes in GM's and IBM's boundaries have been astonishing. Ultimately, the success of GM and IBM will depend on many factors, and not simply on the contributions that knowledge links can make. How much these alliances contribute to the two companies' efforts to secure embedded knowledge, extend their capabilities, and transform themselves will depend on how well these alliances are managed and how quickly these longtime citadels can learn from close relationships with outside organizations.

REFERENCES

1. Paul B. Carroll, "IBM Joins With Siemens AG," *The Wall Street Journal,* January 25, 1990, p. B4.

2. Michael Polanyi, *Personal Knowledge: Towards a Post-Critical Philosophy* (Chicago: University of Chicago Press, 1948), p. 53.

3. This description of Fanuc and GMF Robotics is based upon an interview with Eric Mittelstadt, president and CEO of GMF Robotics, November 1987; Fanuc Annual Reports, 1983–1987; Kuni Sadamoto, *Robots in the Japanese Economy* (Tokyo: Survey Japan, 1981); Centre for Business Research, *The World Market for Industrial Robots* (Manchester, England: Centre for Business Research, 1986); Shinichi Kamata, "GM-Fanuc Joint Venture Will Build Robot Factory in Michigan," *Japan Economic Journal,* May 3, 1983, p. 10; "Next-Century Car Builder," *American Metal Market/Metalworking News,* February 3, 1986, pp. s8–s10; and Gene Bylinsky, "Japan's Robot King Wins Again," *Fortune,* May 25, 1987, pp. 53–58.

4. Ideally, a preemptive strategy secures several important advantages and not just one. The move is difficult for competitors to copy; it exploits rivals' weaknesses; it builds upon the firm's strengths; and the preempting firm can reverse its move, if necessary.

Through its relationships, GM aimed to seize advantages across the full range of critical activities in the auto industry: supplier relations, product design, basic research, manufacturing systems, customer relations, and distribution in service. An analytic overview of preemptive strategies is Ian C. MacMillan, "Preemptive Strategies," *The Journal of Business Strategy* (Fall 1985), pp. 16–26.

5. Niccolo Machiavelli, *The Prince,* translated by George Bull (London: Penguin Books, 1981), p. 51.

6. An operating system is a collection of software that assists and in part controls a computer's basic operations. It coordinates the reading and writing of data between the internal memory and such peripheral devices as disk drives, keyboards, and printers; it also prepares the computer to execute applications programs.

7. This overview of AT&T and its computer efforts is based on Charles P. Lecht, "The Waves of Change," *Computer World,* May 30, 1977, pp. 11–13; David A. Loehing, "Ma Bell vs. IBM?," *Barron's,* February 9, 1976, pp. 3, 14, 16, 22; Michael A. Verespej, "Clash of the Titans," *Industry Week,* May 27, 1985, pp. 64–68; Richard Brandt and John W. Verity, "Unix: The Soul of a Lot of New Machines," *BusinessWeek,* March 14, 1988, pp. 94–96; Brenton R. Schlender, "AT&T, Sun, Looking to Open Windows of Opportunity," *The Wall Street Journal,* April 11, 1988, p. 6; and Jonathan B. Levin, "Will Sun Melt the Software Barrier?," *BusinessWeek,* April 18, 1988, p. 72.

8. This account of IBM Japan's efforts in telecommunications is based on interviews with IBM Japan executives and on "NTT Signs Pacts with IBM," *Electronic News,* March 4, 1985, p. 40; "Mitsubishi's New Communication Adviser Lays Plans for Data Services," *Data Communications,* March 1984, pp. 115–116; and Carla Rapoport, "NTT, IBM Japan Agree Software Systems Venture," *The Financial Times,* September 26, 1985, p. 4.

9. Howard Anderson, "The IBM-MCI Merger: An Evaluation," *Telecommunication Products and Technology* (August 1985), pp. 21–25; and Frances Seghers, "Now If MCI Can Just Keep the Party Going," *BusinessWeek,* May 16, 1988, p. 39.

10. This overview of IBM's efforts in software and systems integration is based on interviews with IBM executives; "Computer Industry Trend: System Integration," *Nikkei Computer,* April 1, 1988, pp. 42–58; Edith Myers, "Risk and Responsibility," *Computer World,* November 18, 1987, pp. 43–45; Paul Gaskell, "Alien Connection," *Systems International* (September 1987), pp. 35–37; "IBM, Mitsubishi Bank in Software Effort," *Electronic News,* October 19, 1987, pp. 12, 20; Peter Freeman, "Software Development Systems," *Computers and People* (September–October 1987), pp. 11–27; and "Nissan and IBM Japan Agree to Jointly Set Up New Company," press release, IBM Japan, January 14, 1987.

11. For an extended and critical assessment of IBM's long-term prospects in telecommunications, see Richard T. DeLamarter, *Big Blue: IBM's Use and Abuse of Power* (New York: Dodd Mead, 1986), Chapter 5.

12. The overview of Saturn's technology and systems is based on an interview with Richard LeFauve, President, Saturn Corporation, October 5, 1988; personal communications with GM managers John Barry DuVall and William McPherson; "Till the Magic Goes," *Manufacturing Systems* (September 1986), pp. 32–36; Bryan H. Berry, "It's Now or Never for World-Class Auto Making at GM," *Iron Age,* November 7, 1986, pp. 34A1–35; Dale D. Buss and Melinda G. Guiles, "GM Slows Big Drive for Saturn

to Produce Small Car in Five Years," *The Wall Street Journal,* October 30, 1986, p. 1; and "Saturn: It's on Target for '90 Introduction," *Automotive News,* April 25, 1988, pp. 1, 64.

13. Roger B. Smith, "A New Age of Almost Cosmic Industrial Achievement," *The Journal of Business Strategy* (March 1984), p. 80.

14. Anne B. Fisher, "Behind the Hype at GM's Saturn," *Fortune,* November 11, 1985, p. 44.

15. David Whiteside, "How GM's Saturn Could Run Rings Around Old-Style Car Makers," *BusinessWeek,* January 28, 1985, p. 126.

16. "Developments in Industrial Relations," *Monthly Labor Review* (October 1985), p. 49.

17. Stewart Brand, *The Media Lab* (New York: Viking, 1987), pp. 1–16.

18. See Michael E. Porter, *The Competitive Advantage of Nations* (New York: Free Press, 1990), pp. 152–165.

9

Strategic Alliances, Organizational Learning, and Competitive Advantage: The HRM Agenda

Vladimir Pucik

STRATEGIC ALLIANCES AND COMPETITIVE COLLABORATION

Partnerships and alliances between two or more multinational firms are becoming increasingly common. Recent examples include AT&T's cooperation with Olivetti and IBM's links with Matsushita in office automation equipment; a tripartite venture of Honeywell, Bull, and NEC in computer mainframes; Philips and AT&T's alliance in telecommunications; Toyota and General Motors' joint manufacturing at NUMMI; or General Electric and Fanuc's worldwide collaborative network in robotics. New strategic alliances are not limited to the manufacturing sector, they are increasingly frequent in the financial sector (e.g., the joint venture of Credit Suisse and First Boston Corporation or the tie-up of Nippon Life and Shearson Lehman) and other service industries as well.

Some of the new alliances are clearly short-term in nature (e.g., General Motors and Toyota); others aim for a long-term strategic synergy between the partners (e.g., AT&T and Olivetti). While international alliances are intrinsically difficult to manage (Killing, 1983), many experts argue that, as business risks soar and competition grows more severe, firms are expected to rely on such alliances with increasing frequency (Harrigan, 1985; Perlmutter and Heenan, 1986). The rationale and the scope of international alliances are becoming increasingly complex (Contractor and Lorange, 1988; Root, 1988).

In the past, alliances were seen primarily as a means to reduce capital investment and lower the risks associated with entry into new markets. Ties between firms were also formed in order to secure fast and reliable access to previously

"Strategic Alliances, Organizational Learning, and Competitive Advantage: The HRM Agenda," Vladimir Pucik, *Human Resource Management,* Vol. 27, No. 1: pp. 77–93. Copyright © 1988 by John Wiley & Sons, Inc. Reprinted by permission of John Wiley & Sons, Inc.

closed markets, or to respond to a government's preference (formal or informal) for local participation in the business (Leontiades, 1985). Today, the rationale behind the formation of new alliances in most cases is related to the increasing speed of technological change and the rapidly growing competitiveness in global markets. Partners join in order to diversify risks inherent in developing new technologies or to take advantage of the complementarity of each partner's developmental skills (Hergert and Morris, 1988). The new partnerships can also provide essential economies of scale and market power to withstand a dominant competitor whom neither partner can challenge individually (e.g., international alliances in the computer industry targeted at IBM).

Strategic alliances can take many forms: technical exchange and cross-licensing, co-production and OEM agreements, sale and distribution ties, joint product development programs, or creation of joint venture firms with equity distributed among the partners. Such a functional classification of alliances, however, does not say much about their competitive context. To understand the strategic logic of the new partnerships and the implications for human resource management, it is essential to consider the changing patterns of global competition. In contrast to traditional single-market joint ventures between large multinational firms and much smaller local firms, the new alliances are often formed by partners of comparable strength whose activities are often global and who are or may become direct competitors (Contractor and Lorange, 1988).

The rapid increase in international partnerships among competitors does not necessarily imply the heralded dawn of a new cooperative era in the global economy (Ohmae, 1985; Perlmutter and Heenan, 1986). The change from competitive to collaborative strategies is often merely a tactical adjustment aimed at specific market conditions. Many of these new partnerships should be viewed as a hidden substitute of market competition, not its dissipation. The objective is similar: attaining the position of global market leadership through internalization of key value-added competencies. The potential competitive relationship between partners distinguishes strategic alliances that involve *competitive collaboration* from more traditional complementary ventures (Doz et al., 1986).

The strategic and managerial implications of the two types of alliances are fundamentally different. In a truly cooperative relationship the underlying assumption is the feasibility (and desirability) of long-term win/win outcomes. In the partnerships that involve competitive collaboration, the strategic intent of achieving dominance makes the long-term win/win outcome highly unlikely. This does not imply that all partnerships between multinational firms are always competitive in nature. However, many of them are, especially when seen in a long-term dynamic context. Partnerships that involve competitive collaboration are dynamic in nature. The relative endowment of resources, skills, and competencies and the sources of bargaining power can change over time. For one firm to be able to sustain its long-term competitive advantage, the organization and control of the partnership has to reflect its competitive context.

Another way to look at strategic partnerships is to examine the source of leverage exercised by the individual partners. In this sense, strategic alliances may be classified into those leveraging *resources* and those leveraging *competencies*.

The cross-licensing, technical agreements, joint development programs (pooling of resources), and co-production or co-distribution (resource economies of scale) are examples of alliances that focus primarily on resource leverage. The resources contributed to a partnership usually have a specific market value, be it land, equipment, labor, money, or patents. Both the contribution and withdrawal of resources are explicit and thus relatively simple to control.

In contrast, competencies are fundamentally information-based invisible assets (Itami, 1987) that cannot be readily purchased and their market value is difficult to ascertain. Examples are management and organizational skills, knowledge of the market, or technological capability. Invisible assets are embodied in people within the organization. These assets represent a tacit knowledge that is difficult to understand and that only can be appropriated over time, if at all (Teece, 1987). Accumulation of invisible assets is seen as the foundation for a sustainable competitive advantage (Itami, 1987).

Invisible assets are closely linked to information, its stock as well as its flow. To increase invisible assets is to increase the amount of information available in the firm as well as its capacity to handle the information. Invisible assets can be accumulated through an explicit action, such as training, or implicitly as a by-product of daily operations (Itami, 1987). Alliances that leverage competencies usually take the form of an OEM supply agreement or a joint venture aimed at a specific market. Superior competencies in different parts of a value chain are combined to achieve a distinct competitive advantage in the market, or at least to protect market position against a superior joint competitor.

Table 9-1 summarizes a classification of international partnerships that considers the competitive context and the source of leverage. While the issue of strategic control as related to the distribution of benefits from the alliances is important in all four quadrants of the strategic alliance matrix, it is especially critical in quadrants III and IV that represent conditions of competitive collaboration. Implicit in a competitive collaboration is the risk that benefits from the alliance may be accrued asymmetrically by the respective partners. The process of appropriation is influenced by the characteristics of organizational assets leveraged in the partnership.

Obviously, in most cases, strategic alliances involve the contribution and leverage of both visible and invisible assets. The type of contribution can be different for each partner. Nevertheless, the traditional management focus is concentrated

TABLE 9-1 Strategic Alliances, Strategic Context, and Source of Leverage

	Source of Leverage	
Strategic Context	Resources	Competencies
Complementarity	I.	II.
Competition	III.	IV.

on the control of visible assets. In complementary partnerships, lack of attention to the accumulation of invisible assets may erode the competitive advantage derived from the venture. However, in the context of competitive collaboration, where competencies provide the critical leverage (quadrant IV), lack of attention to invisible assets may result in a loss of control over the direction of the alliance. It is for this reason that management processes that support accumulation and control of invisible assets are of such critical importance.

The distribution of benefits related to visible assets, such as new products or profits, is relatively easy to monitor. Protection against asymmetry can be instituted through administrative protocols and rules regarding the implementation of the partnership agreement. However, the asymmetric appropriation of invisible benefits—such as the acquisition of product or market know-how for use outside of the partnership framework, or even to support a competitive strategy targeted at the partner—cannot be easily protected. The asymmetry results from the internal dynamics of the strategic alliance. Benefits are appropriated asymmetrically due to differences in the *organizational learning capacity* of the partners. The shifts in relative power in a competitive partnership are related to the speed at which the partners can learn from each other. Not providing a firm strategy for the control of invisible assets in the partnership, and delegating responsibility for them to operating managers concerned with short-term results, is a sure formula for failure.

A good illustration of such a process is the reversal in the competitive relationship between Japanese and Western firms in many industries over the last several decades. The asymmetrical distribution of benefits from these alliances often was the fundamental cause of such a reversal. Japanese firms used access to technology through licensing or joint ventures to master new competencies, and then used the newly acquired knowledge to gain sole control of the market in Japan and even penetrate markets previously dominated by the Western partners with their own superior products. The list of firms (e.g., Allied/Bendix, General Electric, General Foods, International Harvester, Philips, Renault, USX, Westinghouse) that gave up more than they gained is long and is not limited to a single country or industry.

While other factors contributed to the high failure rate of Western joint ventures in Japan (Wright, 1979; Zimmerman, 1985)—such as policies of the Japanese government that at least until the mid-1970s made it difficult for Western partners to achieve bargaining power parity—much of the imbalance in the appropriation of benefits was caused by disparities in learning between Japanese and Western partners. Many Japanese firms have developed a systematic approach to organizational learning (Cole, 1985; Nonaka and Johansson, 1985). This approach involved more than an explicit rejection of the parochial "not-invented-here" syndrome. Japanese firms put in place managerial systems that encourage extensive horizontal and vertical information flow and support the transfer of know-how from the partnership to the rest of the organization. The policies guiding the management of human resources at all levels and functions constituted a vital part of such a learning infrastructure (Pucik, 1983).

The organizational capability to learn is the key to protect competitive advantage in competitive collaboration and to control the strategic direction of the cooperative venture. An organization has many tools to manage the process of learning (Hedberg, 1981), but in principle, the learning ability of an organization depends on its ability to accumulate invisible assets. As invisible assets are embodied in people, policies regarding human resources are critical to organizational learning. The objective of the HRM activities is to complement line management in providing a supporting climate and appropriate systems to guide the process of learning. Organizational learning results from a combination of hard and soft organizational practices anchored in specific HRM techniques.

HUMAN RESOURCE MANAGEMENT AND OBSTACLES TO ORGANIZATIONAL LEARNING

Organizational learning is not a random process. Preventing an asymmetry (or creating an asymmetry in one's favor) in organizational learning must be the key strategic priority for human resources executives in multinational firms engaged in strategic alliances. Removing the organizational obstacles to learning is closely linked to the strategic priorities of the Human Resource function and its involvement in the design and management of the strategic partnership. However, this strategic priority is often buried under the pressure of daily operational concerns. The key obstacles to organizational learning identified from research on Western joint ventures in Japan (Pucik, 1988) are listed in Table 9-2.

The obstacles to organizational learning reviewed in greater detail below are not limited to a specific organizational climate that can easily be changed. Rather, they result from a complex set of HR practices and policies that, while often rational in the short-term, may ultimately lead to a loss of control over the destiny of the partnership, if not to the loss of the entire business. Understanding the obstacles to learning is the first step in the process of restoring competitive balance.

Human Resource Planning

Strategic intent not communicated throughout the firm. Most alliances take place in a highly complex competitive environment. The desirability of cooperation may easily be perceived differently among various parts of the organization, depending on their level of involvement in the creation of the alliance and their responsibility in executing the strategy. Top management often emphasizes the cooperative nature of the new alliance, partly to set the right tone for the partnership, partly to break down any resistance from those opposed to the cooperative strategy. What is often not made clear are the boundaries of cooperation and the specific nature of the missing competencies that led to the alliance in the first place.

TABLE 9-2   Obstacles to Organizational Learning in International Strategic Alliances

HR Function	Key Obstacles
HR planning	• Strategic intent not communicated • Short-term and static planning horizon • Low priority of learning activities • Lack of involvement by the HR function
Staffing	• Insufficient lead-time for staffing decisions • Resource-poor staffing strategy • Low quality of staff assigned to the alliance • Staffing dependence on the partner
Training and development	• Lack of cross-cultural competence • Uni-directional training programs • Career structure not conducive to learning • Poor climate for transfer of learning
Appraisal and rewards	• Appraisal focused on short-term goals • No encouragement of learning • Limited incentives for transfer of know-how • Rewards not tied to global strategy
Organizational design and control	• Responsibility for learning not clear • Fragmentation of the learning process • Control over the HR function given away • No insight into partner's HR strategy

Short-term and static planning horizon. Planning of the alliance is often driven by short-term contingencies, such as an improvement of profitability by cutting production costs through an OEM arrangement, without considering long-term effects on the sustainability of the firm's competitive advantage. General Electric's recent withdrawal from the consumer electronics field was forced by a series of "correct" short-term decisions during the previous two decades that led to a transfer of critical product and process competencies from GE to its competitors. The logic behind many short-term decisions assumes that the existing balance of competencies in the alliance will not change with time.

Low priority given to learning activities. The traditional focus of business plans is on the utilization of and the return on tangible assets. The projected outcomes from the partnership are scrutinized in terms of returns on equity invested, savings from pooled research and development, cost reductions from outsourcing components and products, and/or increases in sales from added distribution channels. However, the accumulation of invisible assets, such as experience regarding the production process, intimate knowledge of the market or relationship with customers, is not evaluated, as traditional planning systems cannot assign a financial value to these outcomes. Activities that can't be evaluated in financial terms are generally not funded. Organizational learning is left with no support.

Lack of involvement by the Human Resource function. In the rush to launch the alliance, insufficient attention is given to a critical evaluation of the learning capacity of the organization and to the steps necessary to upgrade the learning skills and learning climate appropriate for the new venture. Often, the Human Resource function does not play any role in the negotiation process or becomes involved only at a very late stage. The compatibility of philosophies regarding the management of human resources between the partners and its implications for organizational learning are seldom a factor in the decision-making process.

Insufficient lead-time for staffing decisions. When the alliance involves a creation of a new organization, staffing decisions regarding the key representatives should be made well in advance of the conclusion of the agreement; all relevant future players can thus be involved in the negotiation process. Institutional memory breaks down when negotiators are replaced by implementators without continuity. Insufficient lead time also forces short-cuts in training for the managers to be assigned to the partnership. In general, everyone agrees with the idea of training, but many firms are reluctant to invest in the preparation of managers for the new venture until the outcome of the business negotiations is clear; yet after the deal is signed, there is no time to train. As a result, what is won laboriously at the front end through long, arduous bargaining is often lost through the inability to control implementation of the partnership agreement.

Resource-poor staffing strategy. As the motivation for the alliance is often driven by cost consideration, firms cut expenses by limiting the size of managerial staff assigned to the partnership. In particular, this can be observed in alliances that have the major location of their activities overseas, where the cost of expatriates seem prohibitive. Yet, while the expense of staffing a position in an overseas venture can be substantial, such economizing does not consider two substantial benefits derived from expatriate posts: improved control over the management process in the venture and ability to transfer skills from the venture into the home organization. Organizational learning often requires at least some slack resources. When an overextended management team just keeps on dousing fires, the last thing on a manager's mind is the transfer of know-how.

Low quality of staff assigned to manage the alliance. It is often the case that after the initial period of high visibility for the new alliance, management positions in the partnership become a dumping ground for sidetracked executives. The emphasis is on "making the deal," not on its implementation. The dispatched managers don't have the necessary learning skills;

they are expected to "watch the books" only. Even if they gain new knowledge, they may lack the credibility to effectively transfer the know-how to the parent firm, especially if this involves challenging existing "sacred cows." The partners in the alliance are generally well aware of the low skill and credibility level of these managers and do not hesitate to freeze them out of the important decisions.

Staffing dependence on the partner. When staffing is considered a cost rather than an investment, it is very tempting to go along with the offer by the partner to assume the responsibility for staffing the new venture. Naturally, there is always a great concern over the composition of the top management team. However, very little learning ever occurs in the board room: learning takes place in the laboratories, on the production floor, and in interactions with the customers. The partner who controls positions critical to the accumulation of invisible assets gains substantial leverage over the direction of the alliance. Short-term excursions will not do, long-term participation is essential. As GM learned at NUMMI, a videotape of new work practices is a far less efficient learning tool than hands-on experience.

Training and Development

Lack of cross-cultural competence. Many managers and staff involved in international partnerships do not have sufficient intercultural skills (language competence, familiarity with partner's culture, etc.). Expatriates are dispatched abroad with no or limited training at best, with the assumption that knowledge of the business should compensate for the lack of cultural understanding. While the partner's perfect fluency may not be essential, the ability to understand the basic flow of a business conversation and to interact informally with the customers and employees should be the minimum prerequisite for an international assignment. This is important for an expatriate's effectiveness, even in a wholly-owned foreign affiliate (Tung, 1984); the price to pay for the lack of cross-cultural skills in an alliance may be higher: both inability to learn and inability to control.

Uni-directional transfer of know-how. One of the most effective means of learning is through temporary personnel exchange between the partners. However, this exchange is often asymmetrical, especially when the partnership takes the form of a joint venture. While the flow of personnel from the Western joint ventures in Japan often includes staff temporarily seconded from the Japanese parent, the training assignments in the opposite direction are infrequent (Pucik, 1988). Even when transfer of personnel into the joint venture occurs on a regular basis, it is seldom for the purpose of skill acquisition. Rather, staff is transferred either to control or manage the joint venture or to serve as a conduit for transferring know-how into the venture. It is often felt that there is no need to learn (and thus expend resources) on knowledge already possessed in the joint venture. Yet, by gaining independent know-how, a firm can avoid becoming hostage to the uncertain future of the partnership.

Career structure not conducive to learning. Personnel exchange can have a positive impact on the amount of accumulated knowledge only if administered in a consistent and planned fashion over a period of time. Unless the firm posts the returnees from the partnership ventures into positions where the acquired know-how can be effectively used and disseminated, the invisible asset accumulation will not be possible. The amount of time spent learning and transferring know-how is the critical constraint. An effective transfer of know-how requires a long-term commitment of qualified personnel, which clashes with expectations of fast mobility among the most promising executives. While many managers (on a personal basis) may benefit even from a relatively short assignment abroad, a single short-term assignment—especially when it comes relatively late in an executive's career—will not do much for the accumulation of invisible assets in the rest of the organization.

Poor climate for transfer of learning. A large amount of critical invisible assets is embedded in the staff involved in the partnership. To what degree these assets are shared with the parent depends largely on the parent's receptivity to new ideas, and on the quality of the interaction between the cooperative venture and the parent firm. When learning from the outside, in particular from abroad, is seen as an admission of weakness, the receptivity will be poor (Westney, 1988). The ossification of the learning infrastructure reflects the low priority given to the accumulation of invisible assets in the execution of a company's strategy. Low receptivity to inputs from the partnership will naturally encourage a passive attitude towards the transfer of knowledge among the partnership staff. This tendency is further reinforced if the socialization activities in the partnership are controlled by the local parent, as is often the case in Western joint ventures in Japan.

Appraisal and Rewards

Appraisal focused on short-term goals. Organizational learning is fundamentally a long-term activity, stretching far beyond a typical one-year appraisal time-frame. Also, the costs associated with learning are immediate, while the benefits (most of them difficult to quantify under standard accounting procedures) are accrued over time. Support for organizational learning thus may have a negative impact on the short-term measurements used to evaluate a manager's performance. The expectation of short tenure in a given job is another critical constraint. The pressure to get immediate results forces managers to economize on expenditures with long-term payoffs, no matter how attractive such payoffs may be. The issue is not sacrificing profits for abstract learning, but forfeiting a long-term superior performance in order to inflate short-term results.

No encouragement of learning. With little or no rewards given for contributions to the accumulation of invisible assets, learning becomes a "hobby," not a prerequisite of the job. In many leading Japanese and Korean firms, the cross-fertilization of skills across functional areas is actively encouraged, and both foreign language ability (tested by the company) and familiarity with principal foreign markets are considered before promotion to an executive position. In contrast, the skill base of typical Western managers is rather narrow, as are their intercultural skills. Even in firms with decades of experience in the Far East, only a handful of managers speak any of the local languages and have a first-hand knowledge of local conditions. In a joint venture, asymmetry in the distribution of skills will result in an erosion of competitive advantage and the loss of leverage.

Limited incentives for transfer of know-how. The reward systems in many multinational firms encourage hoarding of critical information, not sharing it. Information is treated as a source of power, not as a resource. Smart managers assigned to an international joint venture, who otherwise may expect few opportunities for upward mobility, can make themselves indispensable by blocking the flow of information. Such a behavior is not only tolerated, but these "valuable experts" are often rewarded in terms of superior compensation and considerable operational autonomy. Any increase in information concerning the activities of the partnership outside of their own domain is seen by these managers as a threat to their power. In an alliance that involves competitive collaboration, the other parent and some of the company's own managers may share an interest in limiting the transfer of know-how.

Rewards not tied to global strategy. Performance of executives assigned to manage a partnership venture is often appraised solely on the basis of results in a limited business area or market. There is very little incentive for the "core" partnership staff to worry about the competitive conditions facing other businesses of the distant parent. These managers have nothing to gain from allocating scarce resources to organizational learning benefiting an organization in which they have no tangible interest. This tendency is especially pronounced if these managers are actually dispatched from the other "competing" parent. In such a case, their attitude towards transfer of competencies can easily turn from conservative to downright hostile.

Organizational Design and Control

Responsibility for learning not clear. Who gains and who loses from a strategic alliance often depends on the vantage point. A "win-win" partnership strategy on a corporate level often entails a "win/lose" scenario at the business unit or business function level. For example, a shift from captive manufacturing to an OEM partnership may contribute to immediate cost reduction and thus enhance the product's position in the market while the production competence is eroded. Under such conditions, incentives and responsibility for learning may become unfocused. When competencies are lost, operation managers blame faulty strategy while the corporate staff cites incompetent implementation.

Fragmentation of the learning process. In diversified, complex firms, the stakes in organizational learning may differ by business unit and function. Each subunit has only a partial view of the exchange of competencies involved in the partnership. The perceptions of the potential value of the relationship may therefore differ, as will the commitment to support competencies needed to defend the long-term competitive advantage. In firms with decentralized business units (e.g., SBUs), organization-wide learning activities have low priority in comparison to a business unit's immediate needs.

Control of the HR function is given away. The HR function is seen as a cost burden, not as a powerful tool of control over the strategic direction of the partnership. In particular, when the alliance involves a venture inside the new partner's territory, responsibility for the Human Resource function is often delegated to the partner. In fact, the very possibility of utilization of the partner's know-how concerning the local labor market conditions is often a factor leading to the creation of the alliance in the first place. However, what is gained in lowering the cost of entry may be lost over time, as control over human resource deployment enables the partner to control the patterns of organizational learning, thus the distribution of benefits from the partnership.

No insight into partners HR strategy. The learning strategies of the partner can be monitored through the control of personnel exchange between the joint operations and the parent. The objective is not to stop learning, but to gain understanding about the direction of the partner's learning strategies and its long-term impact on the balance of power in the collaborative relationship. However, when personnel control is abdicated in favor of the partner, the logic of the learning process is obscured. The boundary between the partner's organization and the partnership operation becomes fuzzy and impossible to control. Valuable competence may leak without notice and without reciprocity. A learning asymmetry is again likely to occur.

HRM AGENDA IN COMPETITIVE COLLABORATION

The challenge of competitive collaboration creates a new agenda and new priorities for the management of human resources. This challenge can't be avoided by staying away from strategic alliances. The economic forces in the environment will continue to push firms into more complex sets of global relationships. Those who learn from these relationships will survive; the others will perish. The organization's ability to learn (or the lack of it) will influence the shape of the global markets for many years to come.

Experience shows that the competitive balance in strategic alliances, and in joint ventures in particular, cannot be controlled through structural solutions. The successes and failures of the alliances are often embedded in the same organizational context (Killing, 1983). Neither can symmetry in the appropriation of benefits from a partnership be protected through legal clauses. The complexity of international commercial law and rapid technological change make legal protection impractical. In fact, the reliance on legal means to safeguard the company interests can be counterproductive as it encourages "we-are-safe" attitudes and thus decreases the stimuli to learn.

The accumulation of invisible assets, be it manufacturing competence, market know-how, or global coordination capability, should be explicitly recognized as a value-enhancing activity. It is dangerous to act as if the existence of a partnership permits lowering commitment to the maintenance and expansion of core competencies. Such a strategy assumes that the partner is unwilling or unable to learn and thus unable to alter the long-term bargaining power regarding the appropriation of benefits. In the context of competitive collaboration, such an assumption is unsupportable. It also does not make sense to set up barriers to learning. Artificial constraints imposed on information flow in the partnership may hinder its ability to sustain its competitive advantage and thus erode the competitive position of both parents. The only sustainable response is a pro-active policy encouraging organizational learning that, at minimum, matches, if not surpasses the learning ability of the partner. Everything else is an inferior solution.

A number of specific agenda points for the HR function in firms engaged in international strategic alliances can be drawn from the experience of firms that continuously incorporate organizational learning into their competitive strategy:

1. *Get involved early.* The human resource function should be involved in the formation of the strategic alliance from the early planning stages. In a dialogue with the appropriate line functions, HR staff should assume responsibility for the development of a thorough organizational learning strategy. It is essential to precisely identify the critical value-added learning activities in a given business, and the means to control them. The objective is to support and expand core competencies essential to sustain the long-term competitive advantage of the firm.

2. *Build learning into the partnership agreement.* In order to maintain a long-term symmetry in the distribution of benefits from the partnership, both parties have to learn simultaneously. The process of parallel learning can and should be made explicit. An attempt to prevent the partner from learning is most likely fruitless, as organizational learning is impossible to police. Instead, provisions should be made in the agreement to safeguard the reciprocity in the transfer of competencies (e.g., personnel exchange).

3. *Communicate strategic intent.* As a part of its responsibility for corporate communications, HR should cooperate with operational managers to assure that the strategic intent with respect to the partnership is adequately communicated to the employees. Training programs should be developed to prepare managers to deal effectively with the ambiguity and complexity of strategic alliances. The competitive context has to be made explicit: hushing it up does not fool anybody but your own employees.

4. *Maintain HR input into the partnership.* The control of the HR function in partnership operations, such as joint ventures, should not be bargained away, as it is within the boundaries of such an entity that much of the learning occurs. Once the partnership agreement is concluded, the HR function should continuously monitor the congruence between the learning strategy and the operational HR activities related to the launching and the implementation of the agreement. Periodic reviews of the learning process should be set up with the participation of top management.

5. *Staff to learn.* The accumulation of invisible assets should be the key principle guiding the staffing strategy. Staffing and development plans should be established to cover the existing blind spots. Such an approach may require a considerable investment in the development of core competencies within the parent firm through a carefully calibrated transfer policy. Some attrition must be considered inevitable. In joint ventures, this also means the development of a local staff that is fundamentally loyal to the joint venture entity and has no vested interest in blocking the transfer of critical information. While the immediate costs of the "staff to learn" program may be high, they are far smaller than the long-term negative consequences of lost competence.

6. *Set up learning-driven career plans.* From an individual perspective, effective learning and transfer of competencies span the entire career. While cross-cultural learning is most effective during the early career stages, functional learning and its effective application may require considerable business experience. In the context of international partnerships, this may imply a necessity for multiple assignments, which is seldom done at the present time. A greater use should be made of reciprocal trainee programs. The notion that all expatriates should be managers is obsolete.

7. *Use training to stimulate the learning process.* Three kinds of training activities can create a better climate for learning. First, in internal training, managers should be made aware of the subtleties involved in managing collaboration and competition at the same time. Second, open communication and trust within the partnership is essential for the smooth transfer of know-how. Team-building and cross-cultural communication training should be offered regularly at all management levels. Finally, any training program geared to the acquisition of a specific competence should be, in principle, reciprocal. This diminishes the incentives for opportunistic behavior.

8. *Responsibility for learning should be specified.* In order to create a climate receptive to learning, a specific responsibility for learning should be

written into business plans for managers transferred into the partnership operations as well as those in the receiving units. It should be made clear who is responsible that the information actually flows as intended, in necessary quality and speed, and what supporting mechanisms are needed to be put in place. Where appropriate, support for mutual learning should be made explicit in the partnership agreement.

9. *Reward learning activities.* Management behavior that encourages organizational learning, such as sharing and diffusion of critical information, should be explicitly recognized and rewarded. Long-term incentives (e.g., career opportunities) should be provided to managers actively seeking to acquire new skills. The framework of expatriate transfers into critical locations must be restructured to make them more attractive without incurring prohibitive compensation costs. Dead-end assignments are costly to the organization.

10. *Monitor the HR practices of your partner.* Throughout the duration of the relationship, attention should be given to the partner's HR activities. Beginning with an HR audit prior to the establishment of the partnership, much insight can be gained from the continuous monitoring of the partner's staffing and training. In joint ventures, the career records of staff transferred from the partner's organization should be carefully scrutinized, including their assignments after returning to the partner. It must be assumed that the partner is doing the same, as much of the necessary information is actually in the public domain.

In summary, the strategic agenda for the HRM function in firms involved in international alliances must be centered around the process of learning. In the context of competitive collaboration, the competitive advantage of a firm can be protected only through the organization's capability to accumulate invisible assets by a carefully planned and executed process of organizational learning. As this process is embedded in people, many of the necessary capabilities are closely linked to HRM strategies and practice. The transformation of the HR system to support the process of organizational learning is clearly the key strategic task facing the HR function in many multinational firms today.

REFERENCES

Cole, R. E. The macropolitics of organizational change: A comparative analysis of the spread of small-group activities. *Administrative Science Quarterly,* 1985, 30, 560–585.

Contractor, F., and Lorange, P. Why should firms cooperate? The strategy and economics basis for cooperative ventures, in F. Contractor and P. Lorange (Eds.), *Cooperative strategies in international business.* Lexington, MA: Lexington Books, 1988.

Doz, Y., Hamel G., and Prahalad, C. K. Strategic Partnerships: Success or surrender?, paper presented at the Conference on Cooperative Strategies in International Business, The Wharton School and Rutgers University, October 1986.

Harrigan, K. R. *Strategies for joint ventures.* Lexington, MA: Lexington Books, 1985.

Hedberg, B. How organizations learn and unlearn, in P. C. Nystrom and W. H. Starbuck (Eds.), *Handbook of organizational design.* New York: Oxford University Press, 1981.

Hergert, M., and Morris, D. Trends in international collaborative agreements, in F. Contractor and P. Lorange (Eds.), *Cooperative strategies in international business.* Lexington, MA: Lexington Books, 1988.

Itami, H. *Mobilizing invisible assets.* Cambridge, MA: Harvard University Press, 1987.

Killing, J. P. *Strategies for joint venture success.* New York: Praeger Publishers, 1983.

Leontiades, J. C. *Multinational corporate strategy: Planning for world markets.* Lexington, MA: Lexington Books, 1985.

Nonaka, I., and Johansson, J. K. Organizational learning in Japanese companies, in R. B. Lamb (Ed.), *Advances in strategic management.* Greenwich, CT: JAI Press, 1985, 3, 277–296.

Ohmae, K. *Triad power: The coming shape of global competition.* New York: Free Press, 1985.

Perlmutter, H. V., and Heenan, D. A. Cooperate to compete globally. *Harvard Business Review.* 1986, 64 (2), 136–152.

Pucik, V. Management practices in Japan and their impact on business strategy, in R. B. Lamb (Ed.), *Advances in strategic management.* Greenwich, CT: JAI Press, 1983, 1, 103–131.

Pucik, V. Joint ventures with the Japanese: Implications for human resource management, in F. Contractor and P. Lorange (Eds.), *Cooperative strategies in international business.* Lexington, MA: Lexington Books, 1988.

Root, F. Some taxonomies of international cooperative agreements, in F. Contractor and P. Lorange (Eds.), *Cooperative strategies in international business.* Lexington, MA: Lexington Books, 1988.

Teece, D. J. Profiting from technological innovation: Implications for integration, collaboration, licensing and public policy, in D. J. Teece (Ed.), *The competitive challenge: Strategies for industrial innovation and renewal.* Cambridge, MA: Ballinger Publishing Company, 1987.

Tung, R. *Key to Japan's economic strength: Human power.* Lexington, MA: Lexington Books, D.C. Heath, 1984.

Westney, D. E. Domestic and foreign learning curves in managing international cooperative strategies, in F. Contractor and P. Lorange (Eds.), *Cooperative strategies in international business.* Lexington, MA: Lexington Books, 1988.

Wright, R. W. Joint venture problems in Japan. *Columbia Journal of World Business.* 1979, 20 (1), 25–31.

Zimmerman, M. *How to do business with the Japanese.* New York: Random House, 1985.

10

The Numbers

Charles Handy

The numbers are the numbers of people, the numbers working, numbers dying, and numbers growing up. Demography is a boring word for a mesmerizing subject.

THE NEW MINORITY

Less than half of the work force in the industrial world will be in "proper" full-time jobs in organizations by the beginning of the twenty-first century. Those full timers or insiders will be the new minority, just when we had begun to think that proper jobs were the norm for everyone. The others will not all be unemployed, although in every country there will be some people who belong to this "reserve army" as Marx called it. More will be self-employed, more and more every year; many will be part timers or temporary workers, sometimes because that is the way they want it, sometimes because that is all that is available. And then there is, everywhere, another reserve army of women in waiting, those whom the OECD so accurately calls, "unpaid domestic workers," mothers whose talents and energies are not totally absorbed by their families. Add these disparate groups together and *already* they just about equal the numbers of those with the full-time proper jobs.

When less than half the available work force is in full-time employment, it will no longer make sense to think of a full-time job as the norm. Continuous change will have flipped into discontinuous change, and we shall begin to change our views of "work," of "the job," and of "a career."

The reason for the shift is the emergence of the shamrock organization. . . . Essentially, it is a form of organization based around a core of essential executives and workers supported by outside contractors and part-time help. This is not a new way of organizing things—builders large and small have operated this way for generations, as have newspapers with their printers and their stringers, or farmers with contract harvesting and holiday labor. What is new is the growth of this way of organizing in big businesses and in the institutions of the public sector. All organizations will soon be shamrock organizations.

They have proliferated because their way is cheaper. Organizations have realized that, while it may be convenient to have everyone around all the time, having all of your work force's time at your command is an extravagant way of marshalling the necessary human resources. It is cheaper to keep them outside the organization, employed by themselves or by specialist contractors, and to buy their services when you need them.

When labor is plentiful, when you can pick and choose between suppliers, the shamrock organization provides a sensible strategy. It is a sensible strategy when your work ebbs and flows as it tends to do in service industries. Unlike in manufacturing, where any surplus resources of people or equipment can always be turned to good advantage by producing things for stock for the weeks of peak demand, the *service* industries cannot, or at least should not, stockpile their customers. They must therefore flex their work force.

Both these factors currently exist. The labor supply, the potential work force, is growing in all the industrialized countries as the baby boomers of the 1960s, and their wives, join the work force during the 1990s—an extra million or so in Britain, for instance. At the same time the shift to the service sector continues inexorably everywhere. Between 1960 and 1985 the share of employees in the service sector in the USA rose from 56 to 69 percent and in Italy from 33 to 55 percent. It is unlikely to change back. The two factors work on each other; a growing service sector offers greater opportunities to women, which increases the potential work force, which in turn increases the potential for more flexible ways of organizing.

It has been happening slowly, so slowly that most people have not noticed the new dimensions. Before very long the full-time worker will be a minority of the working population. Our assumptions about how the world works, how taxes are collected, families supported, lives planned, and corporations organized will have to change radically. The Universal Declaration of Human Rights, which in 1947 guaranteed a choice of job to everyone, will be a clear anachronism.

THE NEW INTELLIGENTSIA

The second statistic is alarming in a different way. A study by McKinsey's Amsterdam office in 1986 estimated that 70 percent of all jobs in Europe in the year 2000 would require cerebral skills rather than manual skills. In the USA, the figure is expected to be 80 percent. That would be a complete reversal of the world of work some fifty years earlier. Discontinuity indeed!

It is impossible to be precise about such things. There is, to start with, no clearcut distinction between a cerebral job, requiring brain skills, and a manual job, needing muscles. Even simple manual jobs, like gardening, now require a degree of brains to understand the proper use of fertilizers and herbicides, to distinguish plant varieties, and to maintain machinery.

What is more controversial and even more alarming is McKinsey's estimate that one-half of these brain-skill jobs will require the equivalent of a higher education, or a professional qualification, to be done adequately. If that is even approximately true, it means that some 35 percent of an age group should today be entering higher education or its equivalent if the labor force is going to be adequately skilled by the year 2000. McKinsey's estimate may even be on the conservative side. If we look at the new jobs alone, the current expectation is that 60 percent of them will be managerial or professional of some sort.

In spite of these trends the percentage of young people in Britain going on to higher education is currently 14 percent, rising to 18 percent by 1992, but only because there will be fewer teenagers in total. In the rest of Europe the overall figure is around 20 percent, with small national differences. In France, for instance, 36 percent pass their baccalaureate and are therefore entitled to enter university, but nearly half leave, or are asked to leave, at the end of the first year. Only Japan, the USA, Taiwan, and South Korea seem to have university populations of the right sort of size for the future, and in those countries there are concerns about the quantity if not the quality of some of what is called "higher education."

If these estimates of the required levels of education are even partly true, it means that not only will we see alarming numbers of skill shortages but that, more seriously still, we may lack the skills and the wits even to create the businesses and the opportunities which will then encounter skill shortages! It will, of course, be an invisible discontinuity. We will not miss the organizations we have not had, and never thought to have. . . .

THE VANISHING GENERATION

In the nineties, there will be almost 25 percent fewer young people leaving school. At first glance this seems like a timely end to the problem of youth unemployment. A second glance changes the picture because it points to even more pressure on the relatively small percentage who have the brain skills needed by today's work force. The bulk of the newly reduced cohort of young people will still be like those who leave British schools without a proper certificate in even one subject, 43 percent of them in 1986.

A 1988 British report by the National Economic Development Office and the Training Commission, "Young People and the Labour Market, A Challenge for the 1990s," pointed out that in 1987, less than twenty large employers took on half of all the 27,000 school leavers with two or more A-levels who were looking for work. The drop in youth population, therefore, is a problem because, if nothing is done, it means that the supply of brain skills, already inadequate, will be even more inadequate, and that the skills shortages referred to above will become even more severe. The competition for the more educated will intensify, and the rejection of the less educated will be felt even more cruelly. Youth unemployment will *not* be solved, indeed it will be raised a notch or two.

The statistic, 25 percent fewer, is an opportunity, however, if it makes it easier to tackle the task of educating more of our young men and women for life and work in the world of brain skills. Without anyone doing anything, as every government has discovered, the *percentages* of those going on to higher and further education are bound to improve as the base number falls. Doing rather more will, in percentage terms, make a great deal of difference and will set markers for the future.

Those markers are important because they must change a culture. There is no innate reason why Britain should be sixteenth in the OECD league table of young people in education after 16 years of age—above only Portugal and Spain. British teenagers are not innately more stupid or less educable; they are simply the inheritors of a tradition which held that book learning was for the few; that real life, and real money, should begin as soon as possible, and that manual and pragmatic skills were best learnt on the job. The past, as so often in Europe, determines the future, even though the degree to which these beliefs might have been true in the world of work as it used to be is the degree to which they must be less true today.

In Japan, top of the OECD table, 98 percent of young people stay on in formal education until 18 years of age, even though that education is far from stimulating and far from being pragmatic. They are the inheritors of a different cultural tradition, one that just happens to be more attuned to the needs of the future than that of Britain and most of the rest of Europe. In America, too, the young stay on in school, but whether they learn anything there is a question of growing concern.

The information society, after all, uses information, in the form of numbers, words, pictures, or voices—on screens, in books, or in printouts and reports—as its currency. The essential requirement, therefore, of all its workers is that they are able to read, interpret, and fit together the elements of this currency, irrespective, almost, of what the data actually relates to. That is a skill of the brain. It can be taught or at least developed in classrooms. It does not, for most people, happen quickly, easily, or early but requires years of practice, years which are most conveniently and usefully spent at the beginning of adult life rather than inconveniently in the middle. This general skill is akin to riding a bicycle, once learnt it is never unlearnt, and having learnt it, one can then go on to learn its use in particular applications.

It is this conviction that brain skills are of general use and can be developed in youth that has led places like Taiwan and South Korea, following Japan, to put such an emphasis on the formal, even scholastic, education of their youth. It has been said that every second person in Seoul has either been at university or is currently studying or teaching there, while in the 1970s Mr. Goh Thok Tong, then minister for trade and industry in Singapore, was arguing that Singapore needed "to step into the shoes left behind by countries like Germany and Japan as they restructure, they from skill-intensive to knowledge-intensive and we from labor-intensive to skill-intensive." In pursuit of these objectives Singapore proceeded to increase greatly the number of university places and to lower the entry requirements. Britain, who needs to be one step ahead of Singapore, has until recently been doing the reverse.

The opportunity, however, remains and is made more accessible because of the vanishing generation. The smaller population within an age bracket is also good news for those who want to re-enter or enter late the work of the information society. The squeeze on qualified youth will encourage employers to turn to other sources of skill, particularly to women, many of whom have the necessary early education but have been busy working to raise their families and manage their homes. Less convenient as employees because they want and need more flexibility, they have not been wooed too assiduously in the past. In the 1990s they will be. They do, after all, represent nearly half of all university entrants (over half in 1987 in the USA for the first time). They are a neglected resource which few will be able to neglect once the –25 percent factor begins to bite. The NEDO Report cited estimates that four out of five of the 900,000 new workers it foresees in Britain's work force over the next eight years will be women returning to work.

Women have re-entered the work force before, but the numbers and the conditions under which they will return in the 1990s turn this into a significant discontinuity, which will change the way organizations are run, will affect family structures and living patterns quite significantly . . .

THE THIRD AGE

In 1988 the social affairs ministers of the OECD met to contemplate the time when one person in five will be a pensioner and one in ten aged over 75, when there will be only three people of working age to support each pensioner, and when old-age pensions may account for one-fifth of national income. It will be even worse for Switzerland and West Germany where there will be only two people of working age for each pensioner.

It will be 2040 before this scenario fully becomes a reality, but the people who will be old then are alive now, and unless they quickly change their breeding habits, the numbers of their children are quite predictable. This world will happen and it will start to happen before the end of this century.

Once again, there have been old people before, but never before so many of them. I knew only one grandparent—the others had died before I was born. My children knew all four. Their children will almost certainly know a great-grandparent or two. People in their sixties and retired will still be someone's children. The infrequent has become the commonplace, and the world as we know it will inevitably change in some way.

It is happening because, in the richer countries, it is becoming harder to die. Each major cause of death is either diminished, like smallpox or polio and, one day, cancer, or postponed for a few more years or decades, like heart disease. Of course, nature, or man's tampering with nature, may trigger another plague, and some wonder whether AIDS may not be just that plague, but such disasters excepted, there seems little reason why many of today's teenagers cannot expect to live to 100, provided they do not drink, smoke, or drive themselves to death.

The question is, will they want to live that long? When death as an act of God seems to be indefinitely postponed, will we want to make it increasingly an act of mankind? Euthanasia, already quasi-legal in the Netherlands, may become more acceptable to more societies.

More urgent are the questions, "What will they live on?" "What will they do?" "Who will care for them?" By the year 2020, if nothing changes, Italy will be spending over a quarter of its national income on pensions, while Britain's health service will spend ten times as much on a patient over 75 as on one of working age.

Like all discontinuities, however, this one contains opportunities as well as problems if the changes are seen coming and if everyone concerned can indulge in a little upside-down thinking.

The aged will not all be poor, for instance. An increasing number of them will own their own homes, an asset which can be turned into an annual income provided that they do not intend to bequeath it to the next generation (who will by then be in mid- or late career with their own homes bought and paid for). Most of them will be healthy and active. That is, of course, why they are still alive. They are capable of working. One British study found that 43 percent of over-65s regularly helped other elderly people, 25 percent helped the disabled, 11 percent helped neighbors. If we change our view of work to include such unpaid activity, then these people are only retired in a legal or technical sense. After all, in the last century no one had heard of retirement—they worked till they dropped, or, as a farmer said once when I asked him what was the difference between farming at 75 and farming at 50, "The same only slower!" Experience and wisdom can often compensate for energy.

So, many older people will not go unnoticed, particularly when many more of them will have experienced responsibility earlier in life and will not be used to keeping quiet. If we are sensible we will want to use their talents in our organizations, but not full time or on full pay. We shall need, then, to rethink what jobs call for part-time wisdom and experience, and what work can be done at a distance by responsible people. We shall need to revise the tax rules for pensions to make it economic for such work to be done. Many people, active and healthy, will devise their own activities, organizing around their enthusiasms; we must not let too many rules from the past stand in their way. We will need to change the way we talk about them, words like "retirement" will become as antiquated as "servant" today. Words are so often the bridges of social change, the outward signs of a discontinuity at work triggering some upside-down thinking.

Already the linguistic signposts are going up. The Third Age, the age of living, as the French would have it, which follows the first age of learning and the second of working, is already becoming a common term. There is a University of the Third Age, a network of people exchanging their skills and their knowledge. There will soon be more talk of Third Age careers. Soon, no doubt, there will be Third Age societies and, ultimately, ministers for the Third Age in all OECD countries! The "wrinklies," as my children fondly term us, can be assets as well as liabilities, *if* we want them to be.

If words are indeed the heralds of change, then the Third Age language suggests that before too long we shall be referring to people's job-careers as we now do to their educations. "Where did you work?" to a 65-year-old with fifteen years, at least, of life ahead will sound much like "Where did you go to school?" It would all sound strange indeed to my father who died two years after retiring, at the age of 74. For him there was no Third Age worth living, and the second age, of job and career, had long been a burden before he could afford to leave it.

It will be different for us, his children, and for our children. It is change of a discontinuous sort, but it need not be change for the worse if we can see it coming and can prepare for it.

$$\frac{100,000(4)}{2} = J$$

The changes coming to our ways of work and living, indeed the changes already here, are conveniently summed up by this strange equation. When it is unravelled, it suggests that we have, for some time now, been engaged in a massive job-splitting exercise in our society and have not even noticed it.

It will work like this. Thirty years ago when I joined an international company and started my job, I signed on, although I never realized it, for 100,000 hours of work during my lifetime, because I should, if I was anything like everyone else in the developed world at that time, be expected to work for 47 hours a week, including overtime paid or unpaid, for 47 weeks a year for 47 years of my life (from, on average, 18 to 65). $47 \times 47 \times 47 = 103,823$ or 100,000 hours, give or take a few.

My teenage son and daughter, a generation later, can expect their *jobs* to add up, on average, to 50,000 hours. The lifetime job will have been halved in one generation. At first sight this would imply that they would be working half as many hours per week, for half as many weeks and half as many years. But mathematics does not work like that. Just as half of 4^3 (64) is not 2^3 (8), so half of 47^3 is not 23.5^3. In fact, rather bizarrely, half of the three 47s is three 37s, for $37 \times 37 \times 37 = 50,653$.

It is because of this statistical sleight-of-hand that we have not noticed this rather dramatic piece of discontinuous change. It is also, in part, because it is only now beginning to bite as the next generation begin their second age of jobs and careers.

The world is not so neat, however, as to switch uniformly from the three 47s to the three 37s. That is where the (4) comes in. My daughter and my son have four principal options to choose from.

In the first option they will follow in their father's footsteps and look for a full-time job, or at least a sequence of full-time jobs, in the core of an organization or perhaps as a professional of some sort. In this case their working week will not be that different from the one I knew. Statistically, it will average 45 hours per week, with rather less overtime for the hourly paid and fewer Saturday mornings for office workers. Nor will their working year be much reduced; longer annual holidays bring it down to 45 weeks rather than 47.

What will change, however, is the length of their job life. To get one of those increasingly rare jobs in the core or the professions (less than half of all jobs by 2000), they will need to be both well qualified *and* experienced. In Germany today, a six- or seven-year university course is piled on top of eighteen months of military or community service so that the average entrant into the job market is 27 years of age. In the USA, a postgraduate qualification of some sort, after a four-year degree, is increasingly becoming a prerequisite for a good job, making 24 the normal age at which adults begin full-time jobs. Britain still has three-year degree courses (except in Scotland) and no military service, but employers increasingly look for further qualifications of a more vocational or professional nature *and* for relevant experience in vacations or in "gap" years. It has, after all, been the established practice in the older professions of medicine, architecture, and the law for centuries—a long (seven-year) mix of education, experience, and vocational training. We can expect to see it extend to many other occupations, with the result that British parents must increasingly expect to wait until the offspring are 24 or 25 before they are established in a full-time job, if that is what they want.

It is possible that the fall in the numbers of qualified young people in all industrialized countries will tempt organizations and professions to shorten their training requirements in order to get the best of a shrinking supply. The form this will probably take, however, will be to finance them, perhaps under the guise of employment, during their studies. It will be education more generously funded, not a job.

The next generation of full-time core workers, therefore, be they professionals, managers, technicians, or skilled workers, can expect to start their full-time careers later—and to leave them earlier. This is the crucial point. The core worker will have a harder but shorter job, with more people leaving full-time employment in their late forties or early fifties, partly because they no longer want the pressure that such jobs will increasingly entail, but mainly because there will be younger, more qualified, and more energetic people available for these core jobs.

It is true that early in the next century the total number of people in the work force in every country will start to decline and the average age to rise, as the dip in the birthrate of the 1970s works its way through life. However, with the reduced numbers of full timers, employers will continue to place a premium on youth, energy, and qualifications whenever they can get them in combination. It will be a shorter life but a more furious one for the full timers, as the new professionals in business are already discovering.

The net result of these changes will be a full-time job which, on average, will result in 45 hours for 45 weeks for 25 years, totalling 50,000 hours. Work won't stop for such people after 50 but it will not be the same sort of work; it will not be a *job* as they have known it. They will enter their Third Age sooner than others, affluent, no doubt, but still with a good third of their lives to live.

It is happening already. One personnel manager was surprised to discover that only 2 percent of his work force were, as he put it, still there at the official retirement age of 62. What he had done was to look back fifteen years to those who were then 47 and had found that only a few had stayed on with the organization for the remaining fifteen years. Some had moved to new jobs and one or two had died, but the great majority had opted for, or been persuaded into, early retirement in their fifties. "We knew that people were leaving us early," he said, "but we had no idea of the scale of it all until we started counting." An advertising agency, aware that creativity and mental energy tend to decline with the years, would like to see everyone under the age of 50. They have not, so far, been allowed by the tax authorities to make their full pension scheme applicable under the age of 55 but they are confident that it will come down to 50 within the next ten years—well in time for the generation now starting their careers.

There will always be the glorious exceptions of course. Moreover, those who control their own careers—the self-employed, the professionals, and, apparently heads of state—will buck the trend as long as the clients and their supporters will permit it. It is the bigger organizations, in which most full timers still work, who will be most choosy about whom they keep on their full-time books, and they will want the energetic, the up-to-date, the committed, and the flexible. Most of those will be in their thirties and forties, putting in their 50,000 hours in big annual chunks. Full-time work in organizations will, however, be only one of the options and, if the numbers are anything like right, it will be a minority option, perhaps an elite one. Most people will find their place outside the organization, selling their time or their services into it, as self-employed, part-time, or temporary workers.

For them the pattern of hours will be different. They may find themselves working 25 hours a week for 45 weeks of the year (part time) or 45 hours a week for 25 weeks a year (temporary). In either case they will need to keep on working as long as they can, for 45 years if possible, because they will not be able to accumulate the savings through pension schemes or other mechanisms to live on. This will suit the organizations who will look for experience and reliability in their temporary staff, rather than for the energy and certainty of youth. In both temporary work and part-time work, the sum is still $25 \times 45 \times 45 = 50,000$.

We may, therefore, see the national retirement age going in two very different ways at the same time. While for the core workers it will gradually come down toward 50 over the next twenty years, for most of the work force it will go up. For them the questions, "What shall I do in the missing 50,000 hours, and what shall I live on?" cannot be postponed until the Third Age; they need to be answered now. For these people the future is not a generation away—it started yesterday.

My children have a fourth option. They may be able to work full time for ten years, take ten years out to raise a family, then return to the work force at, say, 45 for a further ten or even fifteen years. ($45 \times 45 \times 25$ hours of paid work = 50,000.) It is an option that has traditionally been taken up by women, who have varied the pattern by going part time for some of the intervening years, but it may increasingly be seen as an opportunity by men to vary their lifestyle and to play a bigger role in home and family life.

Re-entry into the full-time work force has always been difficult. It will get easier as the shortage of qualified young people begins to bite organizations in the 1990s. The organization will then turn to that reservoir of talent, the qualified women at home. In order to tempt them back, however, organizations may have to learn to be more flexible, more willing to recognize that they are buying someone's talents, but not necessarily all their time.

THE PRESSURES BEHIND THE NUMBERS

The $\frac{100,000(4)}{2} = J$ equation is, of course, spuriously precise. The numbers will not work out precisely like that. The equation is there to make a point. The world of jobs is changing. It is changing more dramatically than we realize because numbers like this creep up on one unexpectedly when multiplied out over a lifetime.

No one particularly wants those numbers to happen. They are not the result of any policy decisions by government or boards of directors. They are the cumulative result of many instinctive responses to a changing environment. There is now some general agreement about the nature of this changing environment and an acceptance that it is not going to change back again. Some of the main features are these:

A Move Away from Labor-Intensive Manufacturing

Thirty years ago nearly half of all workers in the industrialized countries were making or helping to make *things*. In another thirty years' time it may be down to 10 percent (in the USA it is already down to 18 percent).

To some extent this is because we have all had to export our factories, instead of our goods, to countries where labor is cheaper and more amenable to working in factories. Even Japan has now been forced by the high price of the yen to follow suit. When Britain did not export her factories soon enough, they were replicated in the newly industrialized countries, and the UK lost out. Situations such as the rapid rise of the pound sterling in the early years of Margaret Thatcher's government in Britain only accelerated this process, leaving swathes of abandoned factories throughout Britain. It would have happened anyway. The clever thing would have been to join the unbeatable (rather than competing with them) by exporting the factories not the goods. Discontinuous change can always be turned to advantage with a bit of forethought.

The result is not just fewer jobs, but different organizations. Labor-intensive manufacturing was traditionally managed with a large pool of relatively cheap labor, a lot of supervision, and a hierarchical management structure. There were a lot of people around, most of them full-time employees whose time was bought to be used at the discretion of the organization, subject increasingly to the agreement of the union.

It was a convenient way to run things; everything and everyone you needed was yours. If you want to control it, own it, was the message. It proved, in the end, to be a very expensive message. The Japanese always did it differently, with a small core staff, a raft of subcontractors, heavy investment in clever machines, and enough clever people to instruct them and work with them. The demise of mass manufacturing has led to the end of the mass employment organizations and a redefinition of the job.

A Move Toward Knowledge-Based Organizations

The end of labor-intensive manufacturing leaves us with organizations which receive their added value from the knowledge and the creativity they put in rather than the muscle power. Fewer people, thinking better, helped by clever machines and computers, add more value than gangs or lines of unthinking "human resources." Manufacturing has gone this way. The more obviously knowledge-based businesses of consultancy, finance and insurance, advertising, journalism and publishing, television, health care, education, and entertainment, have all flourished. Even agriculture and construction, the oldest of industries, have invested in knowledge and clever machines in place of muscles.

The result is not only a requirement for different people, but different organizations, organizations that recognize that they cannot do everything themselves, that they need a central group of talented and energetic people, a lot of specialist help and ancillary agencies. They are smaller, younger organizations than their predecessors, flatter and less hierarchical. . . . Their most immediate effect is on the numbers—fewer people inside who are better qualified, more people outside who are contracted, not employed.

A Move Toward Service

Paradoxically, rich societies seem to breed dependency. If you are poor you are forced into self-sufficiency. As you get rich, it is easier and more sensible to get other people to do what you do not want to do or cannot do, be it fixing the roof or digging the garden. It makes economic sense to let others make your clothes and to buy them in the store, that way you get better clothes and more time to do what you are good at. It goes on and on. Convenience foods take the chore out of cooking, and package holidays, the work out of leisure. All of us become more specialized, better at one thing and worse at others. Like knowledge-based organizations we contract out everything we are not good at and so breed a raft of services on which we now depend.

Affluence breeds service industries, and they in turn create affluence. Sometimes it seems as if everyone is taking in everyone else's metaphorical washing and making money out of it, or as in my particular case, that everyone is going to everyone else's conference and being paid for it or paying for it. Affluence is a matter of mood and self-confidence as much as of economics, for dependency has its own imperatives. If you need to buy all these services, you have to find something to do to pay for them, hence some competitive striving. It is a self-fulfilling prophecy which works as long as everyone believes the prophecy of continued affluence.

The service industries of affluence are therefore ephemeral creations, which could always disappear overnight. The point, however, once again, is that the organizations they spawn are of a different kind. Because they are essentially ephemeral, they have to flex with every shift in demand. Small core staff and lots of part-time and temporary help has to be the rule. Many of them are not knowledge-intensive businesses, although some are, of course. Retailing, transport, cleaning, catering, leisure, are all industries with large requirements for the competent but semi-skilled. It is here that you will find most of the 30 percent who do not have the brain skills for the knowledge-based organizations. It is here that you will find the bulk of the part timers and the temporary workers.

It is the growth of the service sector which has transformed the working lives of so many people in Europe and the USA *because* of the kind of organization which it needs and breeds.

These shifts are irreversible. The degree of affluence may increase or wane in each country but labor-intensive manufacturing will not return to Europe, or to the USA, or to Japan. Knowledge-based enterprises have to be the way forward for all our countries, the more and the better the richer, whether they are manufacturing goods or providing services. The service sector will ebb and flow with local prosperity but will never fade away.

If the shifts are irreversible, so are the changes in the patterns of work which they induce, and therefore the numbers with which this chapter began. A dramatic change in the economic climate may slow things down, but it will not stop them. The world of work has changed already. We need to take notice.

11

Motivating Knowledge Workers—The Challenge for the 1990s

Mahen Tampoe

As early as 1970, Peter Drucker, writing about approaches to managing technology-based companies, raised the question of "whether traditional organization structure is going to work tomorrow the way it has worked for the past 40 years." It was his view that organization structures and management styles appropriate for manufacturing industry may be inappropriate for knowledge-based industries which depended on the acquisition and exploitation of knowledge for competitive advantage. It was his contention that "ideas do not observe hierarchical channels of communication" and that therefore hierarchical structures were inappropriate for knowledge-based organizations.

Kantrow (1984) points out that twentieth century manufacturing techniques had succeeded in converting the "idiosyncratic work of artisans, craftsmen and engineers into consistent, predictable and repeatable practice—to utility," and in this way limited the scope for innovation and creativity among its knowledge workers. Sasaki (1991) writing on how the Japanese accelerate new car development cycles, points out that "new product concepts wither in a company which imposes too much bureaucracy on designers and restricts their creativity."

At a recent workshop run by the author at Henley Management College on the management of High-Tech projects, the participants (consultants and R & D managers from industry and government) agreed that of fourteen problems listed, a key problem was that of "specialist clash" which they defined as balancing the need for autonomy of team members with the need to conform to team/organizational norms to achieve effective outcomes. Bailyn (1985) in her research into the management of technologists in R & D Laboratories focused on the management dilemma of line managers between retaining control and allowing their staff adequate autonomy to be creative and innovative. It would appear that new management approaches seemed justified, this view is supported by Wilmot (1987) who

Reprinted with permission from *Long Range Planning,* Vol. 26, Mahen Tempoe, "Motivating Knowledge Workers—The Challenge for the 1990s," 1993, Elsevier Science Ltd., Pergamon Imprint, Oxford, England.

179

points out that the investment gap in R & D is "in management of innovation" and not in the availability of finance for R & D.

Beattie and Tampoe (1990), in their article on the problems of managing and motivating technologists to achieve high performance in ICL, showed how traditional human resource practices had to be modified or replaced with new HRM initiatives to meet the HRM needs of ICL. Kuwahara, Okada and Horikoshi (1989) point out that Hitachi's approach to this same problem was to develop parallel career structures including the institution of a special "status" structure to ensure that technologists and managers enjoyed similar status within their R & D function. In the early 1980s authors such as Peters and Waterman (1982), Rosabeth Moss Kanter (1983) and others focused our attention on organizational cultures and empowered employees as being a means of overcoming some of the problems of managing knowledge workers. However, empowered employees need direction if their efforts are not to be wasted or self-indulgently applied. It seems that the problem identified by Bailyn (1985) remains still unanswered. Perhaps the answer lies in drawing on the inner drive and motivation of these knowledge workers, rather than in better methods of supervision. Herzberg (1966) offers job enrichment as a way to solve this problem on the basis that it will increase job satisfaction by meeting the motivational needs of employees.

This research study sets out to explore the motivational needs and organizational environments best suited to knowledge workers. It was based on motivation models proposed by previous researchers for managers and modified on the basis of information gathered from literature reviews and recent empirical research in related fields specific to knowledge workers in industry. It seemed inappropriate to extrapolate from the motivational needs of managers, clerical and factory staff, as Hunt (1987) in his research has shown that the motivational needs of staff varied with the nature of their work, their skills levels, and their domestic and material circumstances. In the light of this evidence a new look at the motivational and environmental needs of knowledge workers seem justified.

The research identified four key motivators, eight characteristics which impacted on employee effectiveness at work and six predominant current management practices. These are used as the basis for offering guidance to managers on motivators and management methods appropriate to deriving high performance from knowledge workers.

THE RESEARCH PROJECT

The research project began in May 1988. It drew on widely acknowledged views on motivation theory; for example, those proposed by Herzberg (1987), Maslow (1987), and McGregor (1960) and developments in motivation models, for example, the work of Porter and Lawler (1968), Vroom (1964), and Hunt (1986). It also looked at recent research into creativity (Amabile 1988), management practices in R & D establishments, (Bailyn 1985), and the career expectations of recent graduates (Garden 1990). In addition various views on organizational design and management styles were explored. Based on what was learnt from this literature review a research model was proposed and tested using data gathered by distributing a questionnaire which sought to collect information on:

1. How knowledge workers perceived they *were being managed* in organizations today; and how they thought they *should be managed* to be more effective at work, and
2. What characteristics were important to this group of staff at work so that key motivators could be deduced from their answers to the questions posed.

THE RESEARCH MODEL

The model of motivation (Figure 11-1) which formed the basis of the empirical research and the hypotheses, was based on the model proposed by Porter and Lawler (1968) for managers. It also incorporated ideas from the research work done by Amabile (1988).

The model postulated (a) the potency of different rewards which aroused motivated behaviour, and (b) the presence of certain instrumental factors (e.g., task and domain relevant skills, role and goal clarity) which led to performance, with performance leading to rewards and eventually to a sense of psychological success. The model was built on the expectation that performance would result in the expected rewards and that these would satisfy the motivated drives.

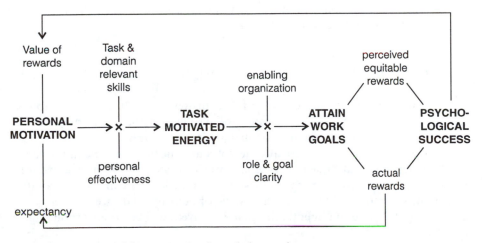

FIGURE 11-1 Model for motivating knowledge workers.

DATA COLLECTION AND ANALYSIS

A questionnaire consisting of 133 questions was prepared and circulated to 800 staff in R & D establishments, software development houses and engineering firms. Smaller samples from many large multinationals in the U.K. were also canvassed. Three hundred and twenty-two staff responded to the questionnaire. Three questions referred to demographic data such as age, sex and qualifications. Ten referred to work related information such as job title, nature of work, team size, years in employment, salary, and job satisfaction. There were 48 identical questions each on current and preferred working conditions and 24 relating to motivators at work. The respondents were required to express the absence or presence of certain characteristics by rating each characteristic against a 7 point Likert scale. The sample comprised 91 managers of knowledge workers, 40 project managers, and 191 team members comprising 44 consultants, 43 researchers, 58 implementors, and 46 designers. Their ages ranged from 20 to 59. Two hundred and thirty of the respondents were below the age of 39, the average age of the sample was 32 years. Two hundred and twenty-one were married, 91 were single and 10 divorced. There were 60 female staff in the sample representing a higher proportion than in industry in general. One hundred and fifty-five of the staff had less than 5 years service with their present employers. Two hundred and seventy had spent less than 5 years in their current jobs. The majority of the sample worked in teams of less than 10 staff, which probably representative of IT and R & D teams.

The responses received were analysed using factor analysis as the main analytical tool along with discriminant and conjoint analysis to differentiate and prioritize the motivators. The data analysis revealed information on what motivators were relevant to knowledge workers and two secondary but related aspects of worklife which the research set out to investigate were also highlighted namely;

1. The way knowledge workers perceived they were managed.
2. The organizational climate which knowledge workers felt they needed if they were to be effective at work.

THE EMPLOYEE

In interpreting the data collected from this research it is important to consider the employees themselves. It would be wrong to assume that they were all interested in the same motivators or that their preferences met the generalized model. It is likely that staff were at different stages in their careers and domestic circumstances and that these factors would affect the strength of their need for the four motivators identified. For the purpose of this article we can propose a different classification of staff based on their stage of personal and career development (see Figure 11-2). We can hypothesize that employees will be at one of four stages, namely;

Stage 1—Fulfilment. These employees will feel a high sense of job satisfaction derived from having achieved a preferred balance of those motivational and reward factors of importance to them. This could lead to a transitional stage.

Stage 2—Transition. These employees have arrived at a crossroads in their career and personal development and are seeking to reposition themselves for the future. This can happen to an employee at any age but is more likely to occur in their late thirties to mid-forties. This can lead to either 3 or 4 below.

Stage 3—Developmental. These employees are seeking to reach their state of equilibrium. They are likely to be in their twenties and early thirties, or moving from one state of equilibrium to another irrespective of age or career position.

Stage 4—Plateaued. These employees are likely to have decided that their level of achievement and personal growth meets their motivational and rewards needs and they are not seeking new challenges.

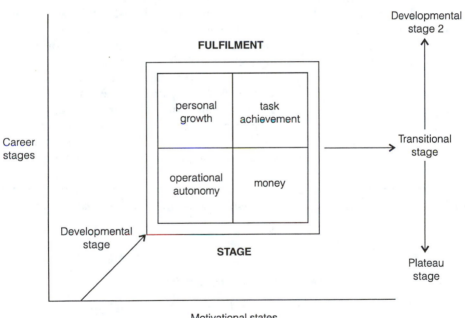

Movement is from fulfilment to transition leading to
either development stage 2 or plateaued stage which in turn
may lead to a state of fulfilment

© Mahen Tampoe

FIGURE 11-2

THE MOTIVATORS

Four key motivators were identified:

1. *Personal growth*—the opportunity for individuals to realize their potential, supporting the hypothesis that knowledge workers were seeking intellectual, personal and career growth.
2. *Operational autonomy*—a work environment in which knowledge workers can achieve the tasks assigned to them within the constraints of strategic direction and self-measurement indices.
3. *Task achievement*—the achievement of producing work to a standard and quality of which the individual can be proud. There is a need for the task undertaken to be relevant to the organization.
4. *Money*—earning an income which is a just reward for the contribution made and enables employees to share in the wealth created by them, through incentive schemes geared to their company's success but related to their personal performance.

To help prioritize these four motivators a new questionnaire was prepared and circulated to 75 knowledge workers. Figure 11-3 below shows how these motivators were prioritized by the sample. It must be pointed out that whilst the majority fitted this general pattern, some showed a very strong preference for one out of the four motivators, emphasising the fact that this generalized data cannot be used without the priorities for each individual being identified and catered to.

This ranking highlights the significantly lower importance placed by the respondents on monetary rewards. No doubt this is due in part to the fact that they all earned well above the national average wage and that money in its varying forms must be considered as having little incremental value as a motivator, even if it is related to individual performance, unless the potential earnings are very significant.

Once the financial rewards offered meet those prevailing in the industry it is the other three motivators, namely personal growth, operational autonomy, and

Motivator	Percentage	Preferred option
Personal growth	33.74%	Significant growth
Operational autonomy	30.51%	Freedom to work within the rules
Task achievement	28.69%	Very high
Money	7.07%	Salary + bonus on personal effort
	100.01%	

FIGURE 11-3 Principal motivators of respondents.

task achievement, which managers should use to achieve motivated behaviour from their staff. When these three motivators are combined in a three circle diagram (Figure 11-4) four motivated states can be identified. These are:

Segment A—motivated behaviour: Achieved by meeting the combination of all three motivators desired by all knowledge workers.

Segment B—Supervised behaviour: This combination of personal growth and task achievement excludes operational autonomy, thus implying that

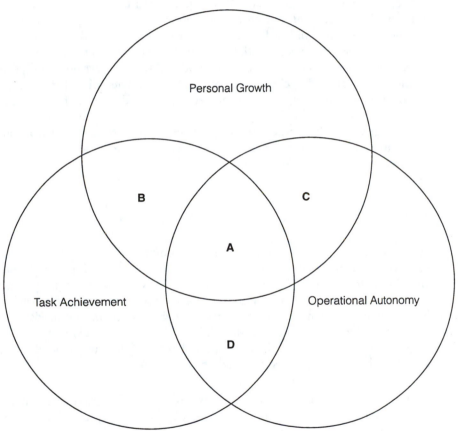

A = motivated behaviour   © Mahen Tampoe
B = supervised behaviour
C = employee-centred behaviour
D = organization-centred behaviour

FIGURE 11-4

staff are within a supervised environment. As two out of the three requirements are met, however, it is still seen as motivational, especially for staff who see themselves as being in a developmental stage or employees who feel they have plateaued.

Segment C—Employee-centred behaviour: This combination of operational autonomy and personal growth excludes task achievement, suggesting that the employee is probably not doing work which he or she feels meets organizational needs. This may be demotivating for some staff, especially those in their developmental phase, but not for those who are in a transitional stage where they may find the independence from strong task dominance useful to reorientate their careers.

Segment D—Organization-centred behaviour: This combination of operational autonomy and task achievement excludes personal growth and is likely to meet the needs of the plateaued employee, especially the more senior ones who have the experience and ability to deliver outcomes, provided they are given clear goals and objectives. They may, for example, trade-off personal growth for job security. The degree of freedom this would give them will compensate for losing out on promotions to the managerial ranks. Others who will benefit from these motivators are likely to be staff in their developmental stage where they may seek to prove themselves at the temporary sacrifice of personal growth.

HOW SHOULD MANAGERS USE THIS DATA?

In this article we have described four states of motivated behaviour and four stages in the career of an employee and have related them to each other offering scope for their effective use. However, progress can only be made if managers are able to identify what career stage employees have or perceive they have reached and then apply a management style which will fit their motivational needs. This means that team sizes and structures should be such that managers can relate to their staff and better understand the motivational needs of their team members. In addition, the following steps need to be taken:

1. Regular appraisals and career discussions with staff so that career stages and motivational needs are understood by both employee and manager.
2. A working environment in which employees can achieve their preferred motivators and rewards.

This second condition is very important as staff must believe that their performance will result in the rewards they seek. This means that the work environment must not only offer these rewards but facilitate their achievement. However, an analysis of current working practices showed they fell short of the conditions considered necessary to satisfy the motivation needs identified earlier.

THE CURRENT WORKING ENVIRONMENT

When the data on perceived management styles was analysed, six current management practices were identified as predominating the working environment of the knowledge workers sampled. These were:

1. *Activity orientation*—a preference shown by management for activity rather then for effective outcomes. This manifested itself in staff having inadequate time to develop and test ideas before implementation due to time pressures for delivery.
2. *Creative autonomy*—the freedom to be creative but a lack of operational autonomy as a result of the bureaucratic bias recorded later. Although staff could think innovatively they were unable to mobilize organizational resources to implement their ideas.
3. *Shared values*—strong corporate cultures.
4. *Bureaucratic bias*—process dominance.
5. *Career stagnation*—lack of promotion opportunities.
6. *Financial rewards focus*—the use of money as a motivator in preference to career opportunities or some of the motivators identified earlier. The perception of staff was that they were unable to share in the financial success of the firm.

When comparing the above list with the sample's own preferences, only *Creative Autonomy* and *Shared Values* were found to coincide. It would appear that current management practices are failing to offer employees a motivating climate and that it is therefore necessary to identify those which would constitute an effective work environment for knowledge workers. This we can do by an analysis of the data on preferred work environments collected from the sample.

BUILDING AN EFFECTIVE WORKING ENVIRONMENT

When the data on effective working environments was analysed, eight requirements were identified, namely:

1. *Commercial relevance* of the job—the need for the assigned task to be relevant and important to the business.
2. *Task competence*—the ability to carry out assigned tasks.
3. *Task consistency*—a stability and consistency in the tasks and goals set so that staff can devote time and energy to their achievement without being required to divert their attention to meet "management crisis" situations.
4. *Directed skills*—role clarity and skills, based on matching individual skills to the assigned tasks and the opportunity to build new competencies.

5. *Creative autonomy*—freedom to pursue the job as seen fit by the employee without detailed supervision or constraint in the way the job is handled.
6. *Resources*—the tools to do the job.
7. *Commitment*—loyalty to the organization rather than to colleagues or the profession.
8. *Peer contacts*—access to information and knowledge which is relevant to the job or specialization.

These eight requirements were seen as being instrumental in enabling staff to perform well at work, and they can be used as the basis for developing the components of the "ideal" empowering work environment. The eight effectiveness factors can be summarized into five main requirements, namely:

Motivated and committed employees.
Individual competence—comprising task competence and creative autonomy.
Facilitative work environment—task consistency and resources.
Purpose—directed skills and commercial relevance of the assigned tasks.
Knowledge exchange—the genuine transmission of information up, down and sideways in a listening rather than speaking organization.

THE MANAGEMENT MODEL

These five elements can be used to develop a management model for knowledge workers as shown in Figure 11-5.

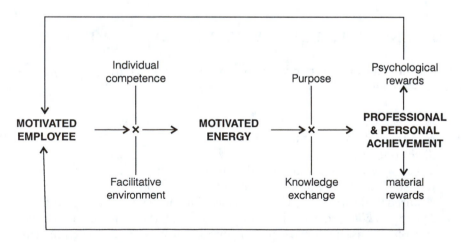

FIGURE 11-5 Model for managing knowledge workers.

Professional and personal achievement is seen as the trigger which, by leading to psychological and material rewards, activates and sustains an individual's motivated drive. The facilitative environment interacts with motivated drive and individual competence to release motivated energy. Motivated energy is directed into professional and personal achievement by ensuring that individuals have a clear sense of purpose and are sustained by access to information and peer contacts. This is essential for the sense of awareness that is critical for success.

REFERENCES

Teresa M. Amabile, A model of creativity and innovation in organisations, *Researchs in Organisational Behaviour,* 10 (1988).

Lotte Bailyn, Autonomy in the industrial R & D lab, *Human Resource Management,* 2, (1985).

D. F. Beattie and F. M. K. Tampoe, Human resource planning for ICL. *Long Range Planning,* 23 (1), (1990).

Peter Drucker, *Technology Management and Society,* Pan, London (1970).

Anna-Maria Garden, Career orientation of software developers in a sample of high tech companies. *R & D Management* 24 (4), (1990).

Frederick Herzberg, *Work and the Nature of Man,* World Publishing Corporation, New York (1966).

John W. Hunt, *Managing People at Work,* McGraw Hill, New York (1987).

Rosabeth Moss Kanter, *The Changemasters.* George Allen and Unwin, London (1983).

Yutaka Kuwahara, Osami Okada, and Hisashi Horikoshi, Planning research and development at Hitachi. *Long Range Planning* 22 (3), (1989).

Abraham Maslow, *Motivation and Personality* (revised edn), Harper & Row, New York (1987).

Douglas McGregor, *The Human Side of Enterprise,* Penguin, London (1960).

Lyman W. Porter and Edward E. Lawler III, *Managerial Attitudes and Performance,* Richard D. Irwin, Inc., New York (1968).

Thomas J. Peters and Robert H. Waterman, *In Search of Excellence,* Harper & Row, New York (1982).

Toru Sasaki, How the Japanese accelerated new car development, *Long Range Planning,* 24 (1), 15–25 (1991).

V. H. Vroom. *Work and Motivation,* Wiley, New York (1964).

Robb W. Wilmot, Change in management and the management of change, *Long Range Planning,* 20 (6), (1987).

12

The Social System at the Shop Level

Michel Crozier

THE SYSTEM OF POWER RELATIONSHIPS IN THE SHOP: ITS EQUILIBRIUM AND ITS LIMITS

The behavior and attitudes of people and groups within an organization cannot be explained without reference to the power relationships existing among them. All the lessons of the past fifteen years' research in organization have brought to light more and more the importance of those problems of power and control that the first attempts at understanding leadership had neglected.[17]

The situation in the Monopoly is especially interesting seen in this perspective. A main rationale of bureaucratic development is the elimination of power relationships and personal dependencies—to administer things instead of governing men. The ideal of bureaucracy is a world where people are bound by impersonal rules and not by personal influence and arbitrary command. The organizational system of the Monopoly has gone a long way toward realizing this ideal. It is primarily characterized by the extent of impersonal ruling. People at the posts of command do not have much leeway. Their response to most eventualities has been fixed in advance; their subordinates know this and can, therefore, act accordingly. The seniority system makes it impossible for the higher-ups to intervene in the careers of their subordinates. Of course, there are many constraints and the usual concomitant punishments; but what is important for our purpose is the impossibility of arbitrary punishment rather than the leniency of the system.

If we re-examine the functioning of the plants we have described in this new light, the system appears, on the one hand, to be very rational in this respect, yet, on the other, to yield unintended results that change the meaning completely, at least at the shop level.

The over-all extension of the rules, the stability and predictability of all occupational behavior, and the lack of interference across hierarchical echelons, all weaken the chain of command considerably. Power is weak down the line, and in its absence there is relative cordiality and lack of concern. Supervisors are passive and workers tolerant. Some provision is still necessary for giving sanctions to the system as a whole, and the roles of the director and assistant director still carry some power. However, it is important that the centralization that has occurred has caused the power of decision to be located at a level where personal influence is difficult to exercise, because of the number of people involved and the lack of immediate reliable information. Thus even the real key relationship—between the workers and the director—is stripped of its power and control function. The director, acting as a judge, remains impersonal. He cannot combine his desires for action and power with his duty as the man who interprets and applies the law.

But if power problems seem eliminated from the official line of command, there remains one group relationship with all the connotations of dependency and attendant emotional feelings. This is the relationship between the maintenance workers and the production workers. We must try to understand how it has come about and how it relates to the system as a whole.

This relationship is centered around the problem of machine stoppages. Machine stoppages . . . occur unusually often because of the difficulties in conditioning the raw material. This is a sore spot in the technological system. However, comparable problems seem to be handled better in other factories in France, and in similar factories working with the same technology in other countries. Elsewhere, at least, they are not considered the crucial events they have become in the Monopoly.

There are apparently two complementary reasons for their being crucial in the bureaucratic organizational setup of the Monopoly. First, machine stoppages are the only major happenings that cannot be predicted and to which impersonal rulings cannot apply. The rules govern the consequences of the stoppages, the reallocation of jobs, and the adjustment of the work load and of pay; but they cannot indicate when the stoppage will occur and how long it will take to repair. The contrast between the detailed rigidity of all other prescribed behavior and the complete uncertainty of mechanical functioning gives this problem disproportionate importance. Second, the people who are in charge of maintenance and repair are the only ones who can cope with machine stoppage. They cannot be overseen by anyone in the shop. No one can understand what they are doing and check on them. Furthermore, a department—a rather abstract services unit—is not responsible. Instead, men are individually responsible, each of them for a number of machines. Thus there is another contrast between impersonality and abstractness on the one side, and individual responsibility on the other.

Production workers are displeased by the consequences of a machine stoppage. It disrupts their work; it is likely to make it necessary for them to work harder to compensate for lost time; and if it lasts long enough, they will be displaced, losing friendship ties and even status.[18]

With machine stoppages, a general uncertainty about what will happen next develops in a world totally dominated by the value of security. It is not surprising, therefore, that the behavior of the maintenance man—the man who alone can handle the situation, and who by preventing these unpleasant consequences gives workers the necessary security—has a tremendous importance for production workers, and that they try to please him and he to influence them. From this state of affairs, a power relationship develops.

The contrast between the power wielded by the maintenance men and the lack of influence of the supervisors explains the advantage that the former have over the latter. Supervisors cannot check on maintenance. They may be competent in the various aspects of their work, but their competence does not extend to the only problem about which the workers care, because only its outcome is uncertain. A supervisor cannot reprimand the mechanics who work in his shop. There is likely to be a perpetual fight for control, and the supervisors will usually be the losers. It is, therefore, natural for them to have low morale, and to adjust to their situation only after having resigned themselves to being the losers—using whatever rationalization they please.

Maintenance workers, on the other hand, have the best of this situation; but their power is contested. It is not an overt, legitimate power. It does not fit the usual expectations of industrial leadership. As a result, maintenance workers still feel insecure. One can understand that their aggressiveness is a way of warding off any attack, of cementing the group solidarity and making individual compromise impossible. It is a value necessary to group struggle—and effective in it. Soul-searching and moderation are qualities the group will definitely refuse to consider; and these qualities tend to make people marginal, if not outcasts.

Production workers resent their dependence, but cannot express their hostility openly, because they need the maintenance men's help and good will individually at the shop, and because, collectively, they know that they can keep their privileges only by maintaining a common front with the other workers' group. Union solidarity and working-class unity are the values in the names of which production workers accept the maintenance workers' leadership. These values are important to them, because of their feelings of insecurity. They feel that they have rights and privileges that are not customary in the usual industrial setups in France, and that they must protect themselves. They fear that they will not be able to keep these assets unless they are prepared to fight. Since the production workers are in this state of mind, the threats of abandoning them which maintenance men make are always successful.[19]

The system of organization we have described may appear quite unworkable. Groups fight endlessly. It seems that there is no way of making changes and adjusting to new conditions. The system appears completely static. Yet it works, with a low but adequate degree of efficiency, and it has incorporated, in one way or another, every stage of technological progress.

One should not, therefore, translate the burden of the opinions expressed and the attitudes revealed into too black-and-white a picture. Conflict, forces discouraging growth, a general conservative system of human adjustment, all put a premium on conformity and conservative values. However, these tendencies cannot develop ad infinitum. There are constant checks that prevent them from going too far and threatening the permanence of the system itself. Behind the struggles there is also, as in any sort of organization, some kind of consensus and organizational commitment.

Keeping these qualifications in mind, we can make a few final remarks about the consequences of the bureaucratic patterns we have observed.

As in the Clerical Agency, the combination of impersonal rules, the absence of promotion from one role to another, and the seniority system, tend to make the hierarchical line progressively weaker. This preserves the personal independence of each employee in respect to the higher-ups, but it produces new kinds of frustration inasmuch as it provides no way of solving immediate problems.

Second, the development of the holders of each separate role into a stratum or an estate-like group has, as its consequence, the submission of each employee to considerable group pressure. In its own way, group pressure replaces the dwindling hierarchical pressure.

In addition, there is a decline in the importance of instrumentality in all personal judgments, accompanied by an increase in the role of affectivity. Human relations, and especially group relations, are likely to be more acute in a bureaucracy than in an organization where sanction is found in relevant measurable results.

Fourth, the initiation of change is made very difficult within an organization where the only kind of leadership is an administrative judicial one. If fairness is the only legitimate value a director can advocate, then whenever there is resistance he is likely to abandon his role as an agent of change. Change will occur only when external pressure becomes impossible to withstand. The company directors will then administer such change in a very impersonal way, without paying due regard—and rightly, if they want to succeed—to the specific requirements of each plant. To counter this kind of action, subordinates will develop a very distrustful and demanding attitude, which will enable them to take full advantage of all the consequent inadequacies.

Finally, new power relationships develop around the loopholes in the regulatory system. Groups fight for control of the ultimate strategic sources of uncertainties, and their fates in the group struggle depend on their ability to control these. New power relationships will have, as a consequence, new kinds of dependencies and frustrations, which will exert pressure for more centralization and reinforce the demand aspect of the subordinate-superior relationship, creating a sort of vicious circle that, at least at this level, it will be impossible to evade.

NOTES

17. This opinion has been more and more frequently expressed since the middle fifties by social psychologists and specialists in the theory of organizations.

18. They are held personally responsible for all stoppages of less than one hour and a half and must compensate for the loss of production; if the stoppage is longer, they will be displaced or may be sent around to do menial jobs if there is no possibility of bumping less senior fellow workers.

19. One of these threats is for a minority of the group to start an autonomous union of maintenance workers. Such attempts are usually temporary, but they impress production workers very much.

13

The Abstraction of Industrial Work

Shoshana Zuboff

In the older pulp and paper mills of Piney Wood and Tiger Creek, where a highly experienced work force was making the transition to a new computer-based technology, operators had many ways of using their bodies to achieve precise knowledge. One man judged the condition of paper coming off a dry roller by the sensitivity of his hair to electricity in the atmosphere around the machine. Another could judge the moisture content of a roll of pulp by a quick slap of his hand. Immediacy was the mode in which things were known; it provided a feeling of certainty, of knowing "what's going on." One worker in Piney Wood described how it felt to be removed from the physical presence of the process equipment and asked to perform his tasks from a computerized control room:

> It is very different now. . . . It is hard to get used to not being out there with the process. I miss it a lot. I miss being able to see it. You can see when the pulp runs over a vat. You know what's happening.

The worker's capacity "to know" has been lodged in sentience and displayed in action. The physical presence of the process equipment has been the setting that corresponded to this knowledge, which could, in turn, be displayed only in that context. As long as the action context remained intact, it was possible for knowledge to remain implicit. In this sense, the worker knew a great deal, but very little of that knowledge was ever articulated, written down, or made explicit in any fashion. Instead, operators went about their business, displaying their know-how and rarely attempting to translate that knowledge into terms that were publicly accessible. This is what managers mean when they speak of the "art" involved in operating these plants. As one manager at Piney Wood described it:

> There are a lot of operators working here who cannot verbally give a description of some piece of the process. I can ask them what is going on at the

far end of the plant, and they can't tell me, but they can draw it for me. By taking away this physical contact that he understands, it's like we have taken away his blueprint. He can't verbalize his way around the process.

In this regard, the pulp and paper mills embody a historical sweep that is unavailable in many other forms of work. Unlike other continuous-process industries, such as oil refining or chemical production, the pulp-and-paper-making process has not yet yielded a full scientific explication. This has retarded the spread of automation and also has worked to preserve the integrity of a certain amount of craft know-how among those operators with lengthy experience in the industry. Like other continuous-process operations, the technological environment in these mills has created work that was more mediated by equipment and dependent upon indirect data than, say, work on an assembly line. However, discrete instrumentation typically was located on or close to the actual operating equipment, allowing the operator to combine data from an instrument reading with data from his or her own senses. Most workers believed that they "knew" what was going on at any particular moment because of what they saw and felt, and they used past experience to relate these perceptions to a set of likely consequences. The required sequences and routines necessary to control certain parts of the process and to make proper adjustments for achieving the best results represented a form of knowledge that the worker displayed in action as a continual reflection of this sentient involvement. Acquired experience made it possible to relate current conditions to past events; thus, an operator's competence increased as the passing of time enabled him or her to experience the action possibilities of a wide variety of operating conditions.

In Piney Wood and Tiger Creek, the technology change did not mean simply trading one form of instrumentation for another. Because the traditional basis of competence, like skilled work in most industries, was still heavily dependent upon sentient involvement, information technology was experienced as a radical departure from the taken-for-granted approach to daily work. In this sense, workers' experiences in these mills bridge two manufacturing domains. They not only illustrate the next phase of technological change within the continuous-process industries but also foreshadow the dilemmas that will emerge in other industrial organizations (for example, batch and assembly-line production) with the transition from machine to computer mediation.

When a process engineer attempts to construct a set of algorithms that will be the basis for automating some portion of the production process, he or she first interviews those individuals who currently perform the tasks that will be automated. The process engineer must learn the detail of their actions in order to translate their practice into the terms of a mathematical model. The algorithms in such a model explicate, rationalize, and institutionalize know-how. In the course of these interviews, the process engineer is likely to run up against the limits of implicit knowledge. A worker may perform competently yet be unable to communicate the structure of his or her actions. As one engineer discovered:

> *There are operators who can run the paper machine with tremendous efficiency, but they cannot describe to you how they do it. They have built-in actions and senses that they are not aware of. One operation required pulling two levers simultaneously, and they were not conscious of the fact they they were pulling two levers. They said they were pulling one. The operators run the mill, but they don't understand how. There are operators who know exactly what to do, but they cannot tell you how they do it.*[1]

Though every operator with similar responsibilities performs the same functions, each will perform them in a unique way, fashioned according to a personal interpretation of what works best. A process engineer contrasted the personal rendering of skill with the impersonal but consistently optimal performance of the computer:

> *There is no question that the computer takes the human factor out of running the machine. Each new person who comes on shift will make their own distinct changes, according to their sense of what is the best setting. In contrast, the computer runs exactly the same way all the time. Each operator thinks he does a better job, each one thinks he has a better intimate understanding of the equipment than another operator. But none of them can compete with the computer.*

These comments describe a particular quality of skill that I refer to as *action-centered*. Four components of action-centered skill are high-lighted in the experiences of these workers:

1. *Sentience.* Action-centered skill is based upon sentient information derived from physical cues.
2. *Action-dependence.* Action-centered skill is developed in physical performance. Although in principle it may be made explicit in language, it typically remains unexplicated—implicit in action.
3. *Context-dependence.* Action-centered skill only has meaning within the context in which its associated physical activities can occur.
4. *Personalism.* It is the individual body that takes in the situation and an individual's actions that display the required competence. There is a felt linkage between the knower and the known. The implicit quality of knowledge provides it with a sense of interiority, much like physical experience.

THE DISSOCIATION OF SENTIENCE AND KNOWLEDGE

Computerization brings about an essential change in the way the worker can know the world and, with it, a crisis of confidence in the possibility of certain knowledge. For the workers of Piney Wood and Tiger Creek, achieving a sense of knowing the world was rarely problematical in their conventional environments. Certain knowledge was conveyed through the immediacy of their sensory experience. Instead of Descartes's "I think, therefore I am," these workers might say, "I see, I touch, I smell, I hear; therefore, I know." Their capacity to trust their knowledge was reflected in the assumption of its validity. In the precomputerized environment, belief was a seamless extension of sensory experience.

As the medium of knowing was transformed by computerization, the placid unity of experience and knowledge was disturbed. Accomplishing work depended upon the ability to manipulate symbolic, electronically presented data. Instead of using their bodies as instruments of *acting-on* equipment and materials, the task relationship became mediated by the information system. Operators had to work through the medium of what I will call the "data interface," represented most visibly by the computer terminals they monitored from central control rooms. The workers in this transition were at first overwhelmed with the feeling that they could no longer see or touch their work, as if it has been made both invisible and intangible by computer mediation.

It's just different getting this information in the control room. The man in here can't see. Out there you can look around until you find something.

The chlorine has overflowed, and it's all over the third floor. You see, this is what I mean . . . it's all over the floor, but you can't see it. You have to remember how to get into the system to do something about it. Before you could see it and you knew what was happening—you just knew.

The hardest thing for us operators is not to have the physical part. I can chew pulp and tell you its physical properties. We knew things from experience. Now we have to try and figure out what is happening. The hardest part is to give up that physical control.

In a world in which skills were honed over long years of physical experience, work was associated with concrete objects and the cues they provided. A worker's sense of occupational identity was deeply marked by his or her understanding of and attachment to discrete tangible entities, such as a piece of operating equipment. Years of service meant continued opportunities to master new objects. It was the immediate knowledge one could gain of these tangible objects that engendered feelings of competence and control. For workers, the new computer-mediated relationship to work often felt like being yanked away from a world that could be known because it could be sensed.

Our operators did their job by feeling a pipe—"Is it hot?" We can't just tell them it's 150 degrees. They have to believe it.

With computerization I am further away from my job than I have ever been before. I used to listen to the sounds the boiler makes and know just how it was running. I could look at the fire in the furnace and tell by its color how it was burning. I knew what kinds of adjustments were needed by the shades of color I saw. A lot of the men also said that there were smells that told you different things about how it was running. I feel uncomfortable being away from these sights and smells. Now I only have numbers to go by. I am scared of that boiler, and I feel that I should be closer to it in order to control it.

It is as if one's job had vanished into a two-dimensional space of abstractions, where digital symbols replace a concrete reality. Workers reiterated a spontaneous emotional response countless times—defined by feelings of loss of control, of vulnerability, and of frustration. It was sharpened with a sense of crisis and a need for steeling oneself with courage and not a little adrenaline in order to meet the challenge. It was shot through with the bewilderment of a man suddenly blind, groping with his hands outstretched in a vast, unfamiliar space. "We are in uncharted water now," they said. "We have to control our operations blind." This oft-repeated metaphor spoke of being robbed of one's senses and plunged into darkness. The tangible world had always been thick with landmarks; it was difficult to cast off from these familiar moorings with only abstractions as guides.

One operator described learning to work with the new computer system in Tiger Creek's pulping area. "The difficulty," he said, "is not being able to touch things." As he spoke, his hands shot out before him and he wiggled all his fingers, as if to emphasize the sense of incompleteness and loss. He continued:

When I go out and touch something, I know what will happen. There is a fear of not being out on the floor watching things. It is like turning your back in a dark alley. You don't know what is behind you; you don't know what might be happening. It all becomes remote from you, and it makes you feel vulnerable. It was like being a new operator all over again. Today I push buttons instead of opening valves on the digester. If I push the wrong button, will I screw up? Will anything happen?

Many other descriptions conveyed a similar feeling:

With the change to the computer it's like driving down the highway with your lights out and someone else pushing the accelerator.

It's like flying an airplane and taking all the instruments out so you can't see. It's like if you had an airplane and you put pieces over each instrument to hide it. Then, if something went wrong, you have to uncover the right one in a split second.

Doing my job through the computer, it feels different. It is like you are riding a big, powerful horse, but someone is sitting behind you on the saddle holding the reins, and you just have to be on that ride and hold on. You see what is coming, but you can't do anything to control it. You can't steer your-

self left and right; you can't control that horse that you are on. You have got to do whatever the guy behind you holding the reins wants you to do. Well, I would rather be holding the reins than have someone behind me holding the reins.

The feeling of being in control and the willingness to be held accountable require a reservoir of critical judgment with which to initiate informed action. In the past, operators like those at Piney Wood derived their critical judgment from their "gut feel" of the production process. Becoming a "good" operator—the kind that workers and managers alike refer to as an "artist" and invest with the authority of expertise—required the years of experience to develop a finely nuanced, felt sense of the equipment, the product, and the overall process. With computerization, many managers acknowledged that operators had lost their ability "to feel the machine." Without considering the new skill implications of this loss, many managers feared it would eliminate the kind of critical judgment that would have allowed operators to take action based upon an understanding that reached beyond the computer system.

Piney Wood's plant manager, as he presided over the massive technology conversion, asked himself what the loss of such art might mean:

In the digester area, we used to have guys doing it who had an art. After we put the computers in, when they went down we could go to manual backup. People remembered how to run the digesters. Now if we try to go back, they can't remember what to do. They have lost the feel for it. We are really stuck now without the computer; we can't successfully operate that unit without it. If you are watching a screen, do you see the same things you would if you were there, face-to-face with the process and the equipment? I am concerned we are losing the art and skills that are not replenishable.

There were many operators who agreed. In one area of Piney Wood, the crew leader explained it this way:

The new people are not going to understand, see, or feel as well as the old guys. Something is wrong with this fan, for example. You may not know what; you just feel it in your feet. The sound, the tone, the volume, the vibrations . . . the computer will control it, but you will have lost something, too. It's a trade-off. The computer can't feel what is going on out there. The new operators will need to have more written down, because they will not know it in their guts. I can't understand how new people coming in are ever going to learn how to run a pulp mill. They are not going to know what is going on. They will only learn what these computers tell them.

Sam Gimbel was a young production coordinator in Piney Wood. Though trained as a chemical engineer, he had been particularly close to the operators whom he managed. He had shepherded them through the technology conversion and construction of the new control room, and worked closely with them as they grappled with new ways of operating:

> We are losing the context where hands-on experience makes sense. If you don't have actual experience, you have to believe everything the computer says, and you can't beat it at its own game. You can't stand up to it. And yet who will have the experience to make these kinds of judgments? It will surely be a different world. You lose the checkpoints in reality to know if you are doing it right; therefore, how will anyone be able to confront the computer information?

Piney Wood's management had approached the technology conversion with the following message: "We are simply providing you with new tools to do your job. Your job is to operate the equipment, and this is a new tool to operate the equipment with." Managers repeatedly made statements such as, "We told them this was a tool just like a hammer or a wrench." One manager even went so far as to say, "We hoped they wouldn't figure out that the terminal we were giving them was really a computer."

As experience with the new operating conditions began to accumulate, many managers began to see that treating the computer system like a physical object, "just another tool," could lead to chronic suboptimization of the technology's potential. A powerhouse worker with over twenty-five years of experience had developed a special way of kicking the boiler in order to make it function smoothly. He used the same approach with the terminal; if he hit a certain button on the keyboard, a particular reading would change in the desired direction, but he did not know why or how. Piney Wood's powerhouse manager put it this way:

> The guy who kicks the boiler is the same guy who mashes the button a certain way just to make the line go down. This person will never optimize the process. He will use too much chemical and too high pressure. He will never make you money because he doesn't understand the problem.

Just as the digester operators had lost their ability to cook manually, other workers throughout the mill felt equally powerless:

> In the old way, you had control over the job. The computer now tells you what to do. There is more responsibility but less control. We lost a boiler that was on computer control. We just had to sit there and stare. We were all shook up.

> Sometimes I am amazed when I realize that we stare at the screen even when it has gone down. You get in the habit and you just keep staring even if there is nothing there.

Ironically, as managers and operators across the mill watched the level of artistry decline, the senior technical designers continued to assume that manual skills would provide the necessary backup to their systems.

The problem was even more acute in Cedar Bluff, where most of the work force lacked the experience base from which felt sense and critical judgment are developed. Managers at Cedar Bluff engaged in a quiet debate as to how much of a problem this lack of experience would ultimately be. On one side of the argument were the "old-timers"—managers with years of experience in the industry:

> *I like to smell and feel the pulp sometimes. It can be slick, it can be slimy, it can be all different consistencies. These are the artistic aspects of making pulp that the computer doesn't know about. Some of the operators have been picking up these aspects, but there are so many numbers so readily accessible, we have to shortcut it at times and solve more problems from the office. The information is so good and rapid we have to use it. . . . You have got to be able to recognize when you can run things from the office and when you have to go and look. Yet, I recognize that I am not as good a pulp maker as the people who trained me, and the new operators are not as good as I am. They are better managers and planners. I am very happy with the new managers, but not with the new pulp makers.*

The younger engineers, schooled in computer-based analytic techniques, had little patience with anxious laments over the loss of the art of pulp making. They were relentlessly confident that a good computer model could reproduce anything that operators knew from experience—only better. Here is how the process engineers articulated the argument:

> *Computer analysis lets us see the effects of many variables and their interactions. This is a picture of truth that we could not have achieved before. It is superior to the experience-based knowledge of an operator. You might say that truth replaces knowledge.*

> *People who have this analytic power do not need to have been around to know what is going on. All you need is to be able to formulate a model and perform the necessary confirmation checks. With the right model you can manage the system just fine.*

Most Cedar Bluff managers agreed that the computer system made it possible to do a better job running the plant with an inexperienced work force than otherwise would have been possible, though some wondered whether the levels of expertise would ever be as high as among workers with hands-on exposure to the pulping process. Yet even as managers argued over the essentiality of action-centered skill, technology was irreversibly altering the context in which the operators performed. The opportunities to develop such skills were becoming increasingly rare as the action context was paved over by the data highway.

Many of Cedar Bluff's managers believed that the traditional knowledge of the pulp mill worker would actually inhibit the development of creativity and flexibility. Under the new technological conditions, the young operators would develop their capacity to "know better" than the systems with which they worked as they struggled with the complexities of the new technology and the data it provided. The data interface would replace the physical equipment as the primary arena for learning.

Yet as months passed, other managers observed a disturbing pattern of interactions between the operators and the computer system. Some believed that the highly computerized task environment resulted in a greater than usual bifurcation of skills. One group of operators would use the information systems to learn an extraordinary amount about the process, while another group would make itself an appendage to the system, mechanically carrying out the computer's directives. These managers complained that the computer system was becoming a crutch that prevented many operators from developing a superior knowledge of the process. One "old-timer" provided an example:

> *When there is a shift change and new operators come on, the good operator will take the process from the computer, put it on manual, make certain changes that the operator thinks are necessary, and then gives it back to the computer. The average operator will come in, see this thing on automatic control, and leave it with the computer. Sometimes that operator won't even realize that things are getting bad or getting worse. They should have known better, but they didn't.*

Most Cedar Bluff operators spoke enthusiastically about the convenience of the computer interface, and some freely admitted what they perceived to be a dependence on the computer system:

> *The computer provides your hands. I don't think I could work in a conventional mill. This is so much more convenient. You have so much control without having to go out to the equipment and adjust things.*

> *We can't run this mill manually. There are too many controls, and it is too complex. The average person can only run four or five variables at once in a manual mode, and the automatic system runs it all. If the computer goes down, we have to sit back and wait. We sit and we stare at the screens and we hope something pipes in.*

Many managers observed with growing alarm the things that occurred when operators neither enjoyed the traditional sources of critical judgment nor had developed enough new knowledge for informed action.

> *In a conventional mill, you have to go and look at the equipment because you cannot get enough data in the control room. Here, you get all the data*

you need. The computer becomes a substitute tool. It replaces all the sensual data instead of being an addition. We had another experience with the feed-water pumps, which supply water to the boiler to make steam. There was a power outage. Something in the computer canceled the alarm. The operator had a lot of trouble and did not look at the readout of the water level and never got an alarm. The tank ran empty, the pumps tripped. The pump finally tore up because there was no water feeding it.

We have so much data from the computer, I find that hard drives out soft. Operators are tempted not to tour the plant. They just sit at the computer and watch for alarms. One weekend I found a tank overflowing in digesting. I went to the operator and told him, and he said, "It can't be; the computer says my level is fine." I am afraid of what happens if we trust the computer too much.

At least since the introduction of the moving assembly line in Ford's Highland Park plant, it has been second nature for managers to use technology to delimit worker discretion and, in this process, to concentrate knowledge within the managerial domain. The special dilemmas raised by information technology require managers to reconsider these assumptions. When information and control technology is used to turn the worker into "just another mechanical variable," one immediate result is the withdrawal of the worker's commitment to and accountability for the work. This lack of care requires additional managerial vigilance and leads to a need for increased automatic control. As this dynamic unfolds, it no longer seems shocking to contemplate an image of work laced with stupefaction and passivity, in which the human being is a hapless bystander at the margins of productive activity. One young operator in Cedar Bluff discussed his prior job as a bank clerk. I asked him if his two employment experiences had anything in common. "Yes," he said, "in both cases you punch the buttons and watch it happen."

As automation intensifies, information technology becomes the receptacle for larger and larger portions of the organization's operating intelligence. Algorithms become the functional equivalent of a once diffuse know-how, and the action context in which know-how can be developed and sustained vanishes. Because many managers assume that more technology means a diminished need for human operating skill, they may recognize the waning of worker know-how without becoming concerned enough to chart a different course. Left unchallenged, these systems become more potent, as they are invested with an escalating degree of authority. Technical experts temporarily serve as resources, but once their knowledge has been depleted, and converted into systematic rules for decision making, their usefulness is attenuated. The analysts and engineers, who construct programs and models, have the capacity to manipulate data and, presumably, to make discoveries. Ultimately, they will become the most important human presence to offer any counterpoint to the growing density and opacity of the automated systems.

NOTES

1. It should be noted that there are other motivations that could account for an operator's inarticulateness in the face of such questioning. Operators, like generations of craftspeople before them, know that as their activities become more explicit, their skills seem less significant. Explication means a loss of power. However, my work in this mill over several years led me to believe that although many operators were aware of these political dynamics, they tended to choose methods of resistance and counter-offense other than deliberately undermining the process engineer's efforts. In most cases I was convinced that operators were not withholding information but, rather, that they had really reached the limits of their explicit understanding.

14

Building Intelligence Networks

Wayne Baker

To manage a business well is to manage its future;
and to manage the future is to manage information.
Marion Harper[1]

Former President George Bush was much better off without John Sununu. When Sununu was Bush's chief of staff, he would indulge in a favorite pastime of subordinates: intercepting information before it could get to the big boss.[2] Helpful John, it seems, would stop letters sent by the president's longtime advisors and keep them from ever reaching the Oval Office. He simply answered the letters himself or referred George's advisors to junior aides. George was the last to know. To get around his chief of staff, George had to establish a back channel—a private post office box in Maine—to which his advisors could send letters directly.

Bush's problem wasn't unusual. And it's not limited to the chief executive; people at all levels suffer from it. The problem just gets worse and worse the higher up you go or the farther away you move from the company's actual operations. The dilemma of indirect management means you rely more and more on information fed to you by others. You get out of touch. And you make poor decisions.

Managers can be their own worst enemies. As they move up, many fall for the management folklore that says they should withdraw from operational affairs and contemplate the big picture. "If he [or she] follows the advice to free himself from operations," warns Ed Wrapp in his famous *Harvard Business Review* article, "he [or she] may soon find himself subsisting on a diet of abstractions, leaving the choice of what he [or she] eats in the hands of his [or her] subordinates."[3]

What can you do? You can't rely on the formal organization to help you out. "The very purpose of a hierarchy," says Kenneth Boulding, "is to prevent infor-

From Chapter 3 of *Networking Smart*. Copyright © 1994 McGraw-Hill, Inc. Reprinted with permission of McGraw-Hill, Inc.

mation from reaching top layers. It operates as an information filter, and there are little wastebaskets all along the way."[4] Information is garbled as it wends its way through formal channels; often it arrives too late to do any good. Conflicting and ambiguous messages create a dull buzz of confusion. Critical details are lost in aggregated summaries. At worst, reports are sanitized, numbers massaged; information is hoarded and withheld, even fabricated.

To get the information you need, you have to take matters into your own hands. Richard Neustadt discovered an important lesson for managers everywhere when he studied the information-collecting habits of Presidents Roosevelt, Truman, and Eisenhower: "It is not information of a general sort that helps a President see personal stakes; not summaries, not surveys, not the bland amalgams. Rather . . . it is the odds and ends of tangible detail that pieced together in his mind illuminate the underside of issues put before him. To help himself he must reach out as widely as he can for every scrap of fact, opinion, gossip, bearing on his interests and relationships as President. He must become his own director of his own central intelligence."[5]

That's what you can do. To get the information you need, you have to build your own intelligence network. Good managers and executives have always done so, but it's more important today than ever, no matter where you are in the organization. Knowledge, says futurist Alvin Toffler, is now the basis of power and wealth creation.[6] We are in the information age. By the mid-1980s, for example, more than half of the U.S. work force already held jobs that were information-related.[7] There's a prodigious increase in the production of information; fast markets and rapid technological change make today's information more perishable than ice at the equator.

This information explosion aggravates the manager's intelligence problem. The information explosion is really the *data* explosion, says Richard Saul Wurman in *Information Anxiety,* and you have to sort and process data to get anything useful.[8] Just getting more data won't help. In fact, psychologists have learned that more data actually hinders good decision making because it makes decision makers feel overconfident.[9] What you need is the *right* information, not more data.

In this chapter, we look at how effective leaders at all levels get the information they need. I describe how personal intelligence systems work and tell you how to build them. Even if you're a seasoned and successful businessperson, there are many things to learn. And, as you'll see, the information theme of this chapter is woven throughout the topics covered in the rest of the book. Managing information well is an essential part of managing relationships and networks in all business areas.

YOUR INTERNAL INTELLIGENCE NETWORK

Effective leaders develop their own independent intelligence networks to keep informed about a wide range of decisions, activities, people, and events. Their personal networks help them to monitor ongoing activities and to spot incipient problems and opportunities. "[E]ach of my heroes," says Ed Wrapp, "has a special talent for keeping himself [or herself] informed about a wide range of operating decisions being made at different levels in the company. As he [or she] moves up the ladder, he [or she] develops a network of information sources in many different departments. He [or she] cultivates these sources and keeps them open no matter how high he [or she] climbs in the organization. When the need arises, he [or she] bypasses the lines on the organization chart to seek more than one version of a situation."[10]

Consider Walter Wriston, the corporate leader who transformed First National Citibank into Citicorp—one of the preeminent financial institutions in the world.[11] Wriston was a master builder of informal intelligence networks. As a fellow executive described in Harry Levinson and Stuart Rosenthal's chapter on Wriston in *CEO:*

> *He relies very heavily on information that comes to him from different parts of the organization. He gets and absorbs the feelings of people who are not only department and group heads but always has a wary ear open to be alert to situations, circumstances within the shop that might not surface in the ordinary routine of management information flows. . . . He's got a very acute sense . . . of the ideas as they float around the organization. . . .*

Wriston understood very well how easy it is to get out of touch. When Jack Welch took the top job at GE, he reports in an interview with *Financial World* that Wriston warned him of this common problem: "Jack, remember one thing, you're always going to be the last one to know the critical things that need to be done in your organization. Everyone else already knows." "He was right," says Welch.[12] Wriston's advice applies to any one, not just those at the top. Without intelligence networks, you're always out of touch, out of the swim of things, out of the loop.

Personal contacts are your direct lines of communication with the various parts of the organization. Building your intelligence network means initiating, cultivating, and maintaining these contacts. You have plenty of opportunities to do so in the course of day-to-day activities. "Managing by Wandering Around"—Tom Peters and Robert Waterman's MBWA principle—offers chance encounters that yield vital information.[13] Merck CEO Roy Vagelos, for example, often takes lunch in the company cafeteria so he can talk informally with scientists.[14] It's a great way to get informed of the latest developments and discoveries. In a similar fashion but a different content, then-governor Bill Clinton regularly visited a local Little Rock McDonald's to sit and chat with people and hear their concerns.[15]

Mobility and movement offer you chances to make personal contacts. Any move you make inside the company—promotions, transfers, temporary details, special projects, committee assignments, relocations, stints in foreign offices—provides great opportunities to develop new information contacts. A pending relocation or reassignment might look brighter if you consider its network-building potential. It might be just the right move if it enables you to meet different people, make new contacts, and build new relationships that'll be helpful down the road.

As a rule, diverse contacts are better than similar or redundant contacts. A large, diverse network of contacts, argues network expert Ronald Burt, gives you the best access to information.[16] You can't stay in the know with a few or a narrow set of contacts. With a diverse set, however, you're better able to quickly discover new opportunities. And broader access to information has its rewards. Burt shows in his impressive study of managers in a high-tech *Fortune* 500 company that those who bridge lots of diverse groups get promoted faster and at younger ages than their peers.

Zigzag career paths are better than linear paths for building the diverse set of connections you need. Vertical paths—moving up rung by rung within the same function—help you build contacts in the same business area. These contacts are useful, of course, but your intelligence network is a mile deep and an inch wide. Zigzag job changes—moving laterally, jumping functions, going abroad—provide the breadth you need. The Japanese have known for a long time about the network-building benefits of zigzagging. That's why Japanese managers have what look to us like inefficient, meandering career paths. All the changes you make, however, are just *opportunities* to build information contacts. You must seize them and actively cultivate contacts. . . .

When I talk to businesspeople about building personal intelligence networks, many raise an objection. You ought to have more respect for the formal hierarchy, they tell me; you shouldn't advise people to go around their subordinates to get to the bottom of a story. When I press them for details, they usually tell me about superiors who circumvent *them* and go straight to the source. They feel undermined, frustrated, caught in the middle. All too often their feelings are justified—many managers throw their weight around and gather intelligence in cavalier and callous ways. If you use your personal intelligence network this way, you're asking for trouble. Your aggrieved subordinates will search for some way to thwart you, and your intelligence network will crumble.

Managing information relationships, just like any sort of relationship, entails ethics and responsibilities. You may need to go around people to get information, but those you go around need to be taken into account. Sometimes just explaining *why* you go directly to an information source is all you need to do. When appropriate, share what you find out. Information dissemination is part of your job. Sharing includes confidential information, though you have to do so judiciously. "The manager is challenged," says management expert Henry Mintzberg, "to find systematic ways to share privileged information."[17] With your diverse set of contacts, you're in a great position to piece together information that can help others do their jobs. Remember that sharing information *empowers* people. A person's power—the ability to get the job done—depends directly on his or her access to information.[18] You empower your people—and yourself—by collecting and sharing information.

Your responsibility to share information extends to your information sources. Reciprocity, the natural give-and-take between people, is one of the basic rules in all cultures and societies.[19] It's essential for building information relationships (or any other kind of relationship for that matter). The reciprocity rule links a future action (repayment) with a present action (a favor, gift, etc.). By linking the present and the future, it activates the fourth networking principle: Repeated interaction encourages cooperation. If you sponge information and never give, your sources will dry up. But give and you shall receive. This doesn't mean you should be an inveterate gossip. Be a tactful, judicious supplier of information and a trustworthy, responsible user of information.

Above all, take what you learn from your personal intelligence system with a grain of salt. You must work hard to gather every tidbit of data, gossip, rumor, and innuendo. Some tidbits are the most timely and accurate pieces of genuine information you'll ever get.[20] A few help you peer into the future. But many pieces of information are irrelevant, others are innocent errors, and more than a few are deliberate disinformation and malicious lies. All, however, are parts of some larger story. You're faced with a balancing act. If you wait until you get the whole story, it'll be too late to act; but if you don't get enough of the story before you act, you'll make bad decisions, alienate your people, and let your organization be ruled by the tyranny of rumor and gossip.

DONUTS WITH DITCH

Donuts with Ditch? OK, here's a more formal-sounding title: information-exchange forum. Donuts with Ditch is the informal communication sessions Allan Ditchfield created ten years ago at AT&T.[21] It was so effective and popular that he imported the practice to MCI when he became chief information officer (CIO) of the long-distance communications company, and then imported it once again when he became CIO of Progressive Corporation, the Ohio-based national auto insurance company. "I do it to break down the hierarchical barriers," he told me. "It's basically a communications meeting." Allan uses these informal meetings to hear everyone's concerns, get and give information, and keep everyone in touch. It's a great way to get at the real issues, the real problems. It gives people a voice and a forum, many of whom have no other means to communicate with or hear from upper-level managers.

Allan holds a Donuts-with-Ditch session at Progressive every two weeks. (He would hold weekly sessions at MCI because the department was much bigger.) The typical meeting lasts about 2 or 3 hours. Attendance is limited to a small number of people. "I have no more than 10 people at a time," he says. "If you have more than 10, people don't like to talk." People are chosen on a random basis for Donuts with Ditch, "but some people ask to be invited, especially if they have a burning issue to discuss." Trust is the most important ingredient for success. "I have a rule—it's a sacred open door—that there will be no retaliation, no one's going to be hurt by [what they say]. I don't tell management."

How has Donuts with Ditch changed over the years? "I have a lot more fruit these days," he says.

Donuts with Ditch is a great example of creating conditions that encourage information flow. Donuts with Ditch comes in all shapes and sizes:

- American Airlines CEO Robert Crandall holds conferences around the country to talk directly with employees.[22]
- Federal Express uses its Open Door policy to encourage employees to communicate directly to management their ideas, questions, or comments about the industry or company; the express courier's Guaranteed Fair Treatment policy makes sure employees can get a fair hearing for any concern or complaint about fair treatment (e.g., questions about a performance review or other personnel matter).[23]
- Royal Bank of Canada establishes conferences to help area managers share expertise, data, and intelligence.[24]
- GE uses its Corporate Executive Council as a forum for leaders from GE's various businesses to get together, exchange information and advice, and to integrate what could be disparate units.[25]
- The U.S. State Department uses the secretary's open forum to encourage "differences of opinion by publishing papers, sponsoring discussions, and inviting critics to speak."[26] State also has a "dissent channel" that lower-level managers can use to send messages directly to the secretary, bypassing the Sununu-type blockade I described earlier.
- Donuts with Ditch, Japanese style, is the regular Friday meeting (*kinyo-kai*) of the presidents of the member companies in the Mitsubishi *keiretsu*, one of Japan's vast and close-knit groups of companies. The Friday meeting has taken place every month for over forty years![27]

Regular operational meetings are another effective variation on the Donuts with Ditch theme. Such meetings are common at Silicon Valley firms, which are role models of the new network organization. Zap Computers, for example, Kathleen Eisenhardt's code name for the large computer maker she studied, relies on frequent operational meetings—two or three a week—to share, relay, and discuss information about sales, inventory, backlog, engineering schedules, new releases, product introductions by competitors, technical developments in the industry, and so on.[28] Zap's top managers use these meetings to relay information they glean from constant phone calls, travel, and business and university contacts.

Lots of meetings, face-to-face interaction—all the variations of Donuts with Ditch—create real-time intelligence networks. Real-time networks help managers accelerate decision making, says Eisenhardt, which is essential wherever the pace of change is fast and furious.[29]

CAN COMPUTER NETWORKING HELP?

Computers are often heralded as the technological cure to the information problem. In a computer-networked company, for example, you *can* find the proverbial needle in a haystack. With electronic mail or an electronic bulletin board, you can query hundreds or even thousands of people all at once. You'd get a few wrong answers, but the odds of getting the right one are tremendous when compared with the luck you'd have with the telephone.

Searching the haystack is just one example of the many ways in which computer technology is revolutionizing communication.[30] Computer technologies free us from the friction of time and space. In 1991, for example, more than 5.5 million people worked as "telecommuters," commuting to work via phone and modem instead of a car. This is a 38 percent increase over the previous year, according to Link Resources National Work at Home Survey.[31] The new advances in networking technologies can help transform and redesign traditional organizations, yielding quicker, more responsive, more effective decision making.[32] Flexible computer networking is often used to support the new network organizations.

But there are serious limitations. Despite great advantages, electronic communication cannot become the cornerstone of your independent intelligence system. To see why, let's begin by looking at the older computer technologies, management information systems (MIS). Part of the folklore about managers, argues Henry Mintzberg, is that senior managers need aggregated information like that produced by MIS. The fact is good managers eschew formal systems that spew forth abstracts and stylized facts.[33] Instead, they obtain and transmit information via all sorts of *verbal* media: face-to-face conversations, phone calls, traveling, meetings, spontaneous and impromptu discussions. "I was struck during my study," Mintzberg said, "by the fact that the executives I was observing—all very competent—are fundamentally indistinguishable from their counterparts of a hundred years ago (or a thousand years ago). The information they need differs, but they seek it in the same way—by word of mouth."[34]

Why do managers prefer word of mouth? MIS provides only aggregated information and old news. Word-of-mouth networks are on-line, real-time systems that give you live, rich, quick, timely information about what's going on. You need this kind of information to get news as it happens, to spot opportunities and problems early. "Every bit of evidence," says Mintzberg, "suggests that the manager identifies decision situations and builds models [mental maps of the organization] not with the aggregated abstractions an MIS provides, but with specific tidbits of data."[35]

Is computer networking better? In some ways, yes. Greater efficiency is one of the benefits companies find when they establish electronic networks: shorter elapsed time for transactions, quicker turnaround, faster group communication.[36] Saving time is important, of course, but electronic networks aren't the appropriate medium for the complex, rich, nuanced communication essential for intelligence gathering. "Proponents of the efficiency benefits of computer-based communication often assume that it delivers the same message as any other medium but simply does so more rapidly," write networking experts Lee Sproull and Sara Kielser in *Connections*. "That view is misleading because a message—even the same 'message'—changes its meaning depending on the forum within which people convey it." Compared with face-to-face interaction, they say, "today's electronic technology is impoverished in social cues and shared experience."[37]

Consider the results of a study by James McKenney and associates at Harvard Business School on how managers use electronic mail versus face-to-face communication.[38] They discovered conspicuous differences in how managers use these media:

- Managers use *electronic mail* for efficient communication in well-defined contexts—monitoring task status, coordinating efforts, exchanging factual information, sending alerts, and broadcasting information.
- Managers use *face-to-face interaction* for defining and discussing problems and solutions, building a shared understanding of the situation, discussing shifting priorities and external pressures, interpreting ambiguous signals, and socialization of members.

Electronic communication is efficient, but only face-to-face interaction provides the richness, interactivity, immediacy of feedback, and social context needed for complex problem solving and fostering a shared set of values, beliefs, and meanings. Former ITT CEO Harold Geneen recognized the difference: "In New York, I might read a request and say no. But in Europe, I could see that an answer to the same question might be yes . . . it became our policy to deal with problems on the spot, face-to-face."[39] Even Allan Ditchfield, who as chief information officer is a champion of electronic communication, relies on informal, face-to-face sessions via his regular Donuts with Ditch.

It is difficult (if not impossible) to initiate or nurture meaningful relationships via electronic interaction. (It's true that some people who meet electronically become friends and even marry, but these are exceptions.) The ritual and ceremonial value of group meetings cannot be simulated with electronic communication.[40] Group meetings, says Stanford University professor Jane Hannaway, "keep a sense of community alive in the organization . . . [and] affirm the place of the individual and others in that community. . . ."[41]

Computer networking can save you a lot of time communicating routine information. But such networking is ill-suited to the rich, sensitive, live, private information you need to be an effective manager. For that, you must build an independent intelligence network based on personal contacts.

YOUR EXTERNAL INTELLIGENCE NETWORK

Along with internal intelligence networks, effective managers build *external networks* of personal contacts. External contacts help you stay informed about what's going on "out there"—changing customer preferences, a competitor's plans and actions, social and economic trends, pending regulations, emergent technologies, and so forth. One reason Ned Tanen of Paramount Pictures was so effective as president of production, for example, was his "dozen Rolodexes of contacts."[42] A colleague who studies the publishing business told me a story about an editor who returned to his office to find his desk taped shut. It seems the publishing house had been taken over abruptly, and the new owners were feeling a touch protective about their new assets. He spotted his rolodex on the desk, snatched it, and walked away saying, "That's all I need."[43]

External intelligence networks help you manage the information problem, the problem of too much data and not enough real information. A few years ago, I was talking with the treasurer of a global high-tech firm about his relationships with investment banks. I commented on the foot-high pile of proposals and brochures on his desk. "It's a problem coping with it all," he said. "I'll look at it eventually; there may be a nugget buried in there. But I don't have time to go through it now." He then told me how he finds out what he really needs to know: the company's senior vice president of finance. "He's talking with Goldman Sachs, Salomon Brothers, Merrill Lynch, Morgan Stanley, and who all else," the treasurer said. "That's what he's paid for—his network of contacts." External contacts provide the right information.

"External networks are reality checks," explains Howard Haas, who was CEO of Sealy Inc. for 19 years. "How do you know the numbers you've got in your own company are correct? You don't know unless you have some way to prove it. Or, I know how my business is, but I don't know how my business is in relation to somebody else's business. How do I find out about that? I say to a competitor, 'How's your business?' He says, 'Terrific! We're 35 percent ahead!' I know the guy's lying through his teeth. So I go out and I call a bunch of dealers and talk to a lot of people. And finally I put together a consensus of the information and say, well, ours is up 5 percent so we're doing a lot better. That's a reality check."[44]

People throughout your organization have special access to the outside world—and it pays to link up with them. "The MIS professional," says Tom Peters, "will be the first to hear that a competitor is developing a sweeping new electronic linkup with hundreds of major customers."[45] Your people in finance have contacts throughout the financial world. Your sales representatives meet your competitor's sales reps every day in customer waiting rooms or at trade shows. They swap stories and gossip (and a few fibs, no doubt!) about you, each other, customers, other competitors, the industry, and so on. Do you have a way of learning what they know? Your scientists and engineers have innumerable contacts in professional and learned societies; they always know what's going on, what's hot, what's new. Do *you* talk with *them?* Remember that *everyone* in your organization has a life outside the company; everyone can be the company's eyes and ears. Recruit them into your external intelligence system.

Just as the daily rounds of business help you make internal contacts, your everyday work life offers plenty of opportunities to make external contacts. Most people think Peters and Waterman's MBWA principle applies only inside the company. But it's just as useful for making outside contacts. Peters advises marketers, for example, to spend more time "hanging out" in the marketplace.[46] It's an idea that Japanese companies have practiced for years. The invention of the Sony Walkman is a great example.[47] The original idea came right from Sony CEO and chairman Akio Morita. But he didn't dream it up sitting in his office. Morita spent lots of time hanging out, observing young people and getting to know their lifestyles and tastes in music. And what he saw was a huge untapped demand for a personal, compact, portable tape player. That's what he conveyed back to Sony designers. The result, as you know, was a smashing success.

Recently, GE instituted the hanging-out principle in its QMI—quick market intelligence technique.[48] QMI is an excellent way to get fast market intelligence and make quick decisions in response. As GE describes in its 1992 Annual Report, "Quick Market Intelligence is our term for the magnificent boundary-busting technique pioneered by Wal-Mart that allows the entire Company to understand, to sense, to touch the changing desires of the customer and to act on them in almost real time."[49] QMI taps the knowledge and insights of people in the field, those who see, touch, and listen to the market daily. Once a week, GE salespeople and managers come in from the field and report what they've learned. "It is a process that gives every salesperson direct access, every Friday, to the key managers and the CEO of the business, to lay out customer problems and needs. The product of the meeting is not deep or strategic in nature, but action—a response to the customer right away."[50] That's networking smart.

Virtually any outside event or gathering—professional meetings, trade conferences and shows, business roundtables, civic activities, charitable work, and so on—provide tremendous network-building opportunities. Michael Mach, CEO of Capital Partners, a very successful commercial real estate development firm, put it this way: "I involve myself in a number of things. Most of them are directly or indirectly related to our business. One reaches the point where one does not deliberately go out and search for things that help one's business. But the important factor is the networking that we all do when you take on one of these other challenges. I take on civic challenges in order to get some form of extra edge in our business, since they are interrelated in some way."

CUSTOMERS AND SUPPLIERS AS EYES AND EARS

Customers and suppliers are some of your best contacts in the outside world. Their networks reach into different nooks and crannies; they have different perspectives; they're steps closer to vital news as it breaks. Your customers, for example, are called on regularly by your competitors. Competitors offer them all sorts of enticements to woo them away from you—new and innovative ideas, special promotions, new marketing strategies. As a result, your customers almost always know before you do what your competitors are up to. Of course, finding out what your customers know is a delicate matter. There are no easy rules. You don't want to put them in an uncomfortable or compromising position; you need to respect their other relationships.* Your customers can't always tell you everything you want to know, but they often can let you know what's in the wind.

Using your customers' eyes and ears is critical if you don't deal directly with the final consumer. If your customers are a link in the chain leading to the final consumer, they are closer than you to information you need. In the soft drink industry, for example, Pepsi, Coca Cola, and other concentrate producers sell most of their output to the bottlers. Bottlers sell to retail stores, who in turn sell to you and me. Because the bottlers stock local retail shelves, they know the nitty gritty details about local markets. Is a competitor making special deals to grab more

---

*You also don't want to solicit price lists or other pricing information which could be construed as attempted price fixing.

shelf space? Is there a last-second change in a competitor's marketing policy? Is a new brand or flavor appearing on the shelves?

Your suppliers are also excellent sources of outside information. Former Sealy CEO Howard Haas, for example, tapped advertising and media types to garner information about competitors. "The people [who] sell us space in the trade papers," he told me, "are the greatest contact people in the world. I would pump them as to what was happening with my competitors."[51] A Midwestern auto dealer uses suppliers' eyes and ears in a very creative way to get customer feedback.[52] He provides free taxicab service for customers who need a ride after dropping off their cars. The cab drivers (his suppliers) converse with riders about their car troubles and the auto dealer's service. The drivers relay this critical information back to the auto dealer.

Lawyers, accountants, bankers, management consultants, advertising agencies, architects, and engineers are all prime information sources. These people sit at the crossroads of complex information flows. By virtue of a diverse client base, they are vast repositories of data. They can provide invaluable information and insights about ongoing developments, events, and business trends. Such informational benefits add a new twist to outsourcing decisions. Many companies try to save money by dropping outside service suppliers and doing it themselves. You can save money this way. The cost of in-house lawyers, for example, is 40 percent lower than the cost of using an outside law firm for the same work.[53] What is not included in these cost calculations, however, is the opportunity cost of lost information: the value of information received from outside suppliers. The lost information can be critical and irreplaceable. Cutting relationships severs information links with the outside world.

You can also incorporate professional intelligence suppliers into your external intelligence system. Chicago-based CombsMoorhead Associates, Inc., for example, is a professional intelligence-gathering service that produces analyses for its clients on such subjects as product trends, environmental issues, sales projections, competitor information, and patents.* The firm systematically combs an array of information sources—industry and government contacts, trade associations, the media, computerized databases, and so on. Companies like this specialize in building information networks, and you tap their extensive networks when you employ them.

HIGH-LEVEL EYES AND EARS

Your company's board of directors is a set of high-level links to the outside world. One of the best-documented findings in organizational research is that top

---

*The principals of the firm, Richard E. Combs and John D. Moorhead, have written *The Competitive Intelligence Handbook* (Metuchen, N.J., Scarecrow Press, 1992) which describes competitive intelligence techniques.

executives and managers use corporate boards to collect critical information from the company's environment. In my study of 1530 companies and their investment banks, for example, I found that many companies invite investment bankers on their boards to gain access to financial advice, ideas, new product developments, investor attitudes, and market intelligence.[54] Northwestern Business School professor Gerald Davis discovered that executives learn the ins and outs of poison pills, golden parachutes, and other tricks from their outside directors.[55] In fact, he learned, if your outside directors already have experience with these tactics, then your company is much more likely to use them as well. It's easy to see why. Your outside directors have direct experience and can tell you exactly how and when to use them.

Because directors are used as high-level eyes and ears, the composition of a company's board can tell you a lot about the kind of environment the company operates in and what information executives feel is important to get. Hospitals, for example, put local community and civic leaders on their boards because they operate in highly politicized environments. Community and civic leaders help them gather the specific kind of political intelligence they need. If financing is especially important, companies populate their boards with commercial bankers, investment bankers, and insurance executives (insurance companies are big lenders).

Some companies invite executives from key customers or suppliers to sit as board directors.* These high-level links can provide information about the outside director's company that helps coordinate and improve the relationship. . . . Other companies invite executives from critical *industries* to serve on their boards. This kind of link provides unbiased information about events, trends, and happenings in the industry.[56]

Trade associations and lobbying organizations can also be your high-level eyes and ears. Sociologists Edward Laumann and David Knoke report a great story about how this can work.[57] When the executive director of a petroleum-industry trade association spotted a *Federal Register* announcement by the Federal Aviation Administration (FAA), he immediately realized the danger to his member firms. The FAA wanted to require the filing of detailed flight plans of noncommercial aircraft as a way to help find downed planes. Under the Freedom of Information Act, however, companies could obtain competitors' flight plans and learn where they were exploring for natural resources. The executive director quickly alerted the membership and mobilized efforts to exempt member organizations.

---

*Of course, one must be careful to avoid so-called tying arrangements, wherein the sale of one product or service is tied to the sale of another. A tying arrangement would occur, for example, if a computer maker hired an investment bank *on the condition* that the bank agrees to buy the computer maker's products.

WHAT YOU CAN DO *NOW*

What you can do now is assess the current state of your personal intelligence system. Are you in the know, or are you the last to know? Do you get news in time to act? Or are you surprised time and time again when decisions are made that affect you and your group? In short, are you the director of your own intelligence network?

The following short quiz will help you assess the current state of your intelligence system. Answer each question yes or no depending on which answer best describes your situation. To score the quiz, simply circle the number of each question to which you answer yes. Count the number of questions that you answered yes. If you answered yes to 15 or more questions, your personal intelligence system's in good shape (though there's always room for improvement!). If you answered yes to 10 or more but fewer than 15, you have substantial room for improvement. And if you answered yes to fewer than 10 questions, well, you've some work to do.

Evaluating Your Intelligence System

1. Do you feel that you're generally "in the know" and typically find out about key decisions, events, and activities inside the organization?
2. Have you stayed in touch with operations as you've moved up?
3. Have you maintained your contacts in other groups or departments as you've moved around the company?
4. Do you regularly supplement reports from management information systems (MIS) with informal word-of-mouth information?
5. Do you prefer to talk face-to-face to define and discuss complex problems and shifting priorities?
6. Do you usually accept contact-building opportunities—transfers, temporary details, committee assignments, relocations?
7. Have you (or would you) accept an assignment abroad?
8. Do you have personal contacts in a wide range of different groups (as opposed to contacts concentrated within the same group)?
9. Do you share actively information with your subordinates, peers, and superiors?
10. Do you provide information *to* your sources? Do you reciprocate?
11. Have you developed real-time intelligence networks, such as your own version of Donuts with Ditch?
12. Do you know people in other groups or departments that have special access to external information that would be useful to you?
13. Do you maintain contacts with lawyers, accountants, bankers, consultants, advertising agencies, and other outside sources?
14. Do you use professional information suppliers?
15. Do you stay in close touch with your customers (including final consumers)?
16. Do you tap suppliers as sources of information?
17. Have you developed fast internal channels to transmit information gathered from outside sources?
18. Do you regularly "wander around" in the outside world, attending trade shows, meetings, civic and charitable events, and so on?
19. Do you know and talk with your peers in other organizations?
20. Do you use board directors, lobbying organizations, and trade associations as high-level eyes and ears?

WHAT YOU CAN DO *SOON*

What you can do soon is figure out how you can improve your personal intelligence network. Even if your personal network's in good shape, still work on it: The best time to build your intelligence network is before you really need it. Times and situations change, and you never really know where the next piece of critical information will come from. By continually augmenting your network, you improve the odds that you'll get the news you need when it breaks. If you wait until you need information, it's too late to develop your network.

The key to creating your personal network is knowing *where* to build contacts, not just *how*. You must figure out *what* critical information you need and *where* it's produced before investing in the establishment of an information network infrastructure. First, look inward and consider your internal information needs:

- What kinds of information do you need? What information is critical to your ability to do your job? What's critical to your group's ability to do its job?
- Where are you (and your group) in the flow of internal information? Who are your internal customers? Who are your internal suppliers?
- Where are your key information uncertainties and threats?[58] Who makes decisions that affect your fate or the fate of your group? Where is information generated that you *really* need to know?

Now look outward and consider the types and sources of information you need from the organization's wider environment:

- What kind of information do you need? What information is critical to your success, your group's, and your organization's?
- Where's your organization located in the production-consumption chain? How far are you from the ultimate consumer?
- Where are your critical uncertainties and threats—customers, suppliers, competitors, regulatory actions, emergent technologies, and so on?

You may find that you can't pin down precisely all the types and sources of information you need. That's OK, because you never really know where the next piece of critical information will come from. You may not even know that a bit of information *is* critical until some time after you get it. People who network smart report that chance encounters, free-ranging and seemingly aimless conversations, tidbits dropped and overheard are frequently the sources of what, in retrospect, was vital information. There's a healthy element of chance in intelligence gathering. That's why a diverse set of information contacts is necessary. Your objective is to be in the right place at the right time—wherever and whenever that is—and you must cast a broad net to make sure you are.

Once you have some idea of the critical types and sources of information, your task is to build contacts. Remember the fifth networking principle: It's a small world. . . . It's your ally in the network-building process. The small-world phenomenon means you're never that far from the information you need. Every time you increase your network of direct contacts by a single person, you tap into a vast network of indirect contacts. This principle may help you see massive restructurings as blessings in disguise. Why? Restructuring means much wider spans of management, and wider spans augment your information network: You get more direct information sources (your additional direct contacts) *and* many more indirect sources (the personal networks your direct contacts bring with them).

Look back at your answers to the 20-question quiz. Is there a pattern to your yes and no answers? If you tended to answer no to questions 2 through 12, then your internal intelligence system is deficient and you should start there. Here are three suggestions for getting started:

- Start your own version of Donuts with Ditch. You don't have to make a big deal about it by making formal announcements. Just extend a casual invitation to chat about "things." Keep it open and free-wheeling. (Be sure to bring your favorite nosh—food is always hard to resist!)
- Reactivate one or two old contacts in groups or departments in which you once worked. Pick up the phone and extend an invitation to coffee or lunch. Or just stop by.
- Share information with a subordinate or team member; let him or her know something that you know. Remember that sharing information empowers people. A subordinate's or team member's power—the ability to get the job done—depends directly on his or her access to information.[59]

If you tended to answer no to questions 13 through 20, then your external intelligence system is deficient and you should concentrate there. (If your no answers appear in both sections, start building your internal network first and then proceed to work on external networks.) Here are three suggestions that can help you begin the process of building your external intelligence system:

- Think of who inside the organization is a natural bridge to a part of the outside world you want more information about. The bridger could be a salesperson, scientist, district manager, computer person, secretary, and so on. Invite that person to your next Donuts with Ditch session.
- Identify an outside supplier who might be a good source of information. It could be your company's law firm, ad agency, banker, and so on. Call them and invite them to lunch.
- Take a trip to an outside conference or trade show. It could be directly related to your business but it doesn't have to be. Attend the sessions, go to cocktail parties, don't eat alone if you can help it. Volunteer to do something at the next meeting.

WHAT YOU CAN DO IN THE *LONG RUN*

What you can do in the long term is manage *conditions:* create the right context that will help you and your organization develop and refine the overall intelligence system. Remember, the more you help others build their personal intelligence networks, the more you multiply your own.

Develop a reward system that encourages network building. Establish a travel budget that lets people attend trade shows, conferences, professional meetings, learned societies, educational seminars, and so on. In fact, make it a formal requirement that *everyone* goes to one such event at least every six months. If you can't afford to send everyone out of town, have them attend local events during the day, evenings, or weekends. And give everyone this chapter to read before they go.

Develop fast internal channels for processing information and getting it to the right people. Internal channels at Tennant Company are a good example. This leading manufacturer of floor maintenance equipment uses the sales force as "quality eyes and ears" in the company's total quality improvement program. "Every time a machine is delivered," say CEO Roger L. Hale and associates, "the salesperson fills out an installation report. If any defects are present, each one is the subject of a separate report. These reports are sent to the warranty and quality departments at company headquarters."[60]

When hiring, ascertain each candidate's *network assets* (the contacts a candidate brings with him or her) and *networking capabilities* (a candidate's motivation and ability to make new contacts). Everyone's personal network is portable. Every time you hire a well-connected person you annex a new network of direct and indirect contacts, new sources of information. (This is one reason behind the federal government's so-called revolving door restriction: a one-year waiting period after leaving a government post before an ex-federal employee can return and lobby for private interests.) When firing, or thinking about it, be sure to consider a person's network. If you don't, you might unwittingly sever important links to the outside.

When accounts are up for review, don't forget that your suppliers have network assets and networking capabilities as well. Are you getting the information you need from your lawyers, bankers, consultants, engineers, advertising agencies, and other professional service suppliers? Because these are easier to change than suppliers of goods . . . , you may want to consider adding or switching suppliers to boost your intelligence networks.

Establish a long-term intelligence trajectory—the directions into which you want to expand the organization's intelligence system. Pick a key uncertainty and establish a plan to build networks in that direction. If you're in an industry noted for fast technological change, for example, work to build information networks of scientists, engineers, university contacts, and so on. If you're in a highly regulated and politicized environment, think of adding political and regulatory contacts to your network. If supply of critical raw materials is a recurrent problem, build networks that will help you monitor supplies, substitutes, and suppliers.

Physical location can be used to create the right intelligence conditions. Edison Electric Institute didn't relocate from New York to Washington, D.C., because real estate was cheaper in the nation's capital.[61] It relocated as a way to become more central in political communication networks. As the major trade association for the electrical utility industry, the Institute had to enlarge its information-collecting and processing capabilities in response to the increasing politicization of energy policy making. Companies locate in close proximity to facilitate the face-to-face exchange of information too ambiguous or sensitive to transmit via electronic media.[62] General Motors' long-time advertising agency, McCann Erickson (now part of The Interpublic Group of Companies), has offices located right in GM's Detroit office building. Similarly, Capital Partners' main architectural firm has its headquarters in Capital Partners' home office.

A few final words. You'll never really be done building your personal intelligence network. Times and situations change. Always look for ways to supplement your intelligence contacts. From time to time, reread this chapter, reassess your situation, and work to become the director of your own intelligence network.

REFERENCES

1. Quoted in Philip Kotler, *Marketing Management,* 6th ed. (Englewood Cliffs, N.J.: Prentice-Hall, 1988), p. 101.

2. Story in *Time*, September 30, 1991, p. 19.

3. H. Edward Wrapp, "Good Managers Don't Make Policy Decisions," *Harvard Business Review,* July–August 1984, pp. 4–11. Quotation from p. 5.

4. From his speech at the Crowell Collier Institute of Continuing Education (New York); reported in *Business Week,* February 18, 1967, p. 202.

5. Richard Neustadt, *Presidential Power: The Politics of Leadership* (New York: John Wiley, 1960).

6. Alvin Toffler, *Powershift* (New York: Bantam Books, 1990).

7. Loy Singleton, *Telecommunications in the Information Age* (New York: Ballinger, 1984).

8. Richard Saul Wurman, *Information Anxiety* (New York: Doubleday, 1989).

9. See, for example, J. Edward Russo and Paul J. H. Schoemaker, *Decision Traps* (New York: Doubleday, 1989).

10. Wrapp, "Good Managers," p. 4.

11. Chapter 3 in Harry Levinson and Stuart Rosenthal, *CEO: Corporate Leadership in Action* (New York: Basic Books, 1984). Quotation from p. 68.

12. Stephen W. Quickel, "Welch on Welch," CEO of the Year, *Financial World,* April 3, 1990, pp. 62–67.

13. Thomas J. Peters and Robert H. Waterman, *In Search of Excellence: Lessons from America's Best-Run Companies* (New York: Harper & Row, 1982).

14. "The CEO Disease/Avoiding the Pitfalls of Power," *Australian Business,* May 1, 1991, pp. 36–41 (which is reprinted from *Business Week,* April 1, 1991).

15. Mitchell Locin, "Little Rock Hops for Local Hero," *Chicago Tribune,* November 4, 1992, sec. 1, p. 5.

16. Ronald S. Burt, *Structural Holes* (Cambridge, Mass.: Harvard University Press, 1992).

17. Henry Mintzberg, "The Manager's Job: Folklore and Fact," *Harvard Business Review,* July–August 1975, pp. 49–61.

18. See, for example, Rosabeth Moss Kanter, "Power Failure in Management Circuits," *Harvard Business Review,* July–August 1979, pp. 65–75.

19. See an excellent discussion of reciprocity in Chapter 2 of Robert B. Cialdini, *Influence: Science and Practice* (Glenview, Ill.: Scott, Foresman, 1985). Anthropologists and sociologists have documented that reciprocity is a rule in *all* cultures and societies.

20. For insights on gossip and decision making, see James G. March and Guje Sevon, "Gossip, Information and Decision-Making," in Lee S. Sproull and J. Patrick Crecine (eds.), *Advances in Information Processing in Organizations,* vol. 1 (Greenwich, Conn.: JAI Press, 1984), pp. 95–107.

21. From interview with Allan Ditchfield, April 23, 1993. Used with permission.

22. "The CEO Disease," p. 40.

23. Described in letter from Kathryn E. Milano, Federal Express, January 18, 1993.

24. Ram Charan, "How Networks Reshape Organizations—for Results," *Harvard Business Review,* September–October 1991, p. 110.

25. Described in Noel M. Tichy and Stratford Sherman, *Control Your Own Destiny or Someone Else Will* (New York: Doubleday, 1993), pp. 156–166.

26. Jane Hannaway, *Managers Managing* (New York: Oxford University Press, 1989), pp. 104–105.

27. See, e.g., "Japan: All in the Family," *Newsweek,* June 10, 1991, pp. 37–39.

28. Kathleen M. Eisenhardt, "Speed and Strategic Choice: How Managers Accelerate Decision Making," *California Management Review,* vol. 32, 1990, pp. 1–16.

29. Eisenhardt, "Speed and Strategic Choice," discusses in detail the concepts of real time information networks and fast decision making.

30. See, for example, Charles Savage, *Fifth Generation Management: Integrating Enterprises through Human Networking* (Digital Press, 1990); and Lee Sproull and Sara Kiesler, *Connections: New Ways of Working in the Networked Organization* (Cambridge, Mass.: MIT Press, 1992).

31. In Brad Schepp, "The 10-Second Commute," *Home Office Computing,* December 1991, pp. 45–48.

32. For example, see Richard L. Nolan, Alex J. Pollock, James P. Ware, "Toward the Design of Network Organizations," *Stage by Stage,* vol. 9, 1989, pp. 1–12, published by Nolan, Norton, & Co.

33. Henry Mintzberg, "The Manager's Job: Folklore and Fact," *Harvard Business Review,* July–August 1975, pp. 49–61.

34. Ibid., p. 167.

35. Ibid.

36. See, for example, Sproull and Kiesler, *Connections,* p. 15, Chapter 2.

37. Ibid., pp. 37, 39.

38. James, L. McKenney, Michael H. Zack, and Victor S. Doherty, "Complementary Communication Media: A Comparison of Electronic Mail and Face-to-Face Communication in a Programming Team," in Nitin Nohria and Robert G. Eccles (eds.), *Net-*

works and Organizations: Structure, Form, and Action (Boston: Harvard Business School Press, 1992), Chapter 10.

39. Quoted in Sproull and Kiesler, *Connections,* p. 40; originally cited in L. K. Trevino, R. Lengel, and R. L. Daft, "Media Symbolism, Media Richness, and Media Choice in Organizations," *Communication Research,* vol. 14, 1987, pp. 553–574.

40. On the importance of symbols, ceremony, and management, see, for example, Harrison M. Trice, James Belasco, and Joseph A. Alutto, "The Role of Ceremonials in Organizational Behavior," *Industrial Management Review,* vol. 23, 1969, pp. 40–51.

41. Jane Hannaway, *Managers Managing* (New York: Oxford University Press, 1989), p. 144.

42. Joshua Hammer, "The Fall of Frank Mancuso," *Newsweek,* May 6, 1991.

43. On networks in publishing, see Walter W. Powell, *Getting into Print* (Chicago: University of Chicago Press, 1985) and Lewis Coser, Charles Kadushin, and Walter W. Powell, *Books: The Culture and Commerce of Publishing* (New York: Basic, 1982), especially Chapter 3, "Networks, Connections, and Circles."

44. Personal interview, Summer 1991.

45. Tom Peters, *Thriving on Chaos* (New York: Harper & Row, 1987), p. 283.

46. Ibid., p. 184.

47. Described, for example, in James Brian Quinn, Henry Mintzberg, and Robert M. James, *The Strategy Process* (Englewood Cliffs, N.J.: Prentice Hall, 1988), pp. 734–735.

48. Described in "To Our Share Owners," 1992 Annual Report, General Electric Co.

49. Ibid, p. 4.

50. Ibid.

51. Personal interview, Summer 1991.

52. Described to me by one of my Executive MBA students.

53. Estimate of cost savings from Anne B. Fisher, "How to Cut Your Legal Costs," *Fortune,* April 23, 1990, pp. 185–192. Based, in part, on Wayne E. Baker and Robert R. Faulkner, "Strategies for Managing Suppliers of Professional Services," *California Management Review,* vol. 33, 1991, pp. 33–45.

54. Wayne E. Baker, "Market Networks and Corporate Behavior," *American Journal of Sociology,* vol. 96, 1990, pp. 589–625.

55. Gerald F. Davis, "Agents without Principles? The Spread of the Poison Pill through the Intercorporate Network," *Administrative Science Quarterly,* vol. 36, 1991, pp. 583–613.

56. See, for example, Linda Brewster Stearns and Mark S. Mizruchi, "Broken-Tie Reconstitution and the Functions of Interorganizational Interlocks: A Re-Examination," *Administrative Science Quarterly,* vol. 31, 1986, pp. 522–588.

57. Edward O. Laumann and David Knoke, *The Organizational State* (Madison, Wis.: University of Wisconsin Press, 1987).

58. Sociologist Arthur L. Stinchcombe argues in *Information and Organizations* (Berkeley, Calif.: University of California Press, 1990) that the organization's main information task is to manage such uncertainties. The organization must be where the news breaks, whenever it breaks.

59. See, for example, Rosabeth Moss Kanter, "Power Failure in Management Circuits," *Harvard Business Review,* July–August 1979, pp. 65–75.

60. Roger L. Hale, Douglas R. Hoelscher, and Ronald E. Kowal, *Quest for Quality*, 2d ed. (Minneapolis: Tennant Company, 1989), p. 56. Used with permission.

61. Based on Edward O. Laumann and David Knoke, *The Organizational State* (Madison, Wis.: The University of Wisconsin Press, 1987), p. 208.

62. I learned this from an excellent study conducted by one of my MBA students, Kenneth A. Posner (MBA '91), "Using Hedonic Models to Examine the Value of Location" (MBA Honors paper, Graduate School of Business, University of Chicago). In the paper, he summarizes Edwin S. Mills' argument in "Sources of Metropolitan Growth and Development" (*The Institute for Urban Economic Development*, 1991) that firms cluster to exchange ambiguous information via face-to-face interaction.

Index